C000199642

For Freddie

BLOOMSBURY
LONDON · OXFORD · NEW YORK · NEW DELHI · SYDNEY

River Cottage

light & easy

Healthy recipes for everyday

Hugh Fearnley-Whittingstall

Photography by Simon Wheeler   Illustrations by Mariko Jesse

CONTENTS

 Suitable for vegans Start to finish in 20 minutes  Ideal for a lunchbox

All recipes are wheat-free and dairy-free Note that 'wheat-free' does not necessarily mean 'gluten-free'.
Recipes using rye flour, for example, contain gluten. Totally gluten-free baking recipes are listed on page 403.

EXPLORING AND EXTOLLING the life-enhancing effects of cooking and eating great food is what I do. And I'm increasingly convinced of a couple of things. Really delicious, satisfying food doesn't have to be time-consuming and complicated. And it certainly needn't be rich and laden with fat. What's more, healthy food doesn't have to be ascetic, restrictive or centred around denial.

I think I've already proved this point with *River Cottage Veg Everyday*. It shows that, lovely and exciting as good meat and fish are to cook with, they make us lazy in the kitchen. Put them on one side – for a while, or for a few days a week – and a torrent of vegetable creativity will be released. I know this approach is now boosting the cooking, and the good health, of families all over Britain and beyond. They are kind enough to keep telling me.

Now I want to encourage another gear change in your cooking – and the phrase *Light and Easy* gets pretty much to the heart of the matter. I'm offering up a set of new recipes that are healthy and well balanced, straightforward to put together, but always, unfailingly, delicious.

You might be wondering if the term 'light' implies that this is a diet book. Well, not if you are into counting calories, or looking for guaranteed weight loss. But in the sense that it might very well change the way you eat – forever, and for the better – then perhaps it is.

Underpinning my idea of 'light' is a notion that might raise a few eyebrows. In much the same spirit as my *Veg* book, I want to address the suspect ubiquity of a couple of very familiar ingredients. They are milk and wheat. My goodness, they are everywhere!

Wheat is in the bread, biscuits, cakes and pasta that get most of us through our busy working lives. Milk – and its derivatives butter, cheese and yoghurt –

are also key elements of the quick-fix fillers, sandwiches and drinks that we keep turning to, day after day. One or other ingredient probably appears in more than half of all published recipes.

My question is, do they deserve to be quite so popular? Are they that good for us, that indispensable, that we must all consume them by the kilo, week in, week out? I've been thinking about this, and exploring alternatives, and I'm convinced the answer is a resounding no!

We need to recognise that wheat and dairy products can be problematic for many of us – and, in excess, perhaps for most of us. The fact that I've been asked many times by many people to write a book that eschews them is perhaps the first clue. So I've been listening.

I am party to a dawning realisation that our increasing dependence on industrially processed dairy and refined wheat is not good for us (or indeed the environment). Our unquestioning reliance on refined white wheat flour is particularly endemic. We fill up our children on pasta and bread. Toast is the unconsidered breakfast option of millions, and 'grabbing a sandwich' has become an entirely un-euphemistic description of the way most of us do lunch. Yet the nutritional profile of today's wheat fails to justify such knee-jerk usage.

Products made with wheat flour – I'm thinking primarily of bread – are among the many that can cause unhealthy short-term spikes in our blood sugar. What's more, modern, high-yielding wheat is very different to wheat grown even 50 years ago. One study has shown a significant decrease in the mineral content in wheat during that time. Another found modern wheat to contain higher levels of a component of wheat protein called 'Glia-A9', which is known to cause a reaction in people with coeliac disease (a condition that is on the increase).

Even people who aren't coeliac can have a severe reaction to wheat – and many more of us have at least some problem with it. I certainly know when I've eaten too much bread or cake. It's that familiar bloated, lethargic feeling, often followed surprisingly speedily by renewed hunger pangs.

Dairy ingredients can also be a challenge to human digestive systems. It's widely recognised that at least 70% of the world's adult population produce low levels of lactase, the enzyme needed to break down the milk sugar, lactose. Some of those people will suffer the unpleasant symptoms of lactose intolerance (including bloating and all kinds of intestinal upsets). Rates are much lower in people of European descent than other ethnic groups, but digestive problems caused by dairy ingredients are a problem everywhere. I bet most of us know someone who struggles with them. And of course there's no question that cream, butter and many cheeses are high in the saturated fats that can contribute to rising cholesterol levels.

The science of diet is complex and remains controversial – especially around wheat and dairy products. This is not least because of the vast vested business interests involved in protecting the industries that produce them. Personal testimony often cuts compellingly through the heated 'scientific' debate. Perhaps, like me, you know people whose bodies and lives were in turmoil, until it was suggested they try giving up wheat. If so, you'll know just how rapid and complete a recovery can follow this simple change of habit.

Few of us have quite such a dramatic relationship with wheat and gluten. But my own view, considered and researched if not exactly expert, is that wheat tolerance/intolerance is not a binary matter either. Rather, in terms of our ability to successfully digest wheat and other glutens, we are all somewhere on a continuum. Having the culinary tools to take a break from wheat now and again will help us find a contented place on that continuum. More of that in a moment.

For my own part, I have a fatty story to tell. I was diagnosed a couple years back with high cholesterol – close to the score when a man of my age is advised to take statins. I really didn't fancy that route, so I decided to cut down on my daily indulgence of generously buttered bread and spuds and regular outings of the cheeseboard. I began to use rapeseed, hempseed and other cold-pressed oils to trickle on veg – and my morning toast.

I didn't give up milk, cream, cheese, butter and yoghurt. I simply chose to recognise when I was consuming them and be conscientious about using them less often, more sparingly, in my cooking. Six months later my cholesterol was smack in the middle of the normal healthy range – which is pretty much where it is today.

I'm not suggesting for a moment that we should all give up wheat and dairy for good. Butter is a lovely, delicious and versatile ingredient, and I still use it often. I know my wife couldn't make her wonderful sourdough bread without good-quality wheat flour. So when she's rustled up a loaf (at its best with a good smear of salty butter, of course) I might opt to have a couple of days when bread, butter and jam are on my menu. But, following that, I'll put a check on the wheat and the butter, and get back to some of my favourite alternatives.

And that's where the fun starts – the range of delicious grains, flours, oils and fats that you can use instead of, or as well as, wheat and dairy products

is impressive. You'll quickly find, as I have, that this way of cooking and eating is not restrictive, but entirely liberating. The world outside wheat and dairy is a place where you can enjoy a much wider repertoire of staples. New ingredients – or familiar ones used in new ways – will bring fresh energy and an uplifting karma to your cooking.

Beyond butter are other natural fats to explore and enjoy. Besides the obvious olive oil (and for me usually preferable to it) is British grown rapeseed oil. Its golden colour, sweet, grassy flavour and high burn point mean it's exceptionally good for both trickling and cooking. I'm also increasingly turning to raw coconut oil – recognised as one of the healthiest fats you can cook with. Besides these stalwarts, all kinds of delicious nut and seed oils – sunflower, pumpkin seed, sesame and hempseed – get their moment in my kitchen. (See also the notes on page 401.)

Putting wheat flour to one side may seem more daunting than giving a new cooking oil a whirl. But, bearing in mind that continuum of wheat tolerance, I think it's worth it. Try taking a holiday for a month or two, just to see how you feel. As you do so, you'll encounter rye, buckwheat and rice flours, along with ground nuts, seeds and pulses.

However you decide to settle in your consumption of wheat and dairy, all these less familiar flours and fats will bring distinctively new and pleasing flavours and textures to your cooking for the long term. They deserve to be part of your daily culinary palette – and this book will help you explore them.

So the word *Light* in my title in large part reflects these recipes' freedom from wheat and dairy. I've also kept my sweeteners (predominantly honey but sometimes sugar) to the minimum I think necessary for the recipes. I guess you could quibble with describing the final chapter of Treats as 'light'. But I just don't think a brownie would be a treat (or even a brownie) if it was completely free of sugar and fat. My strategy has been to make these treats with a panoply of less refined, more digestible flours and oils. The resulting goodies are therefore easier on the system than conventional cakes and biscuits.

The book is not completely gluten-free, as some of the wheat-free ingredients I suggest (rye flour, for example) do contain some gluten, and others (notably oats) may be contaminated with traces of wheat flour. If you are a coeliac, or you're cooking for someone who is, there is plenty of 'safe baking' for you here. For quick reference, see the list on page 403 – and do read my notes on grains and their flours on page 62.

Let's get back to the *Easy* bit. I want to share my ideas about cooking without wheat and dairy in a collection of really straightforward recipes, because I want this kind of eating, which does involve making changes and trying new things, to feel as accessible as possible. These two strands – mindful of health, and free of fuss – come together in an approach to cooking that is now my vernacular.

So what you'll find here are relaxed recipes, without fiddle and fuss or cheffy techniques, recipes with a little margin for error – where a little bit more of this, a little less of that, can usually be absorbed without a problem. That is how I like to cook. Nevertheless, I've applied an extra-vigorous no-faff filter on the dishes gathered here. I've pared down my ingredients lists and honed my labour-saving techniques, so you can enjoy some of my simplest ever recipes.

While 'easy' cooking must, for me, mean uncomplicated, and light on effort and stress, it doesn't *necessarily* mean quick from start to finish. Sometimes a recipe can be thrown together speedily, but then needs a little time to do its thing – that might be fruit macerating in the fridge, veg roasting in the oven to crisp, caramelised loveliness, or meat tenderising slowly in a casserole. Bear in mind that the time taken for these magical things to happen demands nothing from the cook. You're free to do as you please.

Having said that, I like rustling up meals in minutes as much as the next time-poor cook. And so there are plenty of recipes here (almost half the book in fact) that can indeed be ready to eat, from opening this book to dishing up, in no more than 20 minutes. These are marked out with a little stopwatch symbol: ⏱.

Another useful feature of a dish – given the fast lives so many of us lead – is its portability. If you want to eat something delicious and healthy in the middle of your working day, then easy to make *and* easy to move is a winning combination. So I've made sure that 50 recipes are lunchbox or thermos-flask friendly. And I've marked them all with this delightful little lunchbox graphic: 🍱.

I want to make life easy for my vegan readers too. And so there's a healthy dose of recipes that are completely free of animal products. In some cases, you'll need to substitute sugar (or a vegan-friendly sweetener such as agave syrup) for honey. All this is made clear in the text of recipes with the 'v' for vegan tag: Ⓥ.

I'm confident that this book will amply demonstrate that healthy eating – the *Light and Easy* way – is not about denial or abstinence. On the contrary, reducing your dependence on wheat and dairy turns out to be a delicious voyage of discovery. New grains, new oils, new tastes, new combinations: it all adds up to a new zest for life.

MAKE

Breakfast

BRILLIANT!

I'M NOT MAD ABOUT RULES in the kitchen but if I had to apply one to breakfast, it would be this: do it yourself. Eschew the pre-packed and the ready-mixed – mostly 'empty calories' laced with added sugar and salt. Instead, throw simple things together with your own hands and you will start your day more satisfied and better nourished.

The trick is to find delicious, nutritious breakfasts that don't take long to make – good things you can muster while stumbling round the kitchen in that early-morning fug. Luckily, it's not difficult.

A little pre-planning pays dividends. Make a fruity compote (page 20), a batch of granola (page 29) or a tray of oatcakes (page 47) at the weekend and you've got breakfast sorted for the week. Such hearty basics are ripe for customisation. Let everyone add to them as they choose: a splash of almond milk here, a dollop of nut butter there.

Even a scant minute of preparation the night before is time well spent. Put some oatmeal to soak (in water, apple juice or nut milk) last thing before bed, or leave some crushed berries macerating and mingling their lovely juices in the fridge, and you've got a smashing breakfast waiting for you that takes only minutes to bring together.

Chill some fresh fruit overnight and your cool smoothie needs no ice added when you blend it in the morning.

Of course no one – certainly not me – is that organised all the time, which is when really fast, hot dishes such as drop scones (page 45) and omelettes (page 57) come into their own. Or fix a swift fruit salad, like the limey banana one on page 23, that simply involves a bit of rudimentary slicing and perhaps a pinch of surprising seasoning before you tuck in.

Such quick and effortless breakfasting during the week should leave you ready for something a tad more relaxed and 'brunchy' at the weekend – scrambled eggs with kippers perhaps (page 55), or hot potato cakes (page 52) made with last night's leftover spuds. These are the kind of dishes that set the family up for a lunch-skipping Saturday in the garden or down at the beach. With a treat around teatime (something from the final chapter, of course) they'll get you through to supper.

And since it turns out that I am after all laying down a few rules for the first foods of the day, here's a thought to leave you with. How is it that so many of us put up with the same boring breakfast, day in, day out – toast, cereals, toast, cereals…wheat, wheat, wheat, wheat…?

We'd never consider eating an identical dinner or the same salad every day. So let's funk up breakfast a bit. I've made sure this chapter is colourful, varied and full of new ideas – so that breakfast can be something delicious and sustaining that changes with the seasons and your daily desires.

Pepper grapefruit

Sometimes I want my breakfast to start with something palate-piquing and lively. Grapefruit fits the bill – and I've discovered it tastes even better with a pinch of seasoning. The black pepper is magical – it really enhances the fruit's fragrant acidity.

Serves 2

1 large pink or ruby grapefruit

Freshly ground black pepper

Sea salt (optional)

Halve the grapefruit through the 'equator'. Use a small, sharp knife (a special grapefruit knife is handy but by no means essential) to cut around the circumference of the fruit, separating the flesh from the pith. Then use the tip of the knife to cut down both sides of the membranes that separate the segments, releasing each juicy segment but leaving them neatly in place.

Give the grapefruit a generous dusting of black pepper and a tiny sprinkling of salt, if you like, and it's ready to eat.

Spiced berry salad

This lovely raw berry 'compote' is delicately aromatised with Chinese five-spice. You can whip it up in minutes, or make it in the evening for the following day's breakfast.

Serves 2
250g raspberries
1–2 teaspoons runny honey

A pinch or two of ground Chinese five-spice
100g blueberries

Put about 150g of the raspberries in a dish. Mash them to a pulp with a fork, then trickle over 1 teaspoon honey and add a pinch (about ⅛ teaspoon) of five-spice. Stir well, so that the crushed raspberries release their juice and mix with the spice and honey.

Fold the remaining raspberries and the blueberries into the juicy raspberry mixture. Taste and tweak with a trickle more honey and a pinch more five-spice if you like (the berries vary quite a lot in their acidity and a little more sugar and spice will both help counter the tartness).

Eat straight away, or put it in the fridge overnight for tomorrow's breakfast (let it come up to room temperature, or at least de-chill a little, to enjoy the flavours at their fullest).

Limey bananas

This 'carpaccio' treatment turns the good old banana into an elegant breakfast. A trickle of honey or pinch of sugar makes the dish a touch more indulgent, but I actually prefer the pure, fruity flavours of the banana and lime alone. It's best with bananas that are just ripe rather then very ripe. Lime is particularly special here but if you haven't got one to hand, use half a lemon instead.

Per person

1 medium, just-ripe banana (about 150g)

1 lime

A little honey or a pinch of soft light brown sugar (optional)

Peel the banana and slice it into discs, 4–5mm thick. I like to do this on a bit of an angle, so they are oval in cross section rather than completely round.

Spread the banana slices out on a dinner plate, butting them up close to each other or overlapping ever so slightly. Finely grate the zest of the lime over the banana – the fragrant oils in the zest are what make this dish – then squeeze over some of the juice.

Add a tiny trickle of honey or pinch of sugar if you like. That's it – eat without delay, before the banana gets a chance to brown.

Soaked almonds with strawberries

I do a fair bit of nut-soaking these days – almonds for almond milk (page 30), for instance, and cashews for cashew cream (page 394) and ice cream (page 343) – and I've noticed how delicious the nuts are to munch after a few hours in a bowl of water. They taste almost like fresh, straight-off-the-tree nuts, and the soaking helps to unlock their nutrients by making them more digestible. This easy combo – and the variations that follow – pair up these crisp but creamy nuts with very simply prepared fresh or dried fruit. Soak them overnight and they're ready for breakfast the next morning.

Serves 2

About 50g whole, skin-on almonds

About 100g strawberries, quartered or roughly sliced

½ lemon

A trickle of runny honey, to finish

Put the almonds in a bowl, pour on cold water to cover and leave them to soak overnight, or for at least 4 hours. Then drain, rinse and drain again thoroughly. Once soaked they are quite easy to peel with your fingers – but peeling's definitely optional.

Put the soaked nuts, peeled if you like, in a bowl with the strawberries. Add a good squeeze of lemon juice and trickle over a teaspoon or so of honey. Stir, then leave for a few minutes if you have time, and stir again. Divide between two plates and serve.

VARIATIONS

Soaked walnuts with pear and honey Replace the whole almonds with walnut halves. Put the soaked walnuts into two serving bowls. Peel, quarter and core 1 large or 2 small ripe pears, then slice and distribute between the bowls. Finish with a trickle of honey if you like.

Soaked walnuts with prunes Replace the almonds with walnut halves. Put some prunes to soak in orange juice or tea at the same time you start soaking the walnuts – or just put them in the bowl with the soaking walnuts. Drain and serve with the nuts.

Soaked hazelnuts with apple Replace the almonds with whole, skin-on hazelnuts. Remove the skins after soaking if you like – though it's more of a faff than with almonds. Put the hazelnuts into two serving bowls. Quarter and core 1 large or 2 crisp, medium dessert apples, such as Cox's (no need to peel) then slice fairly thinly, distributing the slices between the bowls. Finish with a trickle of honey if you fancy it.

Breakfast crunch

This is a simple but hearty take on muesli, packed with surprising flavours, colours and textures. The tang of raspberries or blueberries and the crunch of the banana make a fun change from the usual muesli dried fruits, while a smattering of really good dark chocolate (optional, but highly recommended) adds an extra, bittersweet dimension. Use the least sweet chocolate you can find. And look out for organic banana chips, which don't contain preservatives.

6–8 servings

300g jumbo oats

25g dark chocolate (at least 70% cocoa solids), chopped

100g hazelnuts, very roughly chopped

100g dried raspberries or blueberries

100g dried banana chips

TO SERVE

Nut milk (bought or home-made, page 30) or oat milk, or apple juice

Honey or maple syrup (optional)

Mix all the dry ingredients together and store in an airtight container until needed.

To serve, spoon some of the dry mix into a bowl. Top with your favourite dairy-free milk – and a trickle of honey or maple syrup if you like things sweet. Alternatively, you can pour a little apple juice over the muesli before tucking in (in this case, it definitely won't need any extra sweetening).

VARIATION

With cacao nibs In place of the dark chocolate, raw cacao nibs make a very interesting and nutritious addition to this muesli. These shards of unsweetened cocoa bean have a bitterness that might not be to everyone's taste but, alongside the sweet banana, I think they're really quite delicious. You'll find them in health food shops and some supermarkets too.

Buckwheat granola

I think everyone should have a good granola recipe up their sleeve – it's great for breakfast but makes a sustaining snack any time of day. You can take some to work in your lunchbox (or keep a jar under your desk!), or add it to a fresh fruit salad or compote for a light and easy pud. Buckwheat flakes are available in health food shops, but this recipe also works with regular porridge oats.

8–10 servings

350g buckwheat flakes (or porridge oats)

150g whole almonds, whole hazelnuts (blanched or not) or cashews, or a mix of nuts, very roughly chopped

150g pumpkin seeds or sunflower seeds, or a mix

A pinch of salt

50ml rapeseed or sunflower oil

150ml maple syrup

2 teaspoons vanilla extract (optional)

TO SERVE (OPTIONAL)

Nut milk (bought or home-made, page 30), or oat milk

Fresh or dried fruit, or a fruit compote (page 20)

Preheat the oven to 150°C/Gas 2 and line two baking sheets (lipped sheets, to keep the granola in) with baking parchment.

Put the buckwheat, nuts, seeds and salt in a large bowl and mix thoroughly. Pour on the oil and mix it in, getting it evenly distributed.

Combine the maple syrup, 50ml water and the vanilla extract, if using. Pour over the buckwheat mixture and mix in thoroughly.

Spread the mixture out on the baking sheets and bake for about 50 minutes, or until golden all over, giving it a good stir halfway through and swapping around the trays in the oven. Then leave to cool and crisp up.

Store the granola in an airtight container where it will keep well for several weeks. Serve it straight up and dry, or with a little dairy-free milk poured over. Or combine it with fresh fruit, dried fruit, or a fruit compote.

VARIATIONS

Seed and nut swaps This granola is easy to customise with some of your other favourite seeds or nuts – try adding a couple of tablespoons of ground flaxseed or shelled hempseeds (good for omega-3 oils) or whole pumpkin seeds before baking.

Zesty version Stir the finely grated zest of 2 lemons and 1 large orange into the mixture before baking.

Almond milk

'Milks' made from blitzed-up nuts and water are extremely useful if you're avoiding dairy. Almond is my favourite – it has a similar creamy sweetness to cow's milk, but with its own subtly nutty notes. It's easy to buy almond milk these days but home-made does taste better – it's rather special, in fact. You'll need a decent blender and a bit of muslin for straining the almond pulp out of the milk – though if you have a very high-powered blender, such as a Vitamix or Omega, you may not even need to do this. These machines should blitz the almonds completely to form a particularly rich and creamy milk.

Makes 400–500ml

250g whole, skin-on almonds

FOR THE SWEETENED VERSION

½ teaspoon vanilla extract

1 teaspoon honey or agave or maple syrup, or to taste

Put the almonds in a bowl, cover with cold water and leave to soak overnight, or for 6–8 hours. This makes the job of blending them easier.

Drain the nuts, then put them in a blender with 600ml fresh cold water. Blitz on the highest speed for at least 30 seconds until the mixture looks thick and creamy and the nuts are broken down to a coarse meal.

Line a large, fine sieve with a large piece of muslin and place it over a bowl. Tip the almond and water mix into the lined sieve. Let this drain for a few minutes, stirring the mixture in the sieve a few times to encourage the liquid to drain through. Then bring up the edges of the muslin around the nut pulp and squeeze, which will press the thicker liquid out. The most efficient way to do this is to twist the ends of the muslin together, forcing the liquor down and out.

If the finished almond milk seems too thick and creamy, just add a little more water. For a sweetened milk, whisk in the vanilla and honey or syrup.

Refrigerate and use within 4 days, stirring well before use.

USING YOUR ALMOND MILK
» Serve it chilled, sweetened or unsweetened, as a refreshing drink
» Pour on muesli, cereal or porridge
» Add to fruit smoothies or shakes
» Use in recipes – it's great in drop scones (see page 45) or try my almond milk rice pudding (on page 364)
» You can use the squeezed-out nut pulp in recipes too, such as the almond and cucumber soup on page 102

VARIATION
You can make cashew milk using exactly the same method.

Polenta porridge with honey

This is my own version of Jamaican cornmeal porridge. The Caribbean dish often includes a lot of sugar or condensed milk, but I prefer to leave the basic porridge unsweetened and trickle it instead with a generous amount of my favourite honey before I tuck in. It's a very quick, filling breakfast, perfect on a cold morning.

Serves 2

200ml coconut milk

A pinch of salt (optional)

75g quick-cook polenta

TO SERVE

Honey

Freshly grated nutmeg and/or sliced banana (optional)

Combine the coconut milk and 300ml water in a pan. Bring gently to a simmer, stirring to amalgamate the two liquids (if your coconut milk has separated into liquid and solid layers, keep stirring until it is smooth).

When the coconut liquid is simmering, add a pinch of salt if you like, then pour in the polenta. Whisk until smooth, then keep whisking as the porridge cooks and thickens. It should take barely a minute to reach a thick but still pourable porridge consistency. Take it straight off the heat at that point, or it will start to thicken too much.

Pour the hot porridge into two bowls straight away. You can add a splash more coconut milk now, if you like, to cool and thin the porridge a little. Add a generous swirl of honey, grate a little nutmeg over the top and/or add some sliced banana if you wish, and eat straight away. If you leave the porridge for long, it will start to thicken and set but you can 'bring it back' by stirring in some more water and/or coconut milk and reheating gently.

VARIATION

Gently spiced version Stir ½ teaspoon ground cinnamon or 1 teaspoon vanilla extract into the polenta as it cooks.

Apple and raisin porridge

(V) Based on classic, oatmeal porridge but using apple juice rather than milk, this is tender and softly sweet. Put the oatmeal and raisins to soak the night before and the porridge takes minutes to cook in the morning.

Serves 2

125g pinhead oatmeal

50g raisins or sultanas

150ml cloudy apple juice
(i.e. not from concentrate)

A pinch of salt (optional)

TO FINISH

A little honey or soft light brown sugar

Ground cinnamon (optional)

Combine the oatmeal and raisins in a bowl or a saucepan, pour over the apple juice and 350ml water, stir well and leave to soak in a cool place (the fridge is fine) overnight.

When you're ready for breakfast, tip the oats and their soaking liquid into a saucepan (if they're not in one already) and add a pinch of salt, if you like. Put over a medium heat and bring slowly to a simmer, stirring often.

When it is simmering, turn the heat down low and let the porridge pop and sputter gently for 5–8 minutes, stirring often, until creamy-textured and thick. Add a splash of hot water from the kettle if it gets too thick. The oat groats should be just tender but still with plenty of nutty texture.

Spoon the porridge into bowls. Top with a little honey or sugar and finish, if you like, with a fine dusting of cinnamon.

Two seasonal smoothies
A fruit-packed smoothie is a light and somehow cheerful way to start the day. These recipes celebrate two of our finest fruits, rhubarb and plums, which I think are both very much under-used as smoothie ingredients.

Rhubarb and orange

Pre-cook the rhubarb for this tangy smoothie the night before and pop it in the fridge, ready to blitz up the following morning. Rhubarb is naturally acidic, so this requires a little sweetening but don't go mad – the tartness makes this drink very refreshing.

Serves 1

200g rhubarb

Juice of 1 medium-large orange (about 100ml)

A little honey or sugar (about 1–2 teaspoons), to taste

A pinch of ground ginger (optional)

Cut the rhubarb into roughly 1cm slices. Put in a smallish pan with 1 tablespoon water over a medium heat. When the water starts to bubble, cover and turn the heat down low. Let the rhubarb simmer in its juices, adding a tiny splash more water only if you need to, for about 10 minutes, stirring often to encourage it to break down. When it is reduced to a purée, take it off the heat. Transfer to a bowl, allow to cool, then chill in the fridge.

Tip the chilled rhubarb purée into a blender, add the orange juice and blitz to a smooth, thin purée. Add honey or sugar to taste, and a pinch of ground ginger if you like, purée again to mix well then serve straight away.

Plum and vanilla

Plums give this drink a wonderful, deep, sweet-tart flavour. Chill both the fruit and almond milk well before you start.

Serves 1

200g ripe plums (3–4 medium ones)

100ml unsweetened almond milk (bought or home-made, page 30)

1 teaspoon vanilla extract

Halve and stone the plums and roughly chop the flesh. Put into a blender, add the nut milk and vanilla and blitz thoroughly for about a minute. Unless you're using a high-powered blender, the smoothie will remain slightly textured and gorgeously plum-flecked. You could add a whisper of honey or sugar, but I doubt you'll need it. Drink straight away.

Three tropical smoothies

A little coconut milk is all you need to turn a blender full of fruit into a thick and creamy – but dairy-free – smoothie. This trio of smoothies makes the most of tropical fruits; they're a great option during our colder months when native berries are out of season. You can use almond milk (bought or home-made, see page 30) instead of the coconut. For a nicely chilled smoothie, refrigerate the fruit the night before, or use a little ice.

Honey piña colada

Serves 1

175g prepared ripe pineapple flesh (about ¼ medium pineapple, skin and core removed), cut into chunks

3 tablespoons coconut milk

2–3 ice cubes or a small handful of crushed ice (optional)

Honey, to taste

Put all the ingredients except the honey in a blender and blend until smooth. Add a little very cold water if the smoothie seems too thick.

Taste and add a little honey until sweetened to your liking, or serve topped with a cheeky trickle of honey. Drink straight away.

Kiwi and banana

The kiwi seeds give this a slightly peppery kick.

Serves 1

2 large, ripe kiwi fruit

½ large, ripe banana

3 tablespoons coconut milk

2–3 ice cubes or a small handful of crushed ice (optional)

A little honey or sugar, to taste (optional)

If your kiwis are very ripe, halve them and scoop the flesh out of the skins with a teaspoon. With slightly firmer fruit, slice off the top and bottom then place them on a board and slice off the skin with a sharp knife. Roughly chop the flesh.

Put the kiwi flesh in a blender with the banana, coconut milk and ice, if using. Blitz until smooth, adding a little cold water if required. Kiwi fruit are naturally sharp and I like this zingy blend just as it is. But if it's too tart for you, add a little honey or sugar. Drink straight away.

Mango and lime

I sometimes add banana to this for a particularly rich and sweet result.

Serves 1

1 large, ripe mango (about 350g), skin and stone removed, flesh cut into chunks

3 tablespoons coconut milk

½ ripe banana (optional)

Juice of 1 large lime

2–3 ice cubes or a small handful of crushed ice (optional)

Put all the ingredients into a blender and blend until smooth. Add a little very cold water or extra lime juice if it seems very thick. Serve straight away.

Two breakfast thickies

If you want to make a fruit smoothie extra satisfying, try chucking in a handful of porridge oats to create a 'thickie'. These are my current favourite examples of the genre. I think they're always nicest when cold, so pre-chill the fruit if you can.

Raspberry and orange

Serves 1

2 tablespoons porridge oats

Juice of 1 orange

100g raspberries

½ large, ripe banana, broken into chunks

2–3 ice cubes or a small handful of crushed ice

A dash of vanilla extract (optional)

Put all the ingredients into a blender and blend on a high speed for about 30 seconds or until you have a smooth drink. Add a little water if it seems excessively thick. Serve straight away.

Apple and banana

Serves 1

2 tablespoons porridge oats

1 ripe, medium banana (about 150g), broken into chunks

½ medium eating apple, peeled, cored and grated or chopped

2–3 ice cubes or a small handful of crushed ice

A pinch of ground cinnamon (optional)

Put the oats, banana, apple, ice and 50ml cold water into a blender. If you don't have any ice, just use 80–100ml very cold water. Blend on a high speed for about 30 seconds or until you have a smooth drink. Add a little more water if it seems excessively thick. Stir in a pinch of ground cinnamon if you like – or dust it on top before drinking. Serve straight away.

VARIATION

Straight banana Simply leave out the apple and sharpen to taste with a little orange or lemon juice.

Pumpkin seed drop scones

I love the crunch of seeds in these delicious breakfast pancakes. Eat them, hot from the pan, with a dollop of marmalade, or a trickle of maple syrup or honey. Add a few strips of crisp-fried bacon for a brunchy treat. If you are avoiding gluten completely, make sure you choose a buckwheat flour that's labelled gluten-free (see page 397).

Makes about 20

250g buckwheat flour

2 teaspoons baking powder

A pinch of salt

250ml unsweetened almond milk (bought or home-made, page 30), or oat milk

2 large eggs

30ml rapeseed or sunflower oil, plus extra for frying

50g honey

50g pumpkin seeds

Put the flour, baking powder and salt into a bowl and combine them with a whisk.

Measure the almond or oat milk into a jug. Add the eggs, oil and honey and whisk together thoroughly so the honey dissolves.

Make a well in the centre of the dry ingredients and slowly pour in the dairy-free milk mixture, whisking as you go. Keep whisking until you have a smooth batter. It should have a slightly gloopy consistency that will pour thickly but easily from a ladle. (If it seems unmanageably thick, add a little water – if very thin, a little more flour.) Stir in the pumpkin seeds.

Place a non-stick frying pan over a medium heat and brush with oil. When hot, drop in puddles of the batter with a ladle, making each one 6–7cm across – you should get 4 or 5 in the pan at a time. Cook for about 1½ minutes until the pancakes start to rise and bubbles are showing on the surface. Flip over and cook for another 1–2 minutes until golden brown on both sides and cooked through. Repeat with the remaining batter, brushing the pan with a little more oil as you go.

Serve the hot pancakes straight away with marmalade, maple or agave syrup, jam or fresh fruit. Alternatively, dish them up with egg and bacon as an alternative to bread or toast.

VARIATIONS

Plain buckwheat drop scones If you don't have any seeds to hand, this recipe makes simple and delicious plain breakfast pancakes.

Buckwheat blinis Leave out the seeds and honey. Add a splash of water to the batter to bring it to the consistency described above, then cook smaller spoonfuls – forming pancakes about 4cm across. Leave to cool before serving topped with smoked fish and a smear of horseradish, or smoked mackerel tartare (page 192).

Poppy seed oatcakes

A variation on a classic oatcake I've been making for years, these are nutty-tasting and delectably crisp – a great alternative to toast. I've used a favourite seedy mix, but you can put in any seeds you fancy, or leave them out altogether to get back to the classic.

Makes about 24

150g medium oatmeal

150g porridge oats (not jumbo oats)

1 tablespoon ground flaxseed

1 tablespoon poppy seeds

1 tablespoon sunflower or pumpkin seeds

½ teaspoon fine salt

75ml rapeseed or sunflower oil

Preheat the oven to 180°C/Gas 4 and line two baking trays with baking parchment.

Put all the dry ingredients into a bowl and mix them well. Make a well in the centre, pour in the oil and mix well so that it coats all the dry ingredients. Add 100ml just-boiled water and stir well, then add a little more hot water, as needed – up to 50ml more – to bring the mix together into a sticky but firm dough. Form it into a ball in the bowl and leave to rest for 5–10 minutes.

Slice the dough in half. Roll out one half between two sheets of baking parchment until 3–4mm thick. Peel off the top sheet, mark the dough into roughly 8cm squares, then slice diagonally across each square to form triangular oatcakes. Repeat with the second piece of dough and re-roll the off-cuts to get more oatcakes.

Transfer the oatcakes to the prepared baking trays. Bake for about 25 minutes (start checking at 20), until very lightly coloured. Transfer to a wire rack and leave to cool. They'll keep in an airtight container for a week.

TOPPING SUGGESTIONS
» A smear of pale, fudgy, set honey
» A little mashed ripe avocado, seasoned with salt and pepper and perhaps a trickle of rapeseed oil
» Marmite topped with chopped boiled egg
» Peanut butter and a few slices of banana
» A spoonful of jam
» Hummus and some quartered cherry tomatoes
» A few flakes of smoked mackerel

Morning tea slice

This scrumptious raw recipe comes from my friend and former River Cottage colleague Nonie Dwyer and the title sums it up nicely – these fruity bars are great with your morning cuppa as an effort-free but energy-packed breakfast or elevenses. Flakes of millet – a nutritious, gluten-free grain, easy to find in health food shops – help to bind these sweet, tasty slabs together.

Makes 10 bars

100g millet flakes

75g whole, skin-on almonds

175g unsulphured dried apricots

200g pitted dates, chopped

100g dried apples

50g raisins

2 dried figs, tough stem ends snipped off

Freshly grated nutmeg (optional)

¼–½ teaspoon ground cinnamon (optional)

Finely grated zest of 1 orange and juice of about ½ the fruit

Line a 19–20cm square tin or dish with cling film or baking parchment.

Put all the ingredients, except the orange juice, into the bowl of a food processor. Pulse until well chopped and combined, stopping once or twice to scrape down the sides so the blades can process all the ingredients. Slowly add the orange juice, pulsing the mixture until it comes together into a very stiff, chunky paste.

Press the mixture firmly into the prepared dish in an even layer, smoothing over the top. Refrigerate for 3–4 hours or, preferably, overnight, then slice into bars. Store in the fridge. These bars will keep happily for at least a couple of weeks.

Fruity soda bread

This is a lighter, more breakfasty soda bread than the one on page 65 – I do love playing with such a simple, gratifying recipe. You can start throwing it together about an hour before you want to eat it. Or you can knock it up the night before the morning after.

Serves 5–6

100g brown rice flour, plus extra to dust

150g light rye flour

A pinch of salt

1½ teaspoons bicarbonate of soda

75g raisins or sultanas

75g unsulphured dried apricots, roughly chopped (or chopped prunes)

Finely grated zest and juice of 1 orange

About 100ml apple juice

50g honey

1 tablespoon rapeseed or sunflower oil

Preheat the oven to 200°C/Gas 6. Line a baking tray with baking parchment.

In a large bowl, thoroughly combine the flours, salt and bicarbonate of soda (sifting them together is a good idea – but giving them a quick whisk does the job too). Stir in the dried fruit and orange zest.

Tip the orange juice into a measuring jug and make it up to 175ml with apple juice. Add the honey and oil to the juice and whisk so that the honey dissolves.

Pour the wet ingredients into the dry and mix together quickly but thoroughly to form a sticky dough.

Scrape the dough on to a floured surface and form into a thick sausage shape (it is a very soft dough, so flour your hands well). Transfer to the baking tray. Dust with a little more rye flour then cut 4 or 5 deep slashes in the top at an angle, at least halfway through the bread. Bake for about 30 minutes, until a rich brown all over.

Transfer to a wire rack to cool or leave on the baking sheet and break along the cuts into 5 or 6 pieces while still warm and crumbly. Trickle with honey, spread with nut butter, dollop with jam or eat just as it comes. It's also delicious with a little extra virgin rapeseed or olive oil trickled over it.

This soda bread will keep for up to 3 days; it's particularly good toasted towards the end of this life-span. You can also freeze it.

Potato cakes

Crisp and golden on the outside and fluffy in the middle, these are a brilliant way to use up leftover mashed potato – although you may find yourself popping a couple of extra spuds in the oven of an evening, just so you can make these the next day. Two large baking potatoes yield enough for this recipe.

Serves 4

250g cold, cooked potato, mashed

2 teaspoons baking powder

20g white rice flour

1 egg yolk

1 tablespoon rapeseed or sunflower oil, plus a little extra for cooking

Sea salt and freshly ground black pepper

Chives, to finish (optional)

Put the cooked mashed potato into a mixing bowl and sift the baking powder and rice flour over the top. If the mash is not already seasoned, add a couple of good pinches of salt and a little pepper. Work these dry ingredients into the potato, then stir in the egg yolk and oil. Mix until all the ingredients are evenly distributed. You may find it helpful to knead the mixture lightly with your hands.

Heat a large, non-stick frying pan over a medium heat. Once hot, add a few drops of oil and tilt or wipe around the pan to get an even film. Divide the potato mix into four portions. Drop each portion into the pan in a little mound then flatten them with the spatula into patties 1–2cm deep. Let them cook for 3–4 minutes or until a golden brown crust has formed on the base.

Gently turn the potato cakes over and cook them for a further 3–4 minutes. If at any point they look like they are browning too quickly, lower the heat. They are ready when they are richly golden on each side, cooked through and fluffy in the centre.

Serve straight away, just as they are or with a generous scattering of chives, or as part of a cooked breakfast (I love them with scrambled eggs).

Scrambled eggs with kippers

Kippers are a fantastic British ingredient and to my mind, even more wonderful with rich, tender eggs than the more conventional – but much less sustainable – smoked salmon.

Serves 2

1 tablespoon rapeseed or sunflower oil

2 kipper fillets

4 eggs, beaten

2–3 spring onions, thinly sliced

Leaves from a few sprigs of parsley, chopped (optional)

Salt and freshly ground black pepper

Rye toast, to serve

Heat the oil in a frying pan over a medium-low heat. Add the kipper fillets and cook them gently for 2–3 minutes on each side, until just done. Remove from the heat and transfer the kippers to a plate. Give them a minute to cool a little, then flake the cooked flesh away from the skin in chunks.

Return the frying pan to a low heat with the kippery oil still in it. Add the beaten eggs to the pan. Cook the eggs very gently, stirring intermittently, for 4–5 minutes or until beginning to scramble. When they're thickened but still looking slightly 'wet' (they will continue to cook off the heat), take them off the heat and gently stir in the kipper flakes, spring onions and chopped parsley, if you like.

Season the scrambled eggs with pepper (they'll probably have enough salt already from the kippers), spoon on to rye toast and serve straight away.

Masala omelette

We're not generally accustomed to spicy foods for breakfast in this country, but for many other cultures it's par for the course. Many millions of Indians eat a masala omelette every day – they're excellent with a cup of tea. Raise the fire factor by upping the amount of green chilli (rather than adding more curry powder). I have recently graduated to a whole (small) green chilli per omelette, seeds and all.

Serves 1

2 large eggs

½ teaspoon curry powder

¼–1 small, hot red or green chilli (or a pinch of dried chilli flakes), to taste

½ medium or 2 cherry tomatoes (about 25g), chopped

1–2 spring onions, sliced, or ½ small onion, finely chopped

Rapeseed or sunflower oil, for cooking

Sea salt and freshly ground black pepper

TO SERVE

A few coriander leaves (optional)

Mango chutney (optional)

Break the eggs into a bowl or jug, add a pinch of salt, a good grinding of pepper and the curry powder and beat together.

Slice the chilli finely, across, into little discs – including the seeds. Add as much as you dare to the beaten egg (or add the chilli flakes), then add the chopped tomato and onion and stir them all in.

Heat a medium (20–22cm) non-stick frying pan over a medium heat and add a trickle of oil. When the oil is hot, pour in the egg mixture. Tilt and swirl the pan a little to spread the egg into a thin omelette. After 15–20 seconds, when the base of the omelette has set, push the edges into the middle in one or two places, so the liquid egg runs back out to fill the spaces. Keep pushing the omelette around a bit, until there's not enough runny egg left to do this again (i.e. the omelette is nearly cooked through but still a bit sticky on the top).

Fold one side of the omelette one-third across and then do the same with the other side, so your omelette becomes a rectangle in the middle of the pan. (This is the most popular way to flip an omelette in India and I have adopted it, but of course you can just fold it in half.)

Serve straight away, scattered with coriander leaves, if you like, and/or with a dollop of mango chutney.

Sweet potato rosti

These quick and easy potato cakes make a sustaining breakfast (and I like nibbling on any leftovers, cold, later in the day). You can serve the rosti just as they come or add accompaniments (see below).

Serves 2–3

1 fairly large orange sweet potato (about 250g)

½ small onion or 1 banana shallot, chopped

1 large egg, beaten

Rapeseed or sunflower oil, for frying

Sea salt and freshly ground black pepper

Peel the potato and grate it coarsely into a bowl. Add the onion, egg, a good pinch of salt and some black pepper and mix well.

Heat a thin layer of oil in a non-stick frying pan over a medium heat. Spoon the potato mix into the pan in four large piles, or six smaller ones (cook the rosti in two batches if your pan is small), flattening the piles out with a spatula to form round, shallow cakes. You may find a little liquid is released by the raw potato mix in the bowl – don't worry about this, just try to leave it in the bowl as you spoon the potato into the pan.

Cook the rosti over a medium heat for about 4 minutes until a golden brown crust has formed on the base, then carefully turn them over and cook for another 4 minutes or so, until golden brown and steaming. The potato should be tender in the middle.

Transfer to warmed plates, sprinkle with black pepper, and a little more salt if you like, and serve.

VARIATIONS

Make more of it A poached egg is delicious on top of these rosti, and makes them into a really filling breakfast – a few crisp rashers of bacon won't go amiss either. I also like them with a few tomatoes – just added to the frying pan for the last few minutes of the rosti cooking time, then seasoned with salt and pepper.

Chilli and garlic rosti Add a fresh red or green chilli, deseeded and finely chopped, and a chopped garlic clove, to the potato and onion mix. These distinctly piquant rosti are good for lunch or supper with sautéed mushrooms or a piece of simply cooked fish.

Baking love, not war

WE'RE HUNG UP ON the idea of yeast-risen, wheat-flour breads, because that's what dominates the market to the exclusion of almost all else. But taking a break from wheat can open your eyes to a whole new raft of bready textures and floury flavours.

Better still, wheat-free breads are usually much quicker and easier to make – there's no kneading required to develop gluten, and no rising time either. You'll see that many of the recipes in this chapter come together very quickly in a bowl and are baked and ready in less than half an hour. Sometimes, when the 'baking' is done the old-fashioned way on a hot pan or griddle, it's a matter of minutes.

In my fave new world of non-wheat baking, I've borrowed and adapted ideas from the cuisines of Ireland, Scotland, India, Mexico, America, Italy, France and Scandinavia. You'll find pancakes and flatbreads, biscuits and soda breads, crisp grissini and chewy, seedy slabs – all ready to make themselves useful at breakfast, lunch, supper and snack time.

My recipes here do not attempt to mimic the texture of conventional 'bread' – in this respect gluten-free or low-gluten flours will always come up short. I'd rather invite you to note and enjoy the *differences* in flavour and texture – while appreciating that they can fulfil the same culinary functions we demand of regular bread. They can be accompaniments to a soup, salad, pâté or hummus, they can be dipped, dunked or spread. Some of them can be rolled or folded around a filling to create a form of sandwich or wrap – and nearly all of them can be enjoyed pretty much as they come, perhaps trickled with a little oil.

I've loved experimenting with a range of non-wheat flours, all of which are much more characterful than standard white wheat flour. Rye is a favourite, with its nutty, toasty tang. It does contain some gluten, so is particularly useful if you want a dough to rise and hold its shape – as in my seedy rye soda bread (page 65) – or in biscuits like my rye-gestives (page 87) where it helps the mix hold together.

Buckwheat flour (gluten-free as long as it is uncontaminated) is now a valuable standby for me too: it has a full, robust flavour and makes very good flatbreads (page 72) and pancakes (page 77). And when I want moisture and tenderness in a bread or pancake, I turn to high-protein, pulse-based flours such as chickpea (aka gram flour).

Sometimes combining different flours gives the best results. A blend of dry, starchy rice flour with nutty-tasting rye and rich, proteinaceous chickpea flour works wonders in my savoury pan scones (page 70), for instance. These recipes feature some tried and trusted flour combinations, which you can make up in bulk and keep standing by for the recipes that you like the most.

You may also want to try using some proprietary gluten-free flour blends – they'll often work well in place of the blends I've suggested. The Dove's Farm organic range is the best I've come across.

You may not think of yourself as having baker's hands, but all these recipes are designed to make you think again. Even without wheat – especially without wheat – you can be more self-sufficient in your daily bread than you ever thought possible.

Seedy rye soda bread

Quick to make and full of nutty flavours, this works well in both savoury and sweet contexts. Serve alongside soups and salads, with a trickle of rapeseed or olive oil. Or enjoy with honey, jam or marmalade for breakfast, elevenses and tea. After a couple of days in the bread bin, you can make breadcrumbs and croûtons with it too. Light rye flour can be sourced from health food shops, or online. Play fast and loose with the seeds and by all means add dried fruit too if you wish.

Makes 1 small loaf

20g sunflower seeds

20g sesame seeds

20g poppy seeds

20g linseeds (flaxseed)

250g light rye flour, plus extra to dust

½ teaspoon salt

1½ teaspoons bicarbonate of soda

100ml apple juice

40g honey

1 tablespoon rapeseed or sunflower oil

Preheat the oven to 200°C/Gas 6. Line a baking tray with baking parchment.

Combine the seeds then set aside about 1 teaspoonful of them for finishing the loaf. In a large bowl, thoroughly combine the remaining seeds with the flour, salt and bicarbonate of soda.

In a jug, combine the apple juice, 100ml water, the honey and oil. Stir well so that the honey dissolves. Pour into the dry ingredients and mix quickly but thoroughly to form a sticky dough.

Scrape the dough on to a floured surface and form into a round (it is a very soft dough, so flour your hands well). Transfer to the baking tray. Sprinkle with the reserved seeds, then dust the dough with a little more rye flour. Cut a deep cross in the dough, going at least halfway down into it. Bake for about 30 minutes, until a rich brown all over.

Transfer the loaf to a wire rack and tuck in as soon as it's cool (or even when it's not quite cool). This will keep well for up to 3 days.

See also my fruity soda bread on page 51.

Carrot cornbread

A chunk of moist, golden cornbread, still warm from the oven, is a great partner to soup or a hearty salad. I've added grated carrot, which keeps the cornbread nice and tender, and contributes a delicious hint of sweetness.

Makes 9–12 pieces

300g fine cornmeal

3 teaspoons baking powder

1 teaspoon salt

2 large eggs

300ml unsweetened almond milk (bought or home-made, page 30)

2 tablespoons rapeseed or sunflower oil, plus extra for greasing

300g carrots, peeled and coarsely grated

Preheat the oven to 190°C/Gas 5. Liberally grease a baking dish, about 20cm square.

Put the cornmeal, baking powder and salt into a large bowl and mix together.

Combine the eggs, almond milk and oil thoroughly, then beat this liquid into the cornmeal to form a fairly loose batter. Stir in the grated carrots.

Pour the batter into the prepared dish and give it a little shake to spread it out evenly. Bake for about 35 minutes until risen and lightly coloured. Leave to cool slightly before slicing into squares. Eat warm or leave to cool completely.

VARIATIONS

Root around This veg-enhanced cornbread can take you right through the year – just swap in other juicy grated veg for the carrot, depending on what's in season. Try autumnal parsnip or squash, summery courgette or, for a delightfully pink cornbread, grated raw beetroot.

Sweeten it up Add a little honey or soft light brown sugar to the batter (around 25g will do it) and a sprinkling of raisins or other dried fruit and you have yourself a delicious, teatime cornbread. Throw in a few seeds too – such as pumpkin, sunflower or linseeds.

Buckwheat and almond scones

These hearty unsweetened scones hit the spot when you need a chunky, bready accompaniment to soup or cold cuts. The sweetened fruity variation (below) makes a cracking tea break treat.

Makes 4 large scones

100g ground almonds

100g buckwheat flour, plus extra to dust

100g white rice flour

2 teaspoons baking powder

¼ teaspoon fine salt

100ml unsweetened almond milk (bought or home-made, page 30), or oat milk

1 large egg

A trickle of extra virgin hempseed or rapeseed oil, to serve

Preheat the oven to 200°C/Gas 6. Line a baking tray with baking parchment.

In a bowl, thoroughly combine the ground almonds, flours, baking powder and salt.

In a jug, beat together the almond milk, 100ml water and the egg.

Pour the wet ingredients into the dry and mix thoroughly to a wet, sticky dough.

Scrape the dough out on to a well floured surface and sprinkle with more buckwheat (or rice) flour. Pat it into a round, 13–14cm in diameter and 3–4cm high. Cut into quarters and carefully transfer each piece to the baking tray. Bake for 30 minutes until risen and lightly coloured.

Transfer to a wire rack and leave to cool completely. Slice in half and trickle with extra virgin oil. Serve with soup, or hummus, pâté or cold meats.

VARIATION

Fruit tea scones Replace the water with more almond or oat milk (i.e. 200ml altogether) and whisk a dessertspoon of honey, or soft light brown sugar into the wet ingredients. Add 50g raisins, sultanas or chopped dried apricots, or a mixture, to the dry ingredients, along with 50g chopped walnuts or pecans if you like, then proceed as above.

Savoury pan scones

These full-flavoured savoury drop scones, made with a very useful flour blend, are a tender, light-textured alternative to a tortilla. Rustled up in minutes, they are best served straight from the pan – with soups, salads, dips and pâtés.

Makes 15–20

100g dark rye flour

100g brown rice flour

100g soya or gram (chickpea) flour

1½ teaspoons baking powder

A pinch of salt

1 teaspoon soft light brown sugar or honey (optional)

1 large egg

1 tablespoon rapeseed or sunflower oil, plus a few drops for greasing the pan

Extra virgin hempseed or rapeseed oil, to finish (optional)

Whisk the three flours together with the baking powder and salt, and the sugar, if using. (If you're using honey, don't add it at this stage.)

In another bowl or a jug, whisk together the egg, oil and 300ml water, and the honey, if using. Make a well in the middle of the flour mix and add the wet ingredients, a third at a time, whisking as you go. Add more water as necessary to create a smooth batter, like very thick paint, that drops obligingly off a spoon.

Heat a large frying pan or pancake pan over a medium heat. Grease with a few drops of oil. Drop spoonfuls of the mixture into the pan. After about 80–90 seconds, when they have risen a little and the bases have got some colour, flip them and cook for a further minute, so they are nicely browned on both sides.

Serve plain, or lightly trickled with extra virgin oil.

VARIATIONS

With dill and black pepper Give these simple scones an aromatic lift by adding a good grinding of black pepper and 2 tablespoons chopped dill to the dry ingredients before adding the liquid. These are delicious served with smoked fish and/or scrambled eggs.

Blini-style pan scones You can also make mini versions using just a teaspoonful of the mixture for each one. These are ideal as a base for all kinds of canapés.

Rye chapatis

Indian chapatis are usually made with wheat flour, so this version is not authentic. It is, however, easy, tasty and just what I want with a saucy curry or even a chunky soup. To make the world's second most eaten flatbread – the Mexican tortilla – see below.

Makes 8

250g light or dark rye flour, plus extra to dust

½ teaspoon salt

1 tablespoon rapeseed or sunflower oil

Combine the flour and salt in a bowl. Add the oil and about 125ml water. Mix together, then work in a little more water, just a few drops at a time, until you have a firm, pliable dough with a texture a little like Play-Doh. Knead for a minute or so until smooth. You can start cooking the chapatis straight away but they will be even better if you cover the dough and leave it to rest in the fridge for 15–30 minutes.

When you are ready to cook, divide the dough into 8 pieces and roll each into a ball. Set a heavy-based frying pan over a high heat. On a lightly rye-floured surface, flatten out one of the balls of dough (with the base of a plate or the palm of your hand), then use a rolling pin to roll it into a disc, about 15cm in diameter and 2mm thick.

When the pan is really hot, drop in the chapati. Cook for about 30–40 seconds. Flip the chapati over (if it's not mottled with a few dark spots the pan's not hot enough). Cook for another 50 seconds or so until the second side is lightly browned too. Flip once more and finish for 30 seconds or so. They may puff up a bit (more likely if using light rye flour).

Wrap the chapati loosely in a tea towel to keep it warm, then repeat with the remaining dough, stacking all the cooked chapatis inside the folded tea towel. (This keeps them warm, soft and pliable.) Eat the chapatis straight away, ideally while still warm. As well as serving with curries, soups and other saucy dishes, they're also delicious for breakfast – trickled with a little rapeseed oil and runny honey, then eaten folded.

VARIATIONS

Buckwheat chapatis Use gluten-free buckwheat flour in place of the rye, for a gluten-free chapati. These can be cooked as above, but are even better if you leave the dough, covered, in the fridge for a little while – up to 8 hours – before cooking.

Cornmeal tortillas Use 250g masa harina (see page 399) instead of the rye flour. It's much more absorbent so you'll need 350ml hand-hot water (half cold and half just-boiled from the kettle), plus 1 tablespoon oil and a pinch of salt. Knead to a smooth, firm dough, adding a little more water if it seems dry. Cover with cling film and rest for 15 minutes. Divide into 8 pieces and roll out as above (or a little thinner) – or use a tortilla press if you have one. Cook as above, until barely coloured, stacking them in a folded tea-towel as you go. They're great with a chilli, stew or curry, or my spiced beef with bashed beans (page 234). Tortillas that have gone cold can be reheated quickly in a dry frying pan.

Socca

Also known as farinata, this is a very simple chickpea-flour pancake – served as street food in Nice and in towns along the Ligurian coast. Cooked hot and fast on a giant griddle, it's devoured straight away, golden and steaming, dressed liberally with extra virgin oil. That's how I like it at home too – on a smaller scale. It's also very good served with stews or curries, such as the lamb cashew curry on page 256.

Serves 6 as a side dish

200g gram (chickpea) flour

¼ teaspoon fine salt, plus extra to serve

1 tablespoon extra virgin rapeseed oil, plus extra for frying and serving

Thyme leaves or chopped parsley, to serve

Put the flour into a large bowl and add the salt. Gradually pour in 400ml water, whisking as you go, until you have a smooth batter. Whisk in the oil. The batter should have a consistency somewhere between single and double cream. Leave it to stand for at least 10 minutes, or an hour or so if you can; this allows the flour to absorb the water and form a silky smooth batter. After resting, whisk again to get rid of any lumps.

Heat a large, non-stick frying pan over a medium-high heat. Add about ½ tablespoon oil and let it get nice and hot. Now scoop up a large ladleful of the batter and pour it into the centre of the hot pan. The batter should spread outwards of its own accord but you can give it a cursory swirl to encourage it into an even circle. Cook over a brisk heat for about 2 minutes, until the underside of the pancake is golden brown. If it needs a bit longer, increase the heat a little. Loosen the pancake with a spatula, then flip it over and cook for another 2 minutes or so, until patched with golden brown on the other side. Transfer to a plate and sprinkle with a pinch of salt.

Repeat with the remaining batter, adding a little more oil to the pan as you go, and stirring the batter well before you ladle it into the pan. You should get about 5 pancakes – but they're nicest served torn into rough pieces so the precise number doesn't matter.

Eat the pancakes straight away or at least while still warm (keep them warm in a low oven if necessary). Trickle them with more extra virgin oil – and scatter with some herbs if you like – or leave them plain if you're eating with a stew or curry.

VARIATIONS

Flavoured socca To enjoy socca on their own, rather than as an accompaniment, try adding some aromatic flavours. You could splash on some garlic-and-chilli infused oil (see page 301) before serving. Alternatively, stir finely chopped herbs, chillies or garlic, or a couple of spoonfuls of pesto, into the batter before frying. (For my latest pestos see pages 275–8.)

Buckwheat galettes

These are particularly satisfying, nutty-tasting crêpes, traditional in northern France. They are delicious with a host of savoury fillings – as well as a few sweet ones. See below for some suggestions on both counts. In fact there's no reason not to make these your go-to pancakes whatever the occasion, be it Shrove Tuesday or a weekend breakfast. As with conventional crêpes, the first one often doesn't come out of the pan quite right but don't worry – it will still taste great.

Makes 4–5 large galettes

125g buckwheat flour

¼ teaspoon fine salt

1 large egg

Rapeseed or sunflower oil, for frying

Put the flour and salt into a large bowl. Roughly whisk the egg together with 300ml water, then whisk the liquid into the flour, working it in gradually, until you have a smooth, thin batter. Leave it to rest for 10 minutes, then whisk again.

Heat a large, non-stick frying pan (about 28cm base measurement) over a very high heat and brush with a little oil. Pour in a large ladleful of the batter and tilt the pan quickly so it spreads out evenly. Cook for about 2 minutes, until the edges begin to curl up a bit. Loosen the edges with a palette knife or spatula, check that the base has some good patches of colour, flip it over and cook for another minute.

Transfer the galette to a warmed plate – or put in a very low oven – while you cook the rest, stirring the batter well each time before you ladle it into the pan.

Spoon some of your chosen filling along the middle of each warm galette and fold the sides over, leaving some of the filling showing at the ends.

FILLINGS FOR YOUR GALETTES

Savoury...
» Sautéed garlicky mushrooms, a fried egg and a handful of rocket
» Sliced or crumbled sausage (wheat-free), with apple sauce or fried apple slices
» Smoked fish and scrambled eggs (page 55)
» Pear and blueberries with thyme and dates (page 140)

and sweet...
» Lemon juice and sugar or honey
» Apple and prune compote (page 347) with cashew cream (page 394)
» Raspberries crushed with a little sugar
» Raspberry, date and lime salad (page 320)
» A generous spoonful of chocolate nut butter (page 392)

Spinachy wraps

These pleasingly green savoury pancakes are superb stuffed with salad and cold meat or hummus, with a smear of something piquant such as chilli sauce or a spiky chutney. They're also a brilliant vehicle for leftovers from dishes like my spiced beef with bashed beans (page 234) or parsnips, chorizo, kale and lentils (page 245).

Makes 4

150g fresh spinach, well washed, tougher stalks removed

4 medium eggs

100g gram (chickpea) flour

Rapeseed or sunflower oil, for frying

Sea salt and freshly ground black pepper

Put the spinach in a large saucepan with a little water – or just the water clinging to the leaves from washing. Cover, put over a medium-high heat and bring to a simmer. Cook for a few minutes until all the spinach has wilted, then transfer to a colander and leave to drain and cool.

When the spinach is cold, squeeze out all the liquid with your hands. Chop the spinach fairly finely.

Put the eggs in a large bowl and beat together. Beat in the gram flour until you have a smooth paste, then add the chopped spinach and a good seasoning of salt and pepper. Stir well, then add enough water (around 50–75ml) to form a loose, spinachy batter with a just-pourable texture like double cream.

Heat a large, non-stick frying pan over a medium heat and add a thin film of oil. When hot, pour one-quarter of the spinach mix into the centre of the pan. Use the back of a spoon to carefully spread out the mixture into an even disc, about 20cm in diameter. Cook gently for a couple of minutes, then use a thin-edged spatula to loosen the pancake in the pan. You should see that the wrap is set on the base but not browned. Flip over. Cook for another minute or so, just to seal the second side. Transfer to a plate to cool and repeat with the remaining mixture.

These pancakes are best eaten as soon as they are cool. Fill generously with whatever tasty bits and pieces you can get your hands on, such as shredded lettuce, olives and hard-boiled egg, or chutney or mayo (try the avocado 'mayo' on page 172) with shredded cold meat.

VARIATION

With frozen spinach These work very well with frozen whole-leaf spinach – keep a bag in the freezer and you can knock up a few wraps at any time. Use about 100g and either leave the frozen chunks to defrost slowly or, to speed things up, put them in a frying pan over a medium-low heat. Either way, squeeze out any excess liquid from the defrosted leaves, chop and add to the batter as above.

Rye and ale crispbreads

These are inspired by some delicious wafer-thin breads I cooked with René Redzepi at Noma in Copenhagen. He cooked his over a charcoal fire, which is quite hairy as you have to take them off just before they go up in flames. A hot dry pan is easier to manage. Smoky and dark, they make a scrumptious pre-dinner nibble. I've also suggested some serving companions, including a quick minty bean dip (see below).

Makes 8

250g dark rye flour,
plus extra to dust

½ teaspoon salt

180–200ml wheat-free beer
(vegan beer, if appropriate)

Combine the flour and salt in a bowl. Mix in enough beer to make a firm, pliable dough. Tip on to a floured surface and knead lightly for a few minutes. Let rest for 10 minutes.

Divide the dough in half, then into 4, 8 and finally 16 portions. Roll one into a fat sausage. On a floured surface, roll this out into a rough-edged rectangle/oval, getting it as thin as you can. Use plenty of flour and keep rolling until the dough is no more than 1mm thick (if not quite paper-thin, then envelope thin). It doesn't matter if it breaks here and there, it all adds to the charm. But if the dough isn't really thin, the crispbreads won't be crisp.

Heat a large, heavy-based frying pan over a high heat. Lay the rolled-out dough in the hot pan – you might get two in at a time. Cook for 2–3 minutes until the underside is dry and patched with brown, then flip and cook for another 2 minutes or so until that side is browned too. To ensure crispness, the breads need to be well cooked. If they curve upwards when you're cooking the second side, press them down with a spatula so as much of the dough as possible is in direct contact with the hot base of the pan.

Remove from the pan and leave to cool while you cook the rest of the crispbreads in the same way. When they have cooled and crisped up, they are ready to serve (if yours are not splinteringly crisp, a few minutes in a hot oven, at 200°C/Gas 6, will finish the job).

TRY SERVING WITH...

» Minty bean dip: into a food processor, tip a drained, rinsed 400g tin cannellini beans (or other plain tinned beans) and add a grated or crushed ½ garlic clove, 2 tablespoons roughly chopped mint, 3 tablespoons rapeseed oil, a good spritz of lemon juice and some salt and pepper. Blitz together, adding enough water to create a loose purée – probably about 3 tablespoons. Add more lemon juice, salt and/or pepper to taste
» A simple guacamole – try the one on page 234
» My smoked mackerel tartare (page 192)

VARIATIONS

Spiced crispbreads For a touch of spice, add 1 teaspoon caraway seeds to the dough for a real Scandinavian savour, or 1 teaspoon cumin seeds for a more Asian taste.

Rye grissini

Rye flour, although it contains some gluten, yields a non-elastic dough. That's a positive boon in this recipe – it makes the dough very easy to roll out into long, slender wands, which, once baked, make irresistible and eye-catching nibbles.

Makes about 30

250g light rye flour

1 teaspoon baking powder

1 teaspoon fine salt

1 tablespoon extra virgin rapeseed or olive oil

Preheat the oven to 220°C/Gas 7. Line two baking sheets with baking parchment.

Put the flour, baking powder and salt into a bowl and mix thoroughly. Add the oil, then gradually stir in about 150ml water – stop when you have a fairly stiff dough. Use your hands to briefly knead the dough until smooth.

Break off a piece of dough about the size of a cherry tomato. Roll it between your palms to form a fat sausage shape. Put this on your work surface then use both hands, palms down, to roll the fat sausage into a long, thin one, applying pressure gently from the middle outwards. Add a little flour to the work surface if you need to – but it's not a very sticky dough, so you may find that's not necessary. Each tomato-sized ball of dough should yield a breadstick about 30cm long and 7–8mm in diameter.

Transfer the breadsticks to the baking sheets as you make them, leaving some space between each one. Once a sheet is full, put it in the oven and bake for about 10 minutes, or until the grissini are lightly browned. Repeat with the remaining dough. Transfer the baked grissini to a wire rack to cool or stand them in a jug for serving.

These grissini keep best if left uncovered, as they tend to soften if stored in an airtight container. Eat them within a couple of days of baking. If they do lose their crispness, simply re-bake at 200°C/Gas 6 for about 3 minutes.

VARIATIONS

Spiced grissini Pep up the dough with some seeds: I love the allium taste of black onion seeds with rye but you could use any small seed – try poppy, sesame, caraway or linseeds. Add 1 tablespoon of your chosen seeds to the dry ingredients before mixing in the oil and water.

Linseed and rosemary crackers

Linseeds, also called flaxseed, are a rich source of omega-3 oils, as well as providing protein, fibre and iron. These crisp, salt-scattered crackers are an irresistible way to eat them. They look wonderful too, with their slightly curled-up form, and random, rough-edged shape. Serve them with dips or soups, or just leave a dish in the kitchen for opportunistic munching.

Makes about 16

50g brown linseeds (flaxseed)

30g ground linseed (ground flaxseed)

20g rice flour (brown or white)

20g buckwheat flour

1½ teaspoons ground cumin

2 teaspoons chopped rosemary

½ teaspoon fine salt

Rapeseed or sunflower oil, for oiling

½ teaspoon flaky sea salt

Preheat the oven to 170°C/Gas 3.

Place the whole linseeds in a heatproof bowl and add 100ml boiling water. Set aside for 10 minutes.

Meanwhile, combine the ground linseed, flours, cumin, rosemary and fine salt in a bowl. After their 10 minutes' soaking, add the linseeds and their water to the dry ingredients and combine into a dough. It should be quite stiff but still hold together. If it seems very dry and crumbly, add a few more drops of water.

Divide the dough in two. Brush a sheet of baking parchment well with oil, or start with a non-stick silicone sheet. Put one portion of dough on the oiled parchment, or silicone sheet. Oil a second sheet of parchment and place, oil side down, on top of the dough. Use a rolling pin to roll out the dough under the parchment. Roll it until it is very thin – only about the thickness of the linseeds themselves – in one, rough-edged sheet.

Carefully peel off the top sheet of parchment and transfer the base sheet, with the dough on it, to a baking tray. Sprinkle with half the flaky salt and bake for about 20 minutes, or until completely dry and slightly curled up. Leave to cool, then very carefully peel away from the parchment. The crackers have a tendency to stick slightly, even to well-oiled parchment (though not to a silicone sheet). Repeat with the second piece of dough.

When the crackers are cool and crisp, break them into pieces to serve. Store in an airtight container for up to 2 weeks.

VARIATIONS

Plain crackers or other flavours Leave out the cumin and rosemary for a plain cracker, or replace with other spices such as paprika, or other dry, woody herbs such as thyme.

Rye-gestives

Rye flour, containing some gluten, behaves very well in a biscuit dough. With oatmeal as well, to help bind the mixture and give it a nutty taste and texture, these are among the nicest and easiest wheat-free biscuits you'll ever make. Like all digestives they're great all rounders – equally good with a cup of tea, or with a slice of pâté or a dollop of hummus.

Makes about 18

125g light rye flour

125g fine oatmeal or oat flour

1 teaspoon baking powder

50g soft light brown sugar

¼ teaspoon fine sea salt

75g coconut oil (raw or odourless), melted

Preheat the oven to 180°C/Gas 4. Line one or two baking trays with baking parchment.

Thoroughly combine the rye flour, oatmeal or oat flour, baking powder, sugar and salt in a bowl. Pour in the melted coconut oil and stir well to combine, then add enough just-boiled water to bring the mix together in a firm but pliable dough – 2–4 tablespoons should do it. Knead the dough lightly with your hands until smooth.

Working quickly, while the dough is still warm, put it between two sheets of baking parchment and roll out to about a 4mm thickness. Stamp out rounds, using a 7cm cutter (or other size if you prefer). Transfer these to the lined tray(s); bake in two batches if necessary. You'll be able to gather the off-cuts together and re-roll them to get more biscuits – just once. After that, the dough will start to get a little crumbly, but you can still hand-shape the last remnants into rough little biscuits.

Bake for about 12 minutes – checking them after 10 – or until the biscuits are just starting to colour at the edges. Transfer to a wire rack to cool and crisp up completely. They can be stored in an airtight container.

VARIATIONS

Hardly sweet rye-gestives If you haven't any oatmeal or oat flour to hand, make a pure rye-gestive with 250g light rye flour. You can also reduce the sugar to a mere 10g – and they will still be just the sweet side of savoury.

Chocolate rye-gestives Once the biscuits are baked and cooled, melt 150g dark chocolate and dip one half of each biscuit in it – or apply the molten chocolate with a spoon. Place on a silicone mat or sheet of baking parchment and leave to set.

Ginger rye-gestives For a gingery kick, add ½ teaspoon ground ginger and 3 finely chopped balls of stem ginger to the dry ingredients before you add the coconut oil. These are particularly good finished with dark chocolate (as above).

Seedy bars with chilli and rosemary

These seedy slabs are an excellent alternative to those ubiquitous, sugary cereal bars. I've used rice malt syrup to bind the mix together without making it too sweet. If you're avoiding gluten, check the label as some rice malt syrup contains barley. The syrup is available in health food shops, as are quinoa flakes.

Makes 12

125g quinoa flakes

50ml rapeseed oil

300g pumpkin seeds

125g sunflower seeds

1 tablespoon finely chopped rosemary

¼ teaspoon salt

½–1 teaspoon dried chilli flakes, to taste

200g rice malt syrup

Preheat the oven to 170°C/Gas 3. Line a 19–20cm square baking dish with baking parchment.

Put the quinoa flakes into a large, dry frying pan over a medium heat and toast for a couple of minutes, tossing or stirring them often, until they look and smell pleasingly toasty, but only barely coloured. Tip them into a large bowl.

Put 1 teaspoon of the oil into the frying pan, add the pumpkin seeds and increase the heat a little. Cook, stirring frequently, for 3 minutes, or until the seeds are lightly coloured. Tip the pumpkin seeds into the bowl with the quinoa. Repeat the toasting process with the sunflower seeds, and, once nicely coloured, add to the bowl with the pumpkin seeds.

Add the rosemary and salt to the mixture. Now add the chilli flakes to taste – a full teaspoon gives a serious kick so maybe start with a quarter or half. Mix well.

Put the rice malt syrup and the remaining oil in a saucepan and heat gently until the mix just starts to simmer. Add to the bowl with the seeds and mix everything together well. Scrape the mixture into the lined dish, press it into an even layer and bake for 15 minutes or until just golden on top.

Allow to cool completely in the dish, then cut into bars and store in an airtight container. They keep well for several weeks.

VARIATION

Plain seed bars If the savoury spicy notes do not appeal, or you want something a bit more tea-time friendly, then leave out the chilli and rosemary.

Soup IT UP!

FOR ME, SOUPS ARE about satisfaction, pure and simple. They are a fast delivery system for energy, goodness and pleasure (and, as long as you have a stout thermos to keep them either hot or cold, you can take them anywhere too).

Achieving soup greatness is all about balance – of flavours and textures, sweetness and acidity, with a touch of creaminess and luxury when needed. All the recipes that follow – from the fresh, raw and almost instant, to the luxurious, warming and filling – adhere fiercely to these principles.

Some of them, the raw soups in particular, may almost seem like drinks – savoury smoothies. But they are always a little more than that, on account of their well-rounded seasonings and depth of flavour. They merit being savoured from a spoon, rather than glugged from a glass. If the idea of preparing raw soups appeals (and I think the gooseberry gazpacho on page 102 should seal the deal), I'd recommend investing in a high-powered blender. Although not essential, they can turn almost anything to a velvety purée at the flick of a switch. They bring a whole new meaning to the term 'instant soup'.

You'll see a few recurring techniques for enhancing flavour and enriching a soup without adding knobs of butter or spoonfuls of cream. In the absence of dairy ingredients, silkiness can, of course, be created with a dash of oil, and richness added through the use of creamed nuts or coconut milk. But in fact these qualities mostly arrive through the greater-than-the-sum-of-their parts alchemy that is the mark of good soup-making.

I have developed a few little tricks to send soups soaring up the satisfaction scale, and I'm pleased to share them with you. Blending a rice cake into the mix, for example, is an excellent and instant way to conjure up a velvety texture, without having to add potato (which invariably lengthens the cooking time and can make a soup gluey).

The run of 'roasting-tray soups' on pages 122–8 showcases another brilliant way to deepen the flavours of your soups. The caramelised corners of chunky roast roots, the crisp, savoury edges of sweet onions, fennel or celery, or the lightly charred skins of tomatoes or aubergines introduce new and intensified flavours to a soup – flavours you won't get from just boiling and blitzing. Once the veg are roasted, you simply pile them into a blender, add hot stock or water, and purée. Even a modest portion will be a tummy-filling comfort.

You'll also come across a good number of recipes that, instead of asking you to sweat vegetables, add stock, build the soup and then blitz, involve merely dropping good ingredients straight into a pan of simmering stock (or another pleasing medium such as almond milk). In just a few minutes you can bring together fresh crunchy vegetables and some delightful aromatics. Soups made like this are particularly zingy and full of lively flavours.

So if you think you've been there and done that with soups, I'm sure these recipes – so gratifyingly simple and so lovely to eat – will rekindle your cauldron and reboot your blender.

Pea and spinach soup

This is a refreshing and surprisingly filling cold soup. I can't accurately describe it as completely raw (peas are always blanched before being frozen), but I certainly think it's got a raw spirit.

Serves 3–4

400g frozen peas or petits pois

Juice of 1 lemon

½ ripe avocado, peeled and roughly chopped

2 good handfuls (75g) of spinach leaves (baby leaf or larger), well washed

½–1 green chilli, to taste, deseeded and finely chopped

Leaves from a few sprigs of mint

Sea salt and freshly ground black pepper

Extra virgin hempseed or rapeseed oil, to finish (optional)

If you are using a high-powered blender, you can add the peas pretty much straight from the freezer: just rinse them in a sieve under cold water until their frostiness has gone. If your blender is of the conventional type, put the peas in a bowl of cold water for about 20 minutes to soften them but keep them cold, then drain.

Place all the ingredients in a blender, starting with the juice of half the lemon, then adding the avocado, spinach, chilli, mint and peas. If you're using baby leaf spinach, you can just chuck it all straight into the blender; if you're using more mature leaf spinach, strip out the fibrous stalks first.

Add a decent pinch of salt and a good grinding of pepper, along with 300ml cold water, then blitz the soup until smooth. You may need to stop once or twice and give the contents a stir to help it all mix and blend.

Taste the soup and adjust the seasoning, adding more salt, pepper and lemon juice as necessary. Add a little more water if you prefer a thinner consistency. Blend again to mix well after any additions.

Serve straight away (the peas should have chilled the soup nicely) or put it into the fridge until serving, making sure you give it a stir before pouring into bowls. Finish with a swirl of extra virgin oil if you like. I really like serving this with linseed and rosemary crackers (page 85).

VARIATION

Coconutty version I sometimes use coconut water – the thin, clear liquid from inside a coconut – instead of plain water to give this soup a slightly richer, sweeter flavour. You can buy coconut water in cartons – or get it from a couple of freshly cracked coconuts (see page 154).

Raw carrot and Bramley soup

Super-fresh and light, this raw soup also has a delightful creaminess from the cashews. A high-powered blender, such as a Vitamix or Omega, makes short work of it but a decent standard blender will also do the job – as long as you give the soup a good long blitz. Chill the carrots and apple, and/or blend with a couple of ice cubes and you can serve straight from the blender.

Serves 2

200g carrots, peeled and roughly chopped, plus an extra carrot to finish

50g cashew nuts

80g Bramley apple (about ¼ large apple), peeled, cored and roughly chopped

Juice of ½ lemon, plus a few extra drops

Sea salt and freshly ground black pepper

Put the carrots, cashews, apple and lemon juice in a blender. Add enough water to barely cover the ingredients (about 350ml) and purée until smooth, giving it a really good blitz in order to get it as smooth as possible.

Taste and adjust the seasoning with salt and pepper and a little more lemon juice if you like. If the soup is a little thick you can 'let it down' with a splash more water.

Serve at once, garnished with some shaved carrot (pared with a veg peeler) tossed in lemon juice, or chill the soup lightly before serving if necessary.

Bloody beetroot soup

I love the tangy, savoury flavours of a Bloody Mary and I like playing with them in the kitchen (see also the salad on page 240). In this very quick soup, they form the perfect counterpoint to the earthy sweetness of beetroot. The soup tastes best lightly chilled but if you start with beetroot and tomato juice from the fridge, you should be good to go straight from the blender. Be aware that Worcestershire sauce may contain gluten.

Serves 4

200g cooked, skinned beetroot (vac-packed is fine, but not pickled!), roughly chopped

500ml tomato juice (from a carton or home-juiced)

2 tablespoons Worcestershire sauce

A healthy shake of Tabasco

Juice of 1 lemon

A good pinch of celery salt

Freshly ground black pepper

1–2 shots vodka (optional!)

TO SERVE

Ice cubes (optional)

Tender inner celery stalks

Lemon wedges

Put the beetroot, tomato juice, Worcestershire sauce, Tabasco, lemon juice, celery salt and some black pepper in a blender and blitz to a smooth consistency (add the vodka too, if you fancy it).

As with the best Bloody Mary cocktails, a bit of customised mixology can make all the difference. Taste the soup and tinker with the seasoning, adding more Worcestershire sauce, Tabasco, lemon, salt or pepper to suit your taste.

Pour the soup into bowls and add a few ice cubes if you like. Serve with celery stalks, lemon wedges and seasonings on the table.

VARIATION

Beetroot and horseradish soup For a creamier but no less peppy spin on this soup, leave out the Worcestershire sauce, Tabasco and celery salt, but season generously with the lemon juice and plenty of salt and pepper. Add 2–3 teaspoons grated horseradish (from a jar or fresh from the root) and 4 tablespoons cashew cream (page 394) and blitz thoroughly. Serve lightly chilled.

Waldorf soup

Fast, fresh and raw, this recipe takes the ingredients from a classic Waldorf salad (minus the mayonnaise!) and turns them into a surprisingly rich and creamy-tasting soup. Chill the celery, apples and walnuts in the fridge, and use chilled or freshly drawn cold water, and there's no need to chill the soup after making.

Serves 3–4

200g tender celery stalks, from the heart

2 small eating apples (about 200g)

50g walnuts

2 tablespoons extra virgin rapeseed oil, plus extra to serve

½ small garlic clove, grated or crushed

A squeeze of lemon juice

Sea salt and freshly ground black pepper

TO FINISH

A handful of grapes, (optional)

Saved celery leaves (optional)

Slice the tender celery stalks fairly finely and place in a blender.

Peel and core the apples, slice them and add to the blender. Add the walnuts, oil, garlic, a good squeeze of lemon, 200ml cold water, a good pinch of salt and a couple of grinds of pepper. Blitz to a creamy, pale soup. You'll need to give it a good long blitz to reduce all the ingredients to a purée, but they will get there in the end.

Taste the soup and add more salt, pepper or lemon juice as needed. If it's very thick, add a little more water. Chill lightly before serving.

Finish with a scattering of chopped celery leaves, a few sliced grapes, pips removed, if you like, and a generous extra swirl of golden rapeseed oil.

Gooseberry gazpacho

I love this recipe. The fruity acidity is coming from gooseberries rather than the traditional tomatoes, but it's everything a gazpacho should be: refreshing, cooling and full of vibrant flavours. Serve it lightly chilled on a summer's day. Pre-chill the main ingredients, and/or blend with a couple of ice cubes and you can serve straight from the blender.

Serves 4

200g gooseberries (fresh or frozen and defrosted), topped and tailed

2 medium-small cucumbers (about 700g in total), peeled, deseeded and roughly chopped

Leaves from a 50g bunch of mint

½ Romaine lettuce, roughly shredded

2 tablespoons porridge oats

¼–½ garlic clove, roughly chopped

2 ice cubes (optional)

50ml extra virgin rapeseed oil, plus extra to serve

1 teaspoon sugar

2–3 teaspoons balsamic vinegar (ideally apple balsamic)

½ teaspoon fine salt

Freshly ground black pepper

A few extra gooseberries or edible flowers, to finish

Put all the ingredients into a blender, add 50ml water and process to a purée. You'll probably have to stop a few times initially and tamp the ingredients down to get the purée going and you may need to add a little more water, particularly if you have used fresh gooseberries, to get a thick soup consistency.

Taste and add more salt, pepper, sugar or vinegar if needed. If you've used chilled gooseberries and cucumbers, the soup will already by nicely cool and ready to serve. Otherwise chill it lightly in the fridge and whisk well before ladling into bowls or cups. Give each portion a trickle more rapeseed oil. Some sliced raw gooseberries look lovely on top, or use a few edible flowers – such as borage, nasturtium or marigold petals.

VARIATION

Chilled cucumber and almond soup This is a creamier take on gazpacho – nicely garlicky, with a whisper of sweetness from the vinegar. Peel, deseed and roughly chop 2 medium cucumbers and put into a food processor or blender. Add 150g blanched almonds or 150g almond pulp (see page 30), ½ garlic clove, 1 tablespoon balsamic vinegar, 100ml extra virgin rapeseed or olive oil, ½ teaspoon salt, a little pepper and 50ml cold water. Blend to a thick soup, adding a touch more cold water to thin it a little if you like. Taste and add more garlic or vinegar if needed, then chill. Before serving, taste and adjust the seasoning again, if necessary, with salt, pepper or vinegar. Serve in small bowls, topped with a swirl of rapeseed or olive oil and a few flaked almonds.

Very green soup

Jam-packed with fresh leafy veg, this vividly coloured soup takes all of 10 minutes to make. The rice cake finish is a great trick for making a smooth velvety soup – and one you will use again and again when improvising your own soups.

Serves 2

2 tablespoons rapeseed or sunflower oil

1 small onion (about 75g), sliced

1 large carrot, peeled and grated

½ garlic clove, grated (optional)

100g spinach, any tough stalks removed

100g flat-leaf parsley or watercress (or 50g of each), any tough stalks removed

About 400ml hot vegetable stock

2 plain rice cakes

Sea salt and freshly ground black pepper

Extra virgin hempseed or rapeseed oil, to finish

Put a large saucepan over a medium-low heat and add the oil. When hot, add the onion, carrot and garlic, if using. Sweat gently for 4–5 minutes, stirring regularly, to soften.

Add the spinach and parsley and/or watercress, about three-quarters of the hot stock and some salt and pepper. Bring to a simmer and cook for a couple of minutes until the leaves have wilted. Turn off the heat.

Crumble the rice cakes into the soup, and stir in well. Leave for a minute so they get very soggy. Purée the soup in the pan with a stick blender, or blitz in a free-standing blender, until smooth and velvety. Return to the pan (if necessary) and reheat gently. Add a little more stock if it seems too thick. Taste, add more salt and pepper as needed, then serve, trickled with a little extra virgin oil, if you like.

SIX WAYS TO SOUP IT UP

» Add a good squeeze of orange juice to the puréed soup; finish with grated orange zest
» Sprinkle some toasted flaked almonds over the soup
» Add flakes of smoked fish – hot-smoked mackerel is ideal
» Drop a generous sprinkling of chopped chives on to the soup
» Nasturtium or rocket flowers look beautiful and add a shot of peppery flavour
» Add a freshly poached egg (see page 110) before you tuck in

VARIATION

Spring nettle soup You can use fresh young nettle tops in this soup, either in place of the spinach, or instead of the parsley/watercress. Use just the tenderest leaves at the top of the nettles, and remove any tough stalks. Give the leaves a good wash (wearing rubber gloves!) then add to the pan, with the other greens if using.

Fragrant Asian broth

This clear, cleansing broth is refreshing and light but also satisfying. It's the sort of thing I like to cook when I have some really good home-made stock to hand – but I've also prepared it using ready-made stock and it's still very good. If you can't lay your hands on all the suggested ingredients, don't panic. As long as you have a decent stock to begin with, each aromatic addition is a bonus.

Serves 2

A small bunch of spring onions

A small bunch of coriander

1 lemongrass stem, bashed

2 kaffir lime leaves (fresh or dried), torn or crumbled

A finger-sized piece of ginger (about 25g), sliced

2 garlic cloves, sliced

1 medium-sized, medium-hot green chilli, deseeded and sliced

2 teaspoons Thai fish sauce (optional)

2 teaspoons sugar

1 tablespoon rice vinegar

1 tablespoon tamari

700ml hot chicken or vegetable stock

Juice of 1 lime

Cut the dark green tops off the spring onions, chop them roughly and put in a medium-large saucepan. Slice the pale parts of the spring onions into thin rounds and set aside.

Pick the leaves from the coriander and set aside with the sliced spring onions. Roughly chop the coriander stalks and add to the pan with the onion tops.

Add all the other ingredients, except the lime juice, to the pan. Bring to a gentle simmer and cook, uncovered, for 10 minutes. Turn off the heat and allow to stand for 5 minutes.

Strain the broth through a sieve, squeezing out all the flavour from the contents of the sieve as you do so. Reheat the broth gently if necessary, add a good squeeze of lime, then taste and adjust the seasoning with more lime or tamari if needed. Ladle into warm bowls and finish each bowl with a generous handful of the sliced spring onions and coriander leaves.

VARIATION

Hearty version For a more substantial main course serving of this soup, add cooked noodles, and/or some cubes of tofu. To up the veg element you can also add a small handful of finely shredded chard or spinach leaves.

Cabbage, carrot and caraway broth

This thrifty, pared-down soup is earthy and comforting but still light. I like to think it follows the tradition of the best peasant cookery: using clever seasoning to turn a few humble vegetables into something really tasty.

Serves 4

1 tablespoon rapeseed or sunflower oil

1 large onion, chopped

2 medium carrots (about 150g in total), peeled and sliced about 5mm thick

1 tablespoon caraway seeds

300g cabbage, such as Savoy, core removed, leaves roughly chopped

1 litre hot vegetable stock

Sea salt and freshly ground black pepper

Extra virgin rapeseed or olive oil, to finish

Heat the oil in a large saucepan over a medium-low heat. Add the onion along with a pinch of salt, cover and sweat gently over a medium heat for 7–10 minutes or until translucent and softened.

Add the carrots and caraway seeds to the pan and stir until well combined. Cook, covered, for a further 3 minutes or so.

Add the cabbage, stir well and then pour over the veg stock and season with pepper. Bring to a gentle simmer and cook, uncovered, for about 15 minutes or until the carrots and cabbage are both tender. Taste and add more salt and pepper as necessary.

Ladle into warmed bowls, making sure everyone gets a share of the caraway seeds, which tend to drift to the bottom of the pan. Give each bowlful a swirl of extra virgin oil and serve. If you want to make lunch of it, serve a hunk of carrot cornbread (page 67) or a slice of seedy rye soda bread (page 65) alongside.

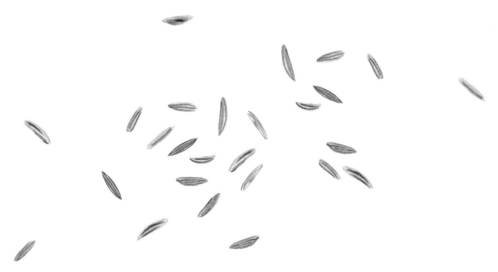

New potato, pea and herb broth

This is exactly the sort of thing I like to eat in early summer (though, to be honest, you can make it later in the year using waxy maincrop potatoes, such as pink fir apple, and frozen peas). Parsley, mint and chives are a great trio but chervil, tarragon and basil are delicious added to the mix too. A little thyme won't go amiss either but be slightly more judicious with this highly aromatic herb.

Serves 4

1 litre vegetable stock

500g new potatoes, scrubbed and cut into roughly 2cm pieces

250g peas or petits pois (fresh or frozen)

1 garlic clove, finely chopped or finely slivered

A large handful of flat-leaf parsley leaves, chopped

A large handful of mint leaves, chopped

A large handful of chives, chopped

Sea salt and freshly ground black pepper

Extra virgin rapeseed or olive oil, to finish

Put the veg stock in a saucepan and bring to a simmer. Add the potatoes, return to a simmer and cook for 6–8 minutes, until tender. If you're using freshly podded large peas, they should go in at the beginning with the potatoes. Frozen peas can go in after 2 minutes of potato cooking, and tiny fresh peas or frozen petits pois should be added just a couple of minutes before the potatoes are done.

When the veg are tender, turn off the heat and stir in the garlic, a good seasoning of salt and pepper and most of the herbs (leaving a few to finish the soup). Taste and add more salt or pepper if needed. Ladle into warmed bowls, top with a generous trickle of good virgin oil, sprinkle on the remaining herbs and serve.

VARIATION

A poached egg to finish I like to serve this broth with a poached egg added – it combines so well with the spuds and herbs, and really makes a meal of it. Break each egg carefully into a cup. Bring a wide pan of water to a rolling boil (while the soup is simmering) and salt lightly. Turn off the heat, immediately but gently tip the eggs into the water, and put a lid on the pan. Leave it on the hob for 3 minutes. By the time you've ladled out the soup, the eggs will be just about ready. Scoop them out of their pan, drain briefly and transfer directly to each bowl of broth.

Sweetcorn and tomato broth

A sunny golden bowlful for late summer, when corn is sweet and tomatoes are bursting with flavour. The tomatoes are barely cooked – just infused briefly in the hot broth so they start to release their savoury-sweet juices.

Serves 4

750ml vegetable stock

2 large or 3 medium cobs of corn (or 250g frozen sweetcorn kernels)

300g cherry tomatoes, quartered (or halved, if very small), or use any really flavourful tomatoes, cut into smallish dice

1 garlic clove, chopped

3–4 spring onions

Sea salt and freshly ground black pepper

Extra virgin rapeseed or olive oil, to finish

Heat the veg stock in a large saucepan over a medium-low heat, until just starting to simmer. While it's heating up, cut the kernels from the corn cobs: hold the cob vertically with the broader end on a board and slice the kernels off downwards. Rotate the cob to target another lot of kernels and slice again.

Add the corn kernels to the simmering stock, bring back to a simmer and cook for 3–4 minutes until the corn is tender. Add the tomatoes, garlic and spring onions and turn off the heat. Leave for a couple of minutes then stir. Taste and add salt and pepper as needed.

Ladle into warmed bowls, top with a splosh of extra virgin oil and some more black pepper, and serve.

VARIATIONS

Bulking with beans If you have some fresh green beans to hand (French or runner), chop into 1–2cm lengths and add to the soup with the corn kernels, cooking them just until al dente.

Herby finish For even more colour and aroma, finish the broth with some chopped fresh herbs such as parsley, chives or basil.

Chickpea soup

This is a fast storecupboard supper that will soothe, sustain and energise. It uses the same ingredients as a classic hummus – with a dash of salty-sour preserved lemon to lift the flavour.

Serves 4

3 tablespoons extra virgin rapeseed or olive oil

4 garlic cloves, sliced

2 tablespoons chopped preserved lemon (rind and flesh, but no pips)

A pinch of dried chilli flakes (optional)

2 x 400g tins chickpeas, drained and rinsed

Up to 800ml hot vegetable stock

1 heaped tablespoon tahini

Leaves from a small bunch of flat-leaf parsley, chopped

Sea salt and freshly ground black pepper

Smoked paprika, to finish

Place a saucepan on a medium heat. Add half the oil, the garlic, preserved lemon and chilli flakes if using. Fry gently for 1–2 minutes, letting the garlic soften but not colour.

Set aside about 5 tablespoons of the chickpeas. Add the remainder to the saucepan, mix well and cook for a further minute. Pour over 750ml hot stock and spoon in the tahini. Bring to a simmer and cook for 2–3 minutes.

Put the contents of the pan into a blender and purée until smooth. Add a little more stock if the soup seems very thick but keep the texture nicely creamy. Season with plenty of salt and pepper to taste. If serving immediately, pour straight from the blender into warmed bowls. Or return to the pan and reheat gently before serving.

Mix the chopped parsley with the reserved whole chickpeas, the remaining extra virgin oil, and some salt and pepper. Spoon the herby chickpeas on top of the soup and finish with a pinch of smoked paprika.

Celeriac, apple and chestnut soup

The combination of earthy root veg and sweet-tart apples is one I keep coming back to. This version is just the thing for an autumn lunch or supper. It tastes even better reheated the day after you've made it.

Serves 4–6

1 tablespoon rapeseed or sunflower oil

1 onion, sliced

1 teaspoon thyme leaves, plus extra to serve (optional)

1 medium celeriac (about 800g), peeled and roughly chopped

2 crisp eating apples, such as Cox's, peeled, cored and roughly chopped

200g cooked chestnuts (vac-packed is fine)

1 litre hot vegetable stock

Extra virgin hempseed or rapeseed oil, to finish

Heat the oil in a large pan over a medium-low heat. Add the onion and thyme and cook gently for 10 minutes or until the onion is soft but not coloured.

Add the celeriac, apples, chestnuts and stock to the onion. Bring to a simmer and cook, uncovered, for about 15 minutes, or until the celeriac is tender.

Blend the soup thoroughly – with a stick blender or in a free-standing blender – adding a little more stock or water if it seems too thick. If necessary, return to the pan and reheat gently.

Add salt and pepper to taste then ladle into warmed bowls and serve, finished with a trickle of extra virgin oil, and a scattering of thyme leaves if you like.

VARIATION

Parsnip swap Parsnips work well instead of the celeriac – or try a mixture of the two.

Swede and smoky bacon soup

You need never again wonder what to do with a swede. In this hearty, belly-filling soup, its pungent earthiness is beautifully balanced with smoky bacon.

Serves 4

2 tablespoons rapeseed or sunflower oil

1 large onion, chopped

2 garlic cloves, crushed

200g smoked streaky bacon, sliced

1 swede (about 750g)

1 litre hot chicken or vegetable stock

Sea salt and freshly ground black pepper

Chopped parsley, to finish

Put most of the oil in a large saucepan over a low heat. Add the onion, garlic, two-thirds of the bacon, plenty of black pepper (which tastes wonderful with swede) but no salt (the bacon is already salty). Cook over a low heat for 10 minutes or until everything is softened and just starting to colour. Meanwhile, peel the swede and cut into 1–2cm dice.

Add the diced swede to the onion, along with the stock, and bring to a simmer. Cook gently for 30 minutes or until the swede is tender.

Meanwhile, fry the remaining bacon separately, with a tiny dash of oil, until crisp. Drain on kitchen paper.

Taste the soup and add a pinch of salt if necessary. Ladle into warmed bowls, top with the extra bacon and some chopped parsley and serve.

Kipper chowder

This smoky fish chowder gets its creaminess from almond, oat or rice milk. With a chunk of carrot cornbread (page 67), it makes a properly filling supper. Waxy and floury potatoes are both suitable but lend a different texture. Floury potatoes will start to collapse and help thicken the soup, while waxy will hold their shape and bite in a lighter liquor.

Serves 4

1 tablespoon rapeseed or sunflower oil

1 large or 2 small leeks, quartered lengthways and sliced

250g potatoes, peeled and diced into 1cm cubes

2 garlic cloves, grated

4 kipper fillets

2 rounded teaspoons cornflour, mixed to a paste with a little water

850ml unsweetened almond milk (bought or home-made, page 30), or oat or rice milk

2 bay leaves

Leaves from a small bunch of parsley, chopped

A small bunch of chives, sliced

Juice of ½ lemon

Sea salt and freshly ground black pepper

Put a large saucepan over a medium heat. Add the oil, followed by the leeks. Season with a little salt and pepper and gently sweat the leeks for a couple of minutes, until softened a little. Add the potatoes and garlic and cook for a further 3–4 minutes, stirring often.

Meanwhile, use a sharp knife to carefully cut the kipper fillets off their skin. Cut the kipper into roughly 2cm pieces.

Stir the cornflour paste into the potato and leek mixture, then pour in the dairy-free milk, add the bay leaves and bring to a simmer. Cook gently for 10–12 minutes until the potatoes are almost tender. Add the kipper pieces and stir them in. Bring back to a simmer, then turn off the heat and put a lid on the pan. Leave to stand for 5–10 minutes. This will cook the kipper and infuse the soup with its smoky flavour.

Add the parsley, chives, lemon juice and salt and pepper to taste, then serve.

VARIATIONS

Smoked fish swaps Replace the kippers with smoked haddock or pollack fillets; you'll need about 300g. You can also use smoked mackerel – peel off the skin with your fingers and tear the fish into chunks before adding to the soup.

Roasted fennel and lemon soup

Over the next few pages, you'll find a selection of roasting-tray soups – thick, hearty bowlfuls made by simply blitzing up roasted veg with some good stock. Roasting intensifies the flavour and sweetness of vegetables with absolutely no effort from the cook, and it's one of my favourite techniques for soup, particularly when I'm in the mood for something very easy.

Serves 4

3 medium-large fennel bulbs (about 1kg), trimmed, tough outer layer removed, roughly chopped

1 large onion, peeled and roughly chopped

1 large potato (about 300g), peeled and roughly chopped

4 garlic cloves, peeled

1 smallish lemon, quartered

3 tablespoons rapeseed or sunflower oil

About 750ml hot vegetable stock

Sea salt and freshly ground black pepper

TO FINISH

Extra virgin rapeseed or olive oil

Fennel seeds (optional)

Preheat the oven to 190°C/Gas 5.

Put the fennel, onion and potato in a large roasting tin. Add the garlic cloves and chunks of lemon. Trickle over the oil, season well with salt and pepper and stir the lot together. Cover with foil and roast for 45 minutes, then uncover the veg, give it a good stir and return to the oven for 15 minutes, by which time everything should be completely tender.

Remove the pieces of lemon, then transfer the remaining contents of the roasting tin to a blender. Pour a little of the hot stock into the roasting tin and use a spatula to swirl it around and scrape up any tasty, caramelised residue from the base of the pan. Tip this into the blender, along with about 500ml of the remaining hot stock. Blitz until you have a smooth, creamy-looking soup, adding more hot stock as needed. Taste and add more salt and pepper as required.

For immediate consumption, pour the hot soup straight from the blender into warmed bowls. Or return to the pan and reheat gently before serving. Top with a trickle of extra virgin oil and, if you like, a pinch of roughly bashed fennel seeds.

VARIATIONS

Extra-fennelly version For a more aniseedy, slightly sweeter soup, leave out the chunks of lemon and add 2 teaspoons whole fennel seeds to the veg before roasting.

Roast celery soup Replace the fennel with a couple of whole heads of celery. Remove the 2 or 3 toughest stalks from the outside of each head – these may have coarse fibres that won't break down in the blender (they're always good for stock though). Save some of the soft leaves from inside the celery heart too – chopped and sprinkled over the finished soup, they are a good alternative to the fennel seeds.

Roasted aubergine and tomato soup

This amazingly simple roasting-tray soup has the tangy intensity of tomatoes, tempered with a subtle, smoky creaminess from the aubergines.

Serves 3–4

1 large or 2 small aubergines (about 400g in total)

1 tablespoon rapeseed or sunflower oil

400g tin whole plum tomatoes, in juice

2 garlic cloves, chopped

1 teaspoon vegetable bouillon powder or ½ veg stock cube

1 teaspoon sugar

½ teaspoon ground cumin (optional)

Sea salt and freshly ground black pepper

Toasted, crushed cumin seeds, or basil leaves, to finish (optional)

Preheat the oven to 190°C/Gas 5.

Halve the aubergine then cut each half into slices 1–2 cm thick. Put them in a deep roasting tray and season well with salt and pepper. Trickle over the oil (it will soak into the aubergine straight away, but don't worry about this). Place in the oven and roast for 20 minutes until the aubergine is tender and starting to brown.

Crush the tinned tomatoes in your hands and add these to the roasting tin, along with their juice (removing any stalky bits) and the garlic. Fill the empty tomato tin with water and add this too, along with the bouillon powder or crumbled stock cube and sugar, and the cumin, if using. Return the tray to the oven for a further 15 minutes.

Pour the contents of the tray into the jug of a blender and purée until smooth. Add a splash more hot water if the soup is too thick for you. For immediate consumption, pour the hot soup straight from the blender into warmed bowls. Or return to the pan and reheat gently before serving. Serve, garnished if you like with a pinch of toasted, crushed cumin seeds, or some torn fresh basil.

Roasted mushroom soup

This has all the earthy flavour and velvety texture that any good mushroom soup should possess – but, because there's no cream or starchy thickeners, it's deliciously light too. Choose well-flavoured mushrooms such as chestnut and dark-gilled, open-cap varieties, rather than white buttons.

Serves 4

1kg mushrooms (ideally a mix of chestnut and open cap)

4 tablespoons rapeseed or sunflower oil

4 garlic cloves, chopped

Leaves from a small bunch of flat-leaf parsley

About 650ml hot vegetable stock

Sea salt and freshly ground black pepper

Extra virgin rapeseed or olive oil, to finish

Preheat the oven to 190°C/Gas 5.

Remove the stalks from the mushrooms then cut the caps into quarters. Put the caps and stalks in your largest roasting tray, or a large, lipped baking tray – ideally they should be no more than one mushroom deep so the liquid they produce can evaporate easily.

Spoon over the oil and season well with salt and pepper. Mix together with your hands. Roast for 25 minutes, then stir in the garlic and return to the oven for 5 minutes to just cook the garlic.

Scrape the cooked mushrooms and any garlicky juices from the roasting tray into a blender. Add most of the parsley leaves (reserving a few to finish the soup) and 650ml stock and purée to a thick, velvety soup. Add a little more stock if necessary.

Taste and add more salt and pepper if needed. For immediate consumption, pour the hot soup straight from the blender into warmed bowls. Or return to the pan and reheat gently before serving. Top each bowl with a trickle of extra virgin oil and a few parsley leaves, roughly chopped if you like.

Creamy roasted tomato soup

The creaminess in this soup comes from a couple of handfuls of cashew nuts, thrown into the roasting tin with the tomatoes. Once puréed, the result is rich and sumptuous. The riper your tomatoes the better – but roasting will sweeten and intensify even less than perfect specimens.

Serves 4

1.2kg tomatoes

4–5 garlic cloves, chopped

3 tablespoons rapeseed or sunflower oil

75g cashew nuts, plus a few extra, to finish (optional)

200ml light vegetable stock or water

A pinch of sugar (optional)

Sea salt and freshly ground black pepper

TO FINISH

Extra virgin hempseed or rapeseed oil

A dusting of paprika (optional)

Preheat the oven to 180°C/Gas 4.

Cut the tomatoes in half and put them in a large roasting tray – they should fit fairly snugly. Scatter over the chopped garlic, trickle over the oil and season generously with salt and pepper. Roast for 25 minutes, then scatter the cashews over the tomatoes. Return to the oven for a further 20 minutes until the tomatoes are soft and pulpy and perhaps a little charred in places.

Scrape the tomatoes, cashews and all the garlicky pan juices into a blender. Add the stock or water and blitz to a purée. Pass this through a sieve, which will remove any pips, or stubborn bits of tomato skin.

When you're ready to serve, reheat gently. You can add a little water if the soup seems very thick or the flavour is too intense. Season with more salt and pepper if needed, and add a pinch of sugar if you think the tomatoey acidity needs tempering slightly.

Ladle into warmed bowls and finish with a swirl of extra virgin oil, plus a few chopped cashews and a dusting of paprika if you like, and a generous sprinkling of pepper.

VARIATION

Chilled version This soup is also very good served cold. Chill in the fridge for a couple of hours, then finish it off with plenty of shredded fresh basil or mint leaves.

Nectarine and raspberry soup

This is a super-quick summer fruit blend. I usually opt for nectarines here because their skins are so thin that they break down easily in the blender – but if you're lucky enough to find some ripe and fragrant peaches, they work well too. Serve it lightly chilled as an elegant and refreshing summer dessert.

Serves 4

1kg ripe nectarines (or peaches)

250g raspberries

½ vanilla pod, split open and cut into 2–3 pieces

About 4 tablespoons honey

Juice of 1 lemon

TO SERVE (OPTIONAL)

Toasted, flaked almonds

Shredded mint leaves

Halve the nectarines and remove the stones. Cut the fruit into chunky pieces and put into a blender or food processor along with the raspberries, bits of vanilla pod, 4 tablespoons honey and the lemon juice. Blend until smooth.

Pass through a sieve to remove the raspberry pips and any fragments of vanilla pod, then taste and add a little more honey if needed.

Serve lightly chilled, sprinkled, if you like, with a few toasted almonds and a little shredded mint.

Pear, blackberry and walnut soup

This cool, fruity, tangy-sweet bowlful of autumn goes down a treat after a meal and also makes a refreshing breakfast. Choose nicely ripe pears that will purée easily and plump, juicy blackberries, rather than very small, pippy ones.

Serves 4

4 medium-sized, ripe pears (about 600g)

150g blackberries (fresh or frozen)

50g walnuts, plus extra to serve

Juice of ½–1 lemon

Maple syrup (or honey or agave syrup), to sweeten

Peel, quarter and core the pears then cut them into chunks and drop them into a blender with the blackberries (frozen ones can go in straight from the freezer, and will give you a nicely chilled soup). Add the walnuts, the juice of ½ lemon and 1 tablespoon maple syrup (or your chosen sweetener).

Blitz everything to a purée – you'll probably need to stop once or twice and stir the fruit around a bit to get it all going. If it seems very thick, add a splash of water.

Taste the soup and add more lemon juice if necessary, and more maple syrup – you may need up to 2 tablespoons more, depending on the sharpness of your blackberries and the bitterness of your walnuts. If the pips bother you, pass the soup through a sieve.

If the soup is not already cold, chill it lightly before serving, sprinkled with a few more chunks of walnut.

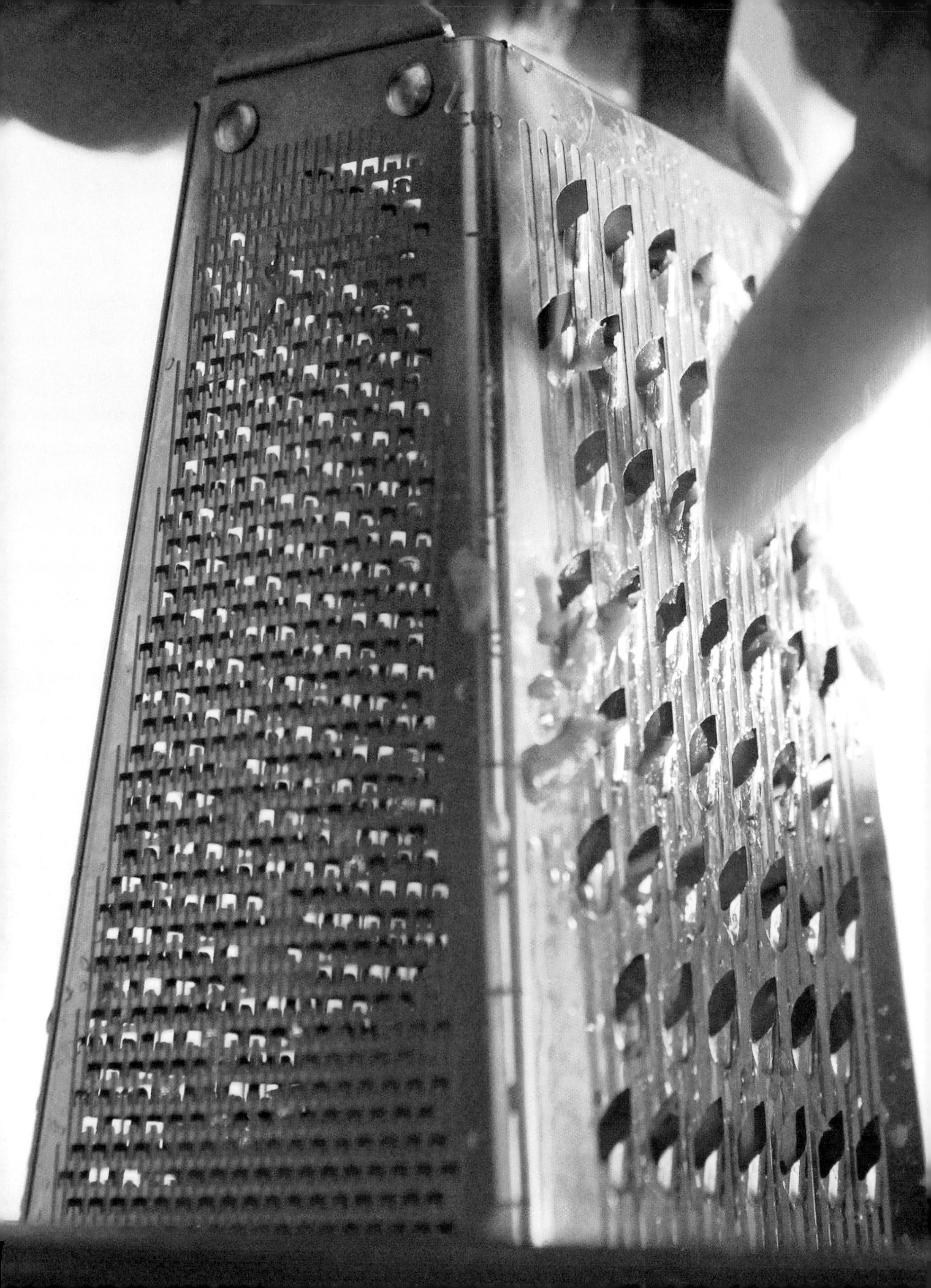

THE FUTURE IS Salad

EVERYONE KNOWS THAT salads are good for you - but that's just the half of it. To me, salads are excitement: a cool culinary concept that you can play with to your heart's (and palate's) content.

My salads are no more and no less than mingled or multi-layered assemblies of tasty things that go together well. There's highly likely to be something raw and crisp in the mix – fresh leaves, sliced stems or grated roots – giving the zest and bite that the word salad should conjure. But you can also expect the unexpected in these recipes. I've been raiding the cupboard and the garden for things that don't often turn up in the salad bowl: surprising spices, juicy fruits (fresh and dried), and all manner of roots and stems, herbs and leaves, nuts and seeds.

I do like salads with a bit of substance. That could be nuts, pulses or grains, or even meat or fish. Used in moderation these give side salads a tempting tweak; used in combination they turn simple sides into sassy starters and moreish mains.

With these elements I 'build' new salads all the time, always exploring surprising but pleasing new contrasts. Nutty raw cauliflower goes brilliantly with silky air-dried ham (page 143), for instance, as do strawberries with spinach (page 144). I might serve up sweet fruits in a savoury dressing (pages 140 and 150) or keep raw something I'd more often cook, as in the squash, cabbage and carrot slaw on page 162. Such wilful experimentation so often bears fruit in the salad bowl.

Dressings – key in bringing a salad together – shouldn't be daunting: they are entirely within your control. Start with a glug of good oil and a much smaller glug of lemon juice or good vinegar. Add salt and pepper, and that's it, a very simple dressing. Add a little more oil if it's too sharp, more lemon if it's too oily, more seasoning if it's bland.

And of course you can extend the idea of seasonings in all directions: mustard, honey, tamari, herbs, citrus, a nip of chilli, different oils and vinegars... all of these can be used in a dressing to harmonise your gathered ingredients.

Salads tend to soften and 'relax' if they are left in their dressing for any length of time. This isn't always a good thing (when fresh leaves and herbs are involved, for example), but with root veg, dried fruits, nuts and seeds it can tenderise textures and mellow flavours. I've borne this in mind in advertising the portability of some of the salads with my lunchbox-friendly symbol:

In fact, please extend a laid-back attitude to the where and when of eating salad across the board. I probably eat something I'd be inclined to call a salad every day: often supper is a salad; when I have guests I like to serve a salad as a starter, but equally often I'll serve it as a second course, after opening with a main. At summer gatherings, especially outdoor ones, the entire meal is often pretty much a smorgasbord of salads. And when the sun shines on them, I couldn't be happier.

Lettuce and pea salad with lemony dressing

At the right time of year (spring and early summer), I like to include pea shoots in this salad. If you grow peas yourself, you can harvest these sweet growing tips when you pick the first little pea pods. Or grow a dedicated row just for cutting the shoots. They increasingly turn up in mixed leaf bags at farmers' markets and delis, and some supermarkets and greengrocers now sell them too. Home pea-growers can also use tiny baby peas, raw, in this dish. Otherwise, blanched petits pois are delicious.

Serves 2, or 4 as a starter

75g mangetout

75g frozen petits pois (or very fresh raw baby peas)

1 Little Gem lettuce, separated into leaves (or a couple of good handfuls of other lettuce leaves)

A couple of handfuls of pea shoots (optional)

About 25g pine nuts, lightly toasted

FOR THE DRESSING

3 tablespoons extra virgin rapeseed or olive oil

Finely grated zest of ½ lemon

1 tablespoon lemon juice

½ teaspoon English mustard

1 teaspoon runny honey

1 tablespoon snipped chives, plus extra to serve

Sea salt and freshly ground black pepper

Bring a pan of water to the boil and add the mangetout and frozen petits pois. Once the water returns to a rolling boil, time 1 minute, then drain the veg in a sieve. Immediately run under cold water to stop the cooking and help fix the colour. Drain thoroughly, then tip the veg into a bowl. If you're using raw peas, add them to the mangetout now.

Meanwhile, put all the dressing ingredients in a jar, adding a pinch of salt and a grinding of pepper, and shake to combine.

Gently toss the mangetout and peas in half the dressing. Arrange the lettuce and dressed veg on individual plates, or one large platter. Scatter over the pea shoots, if using, and trickle over the rest of the dressing. Sprinkle with the pine nuts, finish with a few more chives, snipped into longer lengths, and serve.

Pear and blueberries with thyme and dates

This luscious, super-quick salad makes the most of the late summer overlap between the blueberry and pear seasons. The savoury dressing over the fruit makes for a delightful ambiguity and you can serve this as a starter, a middle course, a light lunch or a pud.

Serves 2, or 4 as a starter

2 ripe pears

50g blueberries

50g soft dates, such as Medjool, halved and stones removed

1 teaspoon thyme leaves

2 tablespoons extra virgin rapeseed or olive oil

Juice of ½ lemon

Salt and freshly ground black pepper

Quarter the pears and remove the core, then cut each quarter in half again. Place the pear slices in a bowl with all the other ingredients. Tumble the ingredients together gently, then divide between plates and serve.

Cauliflower, prosciutto and balsamic dressing

A restrained quantity of salty-sweet, air-dried ham is used almost as a seasoning here – a finishing touch on a plateful of crisp, well-dressed raw veg.

Serves 4 as a starter

1 medium cauliflower (700–800g)

About 75g prosciutto or other good air-dried ham

A handful of flat-leaf parsley, to finish

FOR THE DRESSING

3 tablespoons extra virgin olive oil, plus extra to finish

1 tablespoon balsamic vinegar (ideally apple balsamic)

2 teaspoons runny honey

A spritz of lemon juice

A scrap of garlic (about ¼ clove), crushed or grated

Sea salt and freshly ground black pepper

For the dressing, mix all the ingredients together in a bowl with a fork or whisk, adding a good pinch of salt and a grinding of pepper, to combine.

Trim away the larger leaves and the base stalk from the cauliflower, then cut the cauli into slices, about 5mm thick; work from one side inwards until you reach the stalky core, then turn the cauliflower and start slicing from a different direction. Keep going until you have sliced all the outer part and just have a stump of stalk left. Discard this.

Put the sliced cauliflower in a large bowl with most of the dressing and mix well. Scatter this dressed cauliflower over four plates or shallow bowls. Tear the ham into shreds and distribute over the cauliflower. Add a scattering of parsley, trickle over the remaining dressing and serve.

Spinach, avocado and strawberry salad

Strawberries can be wonderful in a savoury salad – their flavour profile is on the same spectrum as tomato, just a little more towards the sweet/fragrant end of it. Tender spinach, creamy avocado and delicately aniseedy basil partner them very nicely.

Serves 2, or 4 as a starter

2 handfuls of baby spinach leaves

1 small avocado

100g strawberries

50g salted, roasted cashews (or use plain cashews if you prefer)

A small handful of basil leaves, to finish (optional)

FOR THE DRESSING

2 tablespoons extra virgin rapeseed or olive oil

A squeeze of lemon juice

1 teaspoon runny honey

Sea salt and freshly ground black pepper

For the dressing, put the ingredients into a bowl, adding a good pinch of salt and a grinding of pepper, and whisk to combine. Taste the dressing – it should be a little sweet, a little salty and have a hint of acidity from the lemon juice. Adjust as necessary.

Divide the spinach leaves between shallow bowls. Halve, stone and peel the avocado, then cut lengthways into slices roughly 1cm thick at the outer edge. Hull the strawberries and slice them thickly. Arrange the avocado and strawberries over the spinach and spoon over most of the dressing.

Scatter the cashews over the salad. Tear the basil, if using, into small pieces and scatter this over too. Give the salad a trickle more dressing and a grinding of pepper, and serve.

Raw mushrooms with chilli and preserved lemon

Fresh, firm mushrooms have a delicately creamy, almost nutty quality when served raw. The secret is to slice them thinly and season them well, as in this salad, where they're pepped up with preserved lemon, chilli and rocket leaves. Enoki mushrooms, which have long, slender stems and tiny white caps, make a quirky addition here, but the salad is great with any fresh mushrooms.

Serves 2, or 4 as a starter

100g chestnut or open cap mushrooms

75g white button mushrooms

50g enoki mushrooms (optional)

2 tablespoons extra virgin rapeseed or olive oil, plus extra to finish

½ lemon

½ small red chilli, seeds removed, finely chopped

2 good handfuls of rocket leaves

1 tablespoon chopped preserved lemon rind

Sea salt and freshly ground black pepper

Wipe the mushrooms with a damp cloth to remove any dirt. Cut off any tough stem ends. Using a sharp knife, thinly slice the chestnut and button mushrooms. Put them in a bowl with the enoki, if using.

Add the oil, a generous squeeze of lemon, the chilli and some salt and pepper. Toss well and leave for a couple of hours if you can, to allow the flavours to mingle. If you don't have the luxury of time just crack on and it will still be great.

Arrange the rocket and dressed mushrooms on serving plates and scatter over the chopped preserved lemon rind. Give it a final generous trickle of oil, another squeeze of lemon and a touch more salt and pepper, then serve.

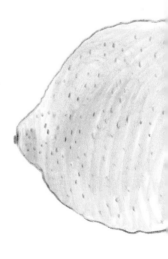

Parsnip, pear and caper salad

Autumnal fare needn't be stodgy. Make this light and elegant dish in September or October when parsnips are young and tender, and pears at their peak.

Serves 2, or 4 as a starter

250g young, firm parsnips (2–3)

3 tablespoons extra virgin rapeseed or olive oil

2 tablespoons lemon juice

2 tablespoons baby capers, rinsed

1 large or 2 small, just-ripe pears (about 200g in total)

Freshly ground black pepper

A scattering of parsley leaves, to finish (optional)

Peel the parsnips and trim off the tips and stalk ends. Then use your veg peeler to shave the roots into long, thin slivers, working down the length of the root, and stopping when you reach the core (you can grate the parsnips if you prefer but I find shaving them just as easy, and it produces elegant, wafer-thin ribbons).

Put the parsnip slivers in a bowl and add the oil, lemon juice, capers and some pepper (no salt as the capers are already salty).

Peel the pear(s), quarter and core them, then cut each quarter into 4 or 5 slim slices. Add to the bowl with the parsnips and toss gently together.

Arrange the salad on plates, finish with a few parsley leaves if you have them, and serve.

Fig, blackberry and walnut salad

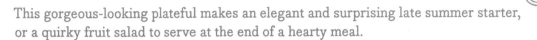

This gorgeous-looking plateful makes an elegant and surprising late summer starter, or a quirky fruit salad to serve at the end of a hearty meal.

Serves 2, or 4 as a starter

3–4 ripe figs

50g walnuts, roughly broken up

About 75g ripe blackberries

3 tablespoons balsamic vinegar (ideally apple balsamic)

1 tablespoon extra virgin rapeseed or olive oil, plus extra to serve

2 teaspoons runny honey

Sea salt and freshly ground black pepper

Slice the figs across into 3–4mm thick slices and spread out on large serving plates. Scatter the walnut pieces over them.

Put the blackberries in a bowl with the vinegar, oil and honey. Use a fork to mix the lot together, crushing the blackberries a little as you go, to get their juices flowing.

Spoon this juicy, berry-stained dressing over the figs and nuts. Give each plate another trickle of extra virgin oil and a scattering of salt and pepper, and serve.

Raw courgette and fennel with peanut dressing

As with any raw courgette dish, this is most delicious when made with young, sweet freshly picked courgettes. If you're not lucky enough to be growing your own, then look for the smallest, firmest, glossiest specimens you can find. Dish this up as a light lunch or starter on its own, or partner it with some protein – lentils, chickpeas, chicken or fish – for something more substantial.

Serves 2, or 4 as a starter

200g young, small courgettes

1 large or 2 small fennel bulbs

A little extra virgin rapeseed or olive oil

1 tablespoon sunflower or pumpkin seeds, or a mix of the two (optional)

A small handful of basil or mint leaves, to finish

FOR THE DRESSING

2 tablespoons smooth or crunchy no-sugar-added peanut butter (or another nut butter of your choice)

Finely grated zest of ½ lemon

1 tablespoon lemon juice

½ teaspoon runny honey

Sea salt and freshly ground black pepper

To make the dressing, put all the ingredients in a bowl, adding salt and pepper as needed, bearing in mind that the nut butter will add salt. Add 2 tablespoons water and whisk until you have a thick mixture, smooth except for any chunks of nut. It should be loose enough to fall off the spoon in thick ribbons – you can whisk in a little more cold water, if necessary, to reach this consistency.

Top and tail the courgettes, then use a veg peeler to shave them lengthways into wafer-thin ribbons. Put into a large wide bowl.

Trim the fennel, removing any tough and fibrous outer layers, saving a few of the fronds if there are any. Then slice the fennel, top to bottom, as thinly as you can, and add to the courgettes. Trickle a little oil over the veg, sprinkle with salt and pepper and toss lightly.

Scatter the seeds, if using, over the veg and spoon on the dressing. Finish with roughly torn basil or mint leaves and fennel fronds if you have them, then serve. For a lunchbox salad, take the dressing separately and add before eating.

Spinach and coconut salad

This beautifully pared-down salad is a great showcase for some lovely fresh leaves. Baby spinach is a winner and rocket is good too but if you can get some very tender, garden-fresh baby kale leaves into the mix as well, so much the better. Prepared chunks of fresh coconut are easy to buy these days but starting with a whole coconut and briefly baking it (in two halves) in the oven renders the flesh delicious to eat and easy to prise from the shell.

Serves 2, or 4 as a starter

50g fresh coconut (pre-prepared or oven-baked as below)

2–3 handfuls of baby spinach, or a mix of baby spinach and rocket, or very tender baby kale leaves, torn from the stalk

50g unsulphured dried apricots, cut into thin slivers, or raisins

FOR THE DRESSING

3 tablespoons extra virgin rapeseed or olive oil

1 tablespoon lime juice (about ½ lime)

½ teaspoon English mustard

Sea salt and freshly ground black pepper

Cut the coconut into fine slices, using a mandoline or veg peeler, or into small chunks.

To make the dressing, whisk or shake the ingredients together in a jar, adding salt and pepper to taste.

Spread the leaves out over a serving platter. Scatter over the apricots or raisins, then the coconut. Trickle over the dressing and serve straight away.

TO PREPARE FRESH COCONUT IN THE OVEN
First pierce the softer of the three 'eyes' with a screwdriver and drain off the coconut water (delicious to drink just as it is, or in smoothies). Hold the coconut in one hand then use the back of a large, heavy knife to tap the shell firmly, working around the 'equator', until it splits open. Bake the coconut halves at 200°C/Gas 6 for about 20 minutes then leave to cool, before prising the flesh away from the shell with a knife.

Super-savoury raw cauliflower

When finely chopped, raw cauliflower functions as a kind of veggie 'rice'. Dress it in some well-flavoured seasonings and it's a lovely fresh base for an unusual salad. Serve it up as part of a picnic or summer lunch spread. It also makes a cracking packed lunch.

Serves 4

1 small-medium cauliflower (700–800g)

A squeeze of lime juice

About 50g roasted, unsalted peanuts, coarsely chopped

20g sunflower seeds

2 teaspoons black onion seeds (optional)

A few mint or coriander leaves, whole or roughly torn

FOR THE DRESSING

A scrap of garlic (about ¼ clove)

A pinch of sugar

1 teaspoon freshly grated root ginger

1½ tablespoons rice vinegar

1½ tablespoons toasted sesame oil

1 tablespoon tamari

A pinch of dried chilli flakes (optional)

Sea salt and freshly ground black pepper

To make the dressing, crush the garlic with a pinch of salt and another of sugar, then combine with the ginger, vinegar, sesame oil and tamari. Add the chilli flakes, if using, and a grinding of pepper, and mix thoroughly.

Trim away the leaves and most of the stalk from the cauliflower and cut the florets into small pieces. Put these in a food processor and process until they are very finely chopped and look a little like fluffy white grains. Transfer to a bowl.

Spread the cauliflower out over a serving plate and trickle over most of the dressing. Give it a squeeze of lime and scatter over the peanuts, seeds and mint or coriander. Spoon on the remaining dressing and serve.

Orange and beetroot salad with toasted seeds

With its strong colours and bold flavours, this salad from River Cottage head chef Gill Meller is a lively, original plateful. It's worth taking the time to prepare the fennel-scented seed mix. You'll find yourself using it on all sorts of other salads, not to mention soups and veg dishes.

Serves 2, or 4 as a starter

3–4 small beetroot (about 250g in total)

2 large oranges

3 tablespoons cider vinegar

1 teaspoon caster or soft light brown sugar

Sea salt and freshly ground black pepper

FOR THE ROASTED SEED MIX

2 tablespoons fennel seeds

½ teaspoon fine salt

1½ teaspoons caster sugar

40g sunflower seeds

40g pumpkin seeds

1 tablespoon extra virgin rapeseed or olive oil

Peel the raw beetroot and slice them very thinly, using a mandoline or veg peeler to create fine discs or wafer-thin ribbons.

To prepare the oranges, take a slice off the top and base of each and stand them on a board. Use a sharp knife to slice away the peel and pith, then cut the oranges across into 1cm thick slices.

Put the beetroot and orange slices into a bowl. Add the cider vinegar, sugar and a little salt and pepper, toss gently to combine and leave to marinate for up to 2 hours.

Meanwhile, make the roasted seed mix. Preheat the oven to 180°C/Gas 4 and line a baking tray with baking parchment. Using a heavy pestle and mortar, grind the fennel seeds, salt and sugar to a fairly fine texture. Put the sunflower and pumpkin seeds in a bowl, add 1 tablespoon water, the oil and the crushed fennel seed mixture and combine thoroughly. Spread this mixture over the prepared baking tray and roast for 6–8 minutes. Leave to cool. You can keep this roasted seed mix in a jar for several days.

Arrange the marinated beetroot and orange on serving plates, spooning over the fruity juices as you go. Scatter over the seeds generously, and serve. You'll have plenty of the seed mix left to play with on other dishes.

Nordic slaw with rye crumbs

With the fresh, crisp flavours of dill, vinegar-sharpened cucumber and toasted rye, I think of this as a kind of Scandinavian slaw. A dish of it does very nicely for lunch. It's also a great accompaniment to fish – perhaps grilled mackerel or sprats (page 196), or smoked trout.

Serves 2, or 4 as a side

1 very large or 2 small cucumbers (500–600g in total)

1 tablespoon cider vinegar

A pinch of sugar

200g celeriac

2–3 tablespoons coarsely chopped dill

FOR THE RYE CRUMBS

1 garlic clove, halved (optional)

100g rye breadcrumbs (see page 65), or use wholegrain gluten-free bread or cheaty crumbs (see below)

1 tablespoon extra virgin rapeseed or olive oil

FOR THE DRESSING

3 tablespoons good mayonnaise

1 teaspoon English mustard

Sea salt and freshly ground black pepper

Cut the cucumber into manageable lengths (10–12cm). Quarter each piece lengthways, scoop out the seeds with a teaspoon, then use a mandoline or veg peeler to shave the cucumber into long ribbons – some of which will include a fine strip of green peel. This is good for the texture of the finished dish. You'll probably have a tricky end bit – it won't look great in the dish, but you can throw it in if you like, or pop it in a Pimms!

Toss the cucumber ribbons with the vinegar, sugar, ¼ teaspoon salt and a good grinding of pepper. Leave to macerate in a cool place for at least an hour, up to 3 or 4.

Meanwhile, prepare the rye crumbs. Preheat the oven to 180°C/Gas 4. Rub the base of a small baking tray with the cut surface of the garlic for a subtle garlicky savour. Tip the rye crumbs on to it, trickle them with the oil and toss together so the crumbs are lightly oiled. Bake for 5–7 minutes, until sizzling and smelling toasty. Leave to cool completely.

Drain the liquid from the cucumber into a small bowl. Whisk this together with the mayonnaise, mustard and, if necessary, some more salt and pepper, to make a dressing. Pour back over the cucumber.

Slice the peel from the celeriac then cut the flesh into thin matchsticks (or coarsely grate it if you prefer). Add to the dressed cucumber and toss well. Stir in the dill.

Pile the slaw into a serving dish, and pour over all its juicy dressing. Scatter with the toasty crumbs and serve.

VARIATION

Quick cheaty rye crumbs Take a good quality rye crispbread (the very thin type is best, and do check it's wheat-free) and break into shards or bash into crumbs.

Squash, cabbage and carrot slaw

Raw squash flesh brings vibrant colour and nutty flavour to this gorgeous-looking slaw, which you can keep in the fridge for a couple of days and dig into as you please. Use a small squash or culinary pumpkin, rather than a swollen Halloween monster. My favourite varieties include butternut, kabocha, onion squash and Crown Prince.

Serves 4–6 as a side

75g sunflower seeds

300g chunk of squash

2 medium carrots (about 150g in total)

½ small red cabbage (about 400g), core removed

Finely grated zest and juice of 1 orange

Sea salt and freshly ground black pepper

FOR THE DRESSING

1 teaspoon English mustard

1 teaspoon runny honey

2 tablespoons cider vinegar

4 tablespoons extra virgin rapeseed or olive oil

If you've got time, lightly toast the sunflower seeds in a dry pan over a medium heat. This isn't essential but it does develop their nutty flavour. Leave to cool.

Peel and deseed the squash and grate it coarsely into a large bowl. Peel and grate the carrots into the same bowl. You can do this with the coarse side of a cheese grater but of course it's much quicker if you use the grating attachment on a food processor.

Use a sharp knife to finely shred the cabbage and add to the bowl. Add the orange zest and juice, sprinkle in the sunflower seeds and mix everything well. Season with salt and pepper.

For the dressing, shake all the ingredients together in a jar with a pinch of salt and a grinding of pepper until emulsified.

Pour the dressing over the slaw and mix well. Taste and add a little more salt and pepper if necessary, then it's ready to eat. This will keep for 2 days in the fridge.

VARIATIONS

Veg swaps Though it looks stunning with red cabbage, this works just as well with finely shredded white cabbage. You can also swap small, firm parsnips for the carrot.

Cucurbit salad

Melons, cucumbers and courgettes are all members of the cucurbit family and here they make a harmonious trio, their lush textures and ample juices nicely enhanced with a piquant scattering of olives and onion. I could happily eat a bowlful of this lovely, summery salad on its own, but it also goes exceptionally well with fish.

Serves 2, or 4 as a side

½ medium-large cucumber (about 200g)

1 medium courgette (about 200g)

¼ small Charentais or Galia melon (about 200g)

50g pitted black olives, such as Kalamata

½ medium red onion, finely chopped

Juice of ½ small lemon

2 tablespoons extra virgin rapeseed or olive oil

Sea salt and freshly ground black pepper

Quarter the cucumber lengthways and scoop out the seeds with a teaspoon. Slice the cucumber into thin quarter-moons – about 2mm thick. Put into a large bowl. Top and tail the courgette, quarter it lengthways and slice into pieces the same width as the cucumber. Add to the bowl.

Scoop the seeds out of the melon. Carefully slice the melon off its skin, then slice it lengthways into 2–3 slender wedges before slicing crossways, as with the cucumber and courgette. Add to the bowl.

Roughly chop the olives and add to the salad with the finely chopped onion. Squeeze over the lemon juice, trickle over the oil, give it a good seasoning of salt and pepper and stir together gently. Taste, add more salt, pepper or lemon juice if needed, and serve straight away.

Tomatoes with tahini

A creamy, earthy tahini dressing is a fine foil to tomatoes – as long as your toms are ripe and flavoursome, you can use any size or variety you like. I love the hot, sweet bite of brine-pickled green peppercorns in this salad too, but they are optional.

Serves 3–4 as a side

About 400g tomatoes

1 tablespoon green peppercorns in brine, drained and rinsed (optional)

4 teaspoons sesame seeds

FOR THE DRESSING

1 tablespoon tahini

A scrap of crushed or grated garlic (about ¼ clove)

1 teaspoon runny honey

4 teaspoons cider vinegar

2 tablespoons extra virgin rapeseed or olive oil

Sea salt and freshly ground black pepper

Put all the ingredients for the dressing in a bowl, adding salt and pepper to taste. Add 1 tablespoon water and combine thoroughly with a whisk or wooden spoon, adding a little more water if it seems very thick. It needs to be thin enough to trickle easily over the tomatoes.

Cut the tomatoes into slim wedges (little cherry tomatoes can be halved or quartered) and divide between serving bowls. Season with salt and pepper, then trickle over the tahini dressing.

Scatter over the green peppercorns, if using, or add a generous extra grinding of black pepper, and finish with a sprinkling of sesame seeds.

Chinese-style bashed cucumber

This is really quick and easy. Giving the cucumber a light pummelling with a rolling pin breaks it down a little inside so that it readily absorbs the garlicky dressing. I like to serve it as part of an Asian-style meal, perhaps with rice and chicken, or with something meaty such as slow-roast pork, where it cuts the richness nicely. Chinese black vinegar lends a lovely, deep, mellow acidity, whereas rice wine vinegar gives a lighter, milder result.

Serves 4 as a side dish

1 garlic clove, peeled and very finely chopped

1 tablespoon Chinese black rice vinegar (or use rice wine vinegar)

1 tablespoon tamari

1 tablespoon toasted sesame oil

1 teaspoon caster sugar

Up to ½ teaspoon dried chilli flakes (optional)

1 large cucumber (about 450g), trimmed

Mix together all the ingredients except the cucumber in a large bowl. Stir until the sugar is dissolved.

Place the cucumber on a board and roughly bash it with a rolling pin until flattened slightly – you are aiming to break the cucumber up a bit on the inside without splitting the skin too much.

Slice the cucumber lengthways into quarters and then slice each quarter on an angle into pieces about 2cm wide. Add to the other ingredients and stir around so all the surfaces of the cucumber are coated. Leave for a few minutes, then stir again and serve.

This salad is best eaten within an hour or so of making, otherwise the cucumber juices can dilute the dressing.

VARIATION
Cucumber and rice noodle salad If you want to make this simple salad into more of a stand-alone dish, toss in some rice noodles – cooked, cooled in cold water, drained then dressed with a little toasted sesame oil. Add some cashew nuts and finish the dish off with lots of roughly chopped coriander leaves.

Green salad with Thai dressing

The zingy flavours of lime, fish sauce and fresh coriander turn a simple green salad into something exotic. I like to use mint and basil in this dish too – or Thai basil if I can get it – but neither is essential.

Serves 4 as a side

2 medium avocados, ripe but not squashy

Juice of ½ lime or lemon

8 spring onions, cut on the diagonal into 1cm slices

2 Little Gem lettuces

About 3 tablespoons coriander leaves, roughly chopped

About 1 tablespoon mint and/or basil or Thai basil leaves, roughly chopped (optional)

Sesame or sunflower seeds, to finish (optional)

FOR THE DRESSING

1 teaspoon toasted sesame oil

1 teaspoon fish sauce

1 teaspoon runny honey

1 teaspoon rice vinegar

1 tablespoon mirin

1 tablespoon tamari

Halve the avocados and remove the stones, then quarter and peel. Cut each quarter lengthways into 2 or 3 slices. Place in a bowl and spritz with a good squeeze of lime or lemon juice. Add the sliced spring onions.

Mix all the dressing ingredients thoroughly together. Tip the dressing over the avocado and spring onions and toss together gently.

Separate the lettuce leaves and split any large ones down the centre. Add to the salad and gently turn again.

Add the herbs, give the salad another good squeeze of lime or lemon, sprinkle with seeds if you have some to hand, and it's ready to serve.

VARIATION

Bulk it up with noodles You can turn this salad into a main dish by tossing cooked, rinsed rice or glass noodles (25g uncooked weight per person) into the finished salad. Or, for a more elegant presentation, hold back a little of the dressing and dress the noodles separately, then serve the noodles in a shallow bowl and pile the salad on top.

Chickpea salad with avocado 'mayo'

This is an easy dish to whip up on a whim with a tin of chickpeas, drained and rinsed, but it's also delicious using sprouted chickpeas – either bought or sprouted at home (see below). The thick avocado dressing is not a mayonnaise in any strict sense, but it has a similar rich creaminess with a piquant seasoning.

Serves 4

1 Cos lettuce, shredded into broad ribbons

400g tin chickpeas, drained and rinsed, or 100g dried chickpeas, sprouted (see below)

25g sunflower seeds

Extra virgin hempseed or rapeseed oil, to trickle

FOR THE AVOCADO 'MAYO'

1 medium-large ripe avocado

2 tablespoons cider vinegar

3 tablespoons extra virgin rapeseed or olive oil

½ teaspoon English mustard

½ garlic clove, grated or crushed

Sea salt and freshly ground black pepper

To make the avocado 'mayo', halve the avocado, peel and remove the stone then put it into a food processor. Add the cider vinegar, oil, mustard, garlic, a good pinch of salt and a few twists of pepper. Process to a smooth green purée.

Spread the shredded lettuce over a large platter or individual plates. Trickle with a little oil and season with salt and pepper. Mix about half the chickpeas (tinned or sprouted) with a couple of tablespoons of the avocado mayo and scatter over the lettuce.

Spoon over the remaining avocado mayo, scatter over the remaining chickpeas and add the sunflower seeds. Add a final trickle of oil, sprinkle with salt and pepper, and serve.

SPROUTING YOUR OWN CHICKPEAS

Sprouted chickpeas are deliciously versatile and bring a lovely nutritious crunch to salads. The process takes 5–7 days.

Take 50g dried chickpeas, put them in a bowl, cover with plenty of cold water (they will swell up a lot) and leave to soak for 24 hours. Drain and rinse the chickpeas well then put them in a sieve or colander suspended over a bowl and cover loosely with muslin or a thin cloth (they need to be able to 'breathe').

The initial soaking will have 'woken up' the chickpeas and they will soon start to sprout. Over the next 3–5 days, you need to thoroughly rinse them a couple of times a day, and return them to their colander, loosely covered. Chickpeas dry out more easily than smaller pulses during sprouting, so keep an eye on them and give them a good rinse whenever they start to look a little dry. When the chickpeas have sprouts at least 2cm long, they're ready to use. Give them a final rinse before using. You can keep them in the fridge for a couple of days.

Quinoa and gooseberry tabbouleh

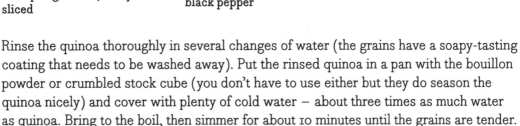

An authentic tabbouleh uses bulgar wheat. Quinoa is an under-explored grain that's quicker to prepare and has a lovely mild, nutty taste. The gooseberry and cucumber give tartness and cool crunch. Try it clean and green, or add the cinnamon and allspice for a warm Middle Eastern note.

Serves 4

200g quinoa

½ teaspoon vegetable bouillon powder or ¼ veg stock cube (optional)

3 tablespoons extra virgin rapeseed or olive oil, plus an extra trickle

A large bunch of flat-leaf parsley (about 100g)

A small bunch of mint (about 20g)

6–8 spring onions, finely sliced

150g gooseberries (fresh or frozen and defrosted), halved or quartered, depending on size

1 medium-large cucumber (about 400g), cut into roughly 1cm cubes

½ teaspoon ground allspice (optional)

½ teaspoon ground cinnamon (optional)

Juice of ½ lemon

Sea salt and freshly ground black pepper

Rinse the quinoa thoroughly in several changes of water (the grains have a soapy-tasting coating that needs to be washed away). Put the rinsed quinoa in a pan with the bouillon powder or crumbled stock cube (you don't have to use either but they do season the quinoa nicely) and cover with plenty of cold water – about three times as much water as quinoa. Bring to the boil, then simmer for about 10 minutes until the grains are tender.

Drain the quinoa well and tip into a large bowl. Add a little salt and pepper and a trickle of oil and toss well, then leave to cool completely.

Pick all the leaves from the parsley and mint, chop them fairly finely and put into a large bowl. Add the sliced spring onions, gooseberries and diced cucumber. Sprinkle over the spices, if using, a good pinch of salt and a few twists of pepper, and mix well.

Add the cooled quinoa, lemon juice and 3 tablespoons extra virgin oil and toss together thoroughly. Leave to stand for at least an hour. Taste and add more salt, pepper and lemon juice if needed before serving.

VARIATIONS

Add nuts or seeds To make the dish even more robust – for a stand-alone lunch or lunchbox – add a handful of your favourite nuts or seeds, ideally lightly toasted. Cashews, sunflower seeds and/or pumpkin seeds are ideal.

Green bean, tomato and lentil salad

Puy lentils are one of my favourite dish-completing ingredients. They soak up the flavours of a dressing brilliantly and give substance to all kinds of salads. This one is particularly satisfying.

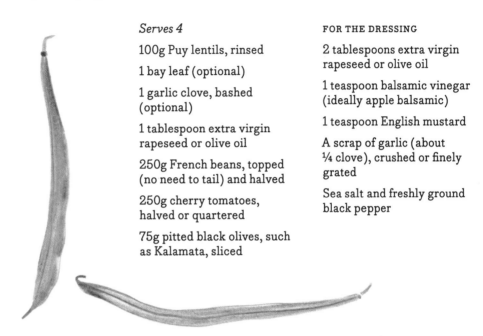

Serves 4

100g Puy lentils, rinsed

1 bay leaf (optional)

1 garlic clove, bashed (optional)

1 tablespoon extra virgin rapeseed or olive oil

250g French beans, topped (no need to tail) and halved

250g cherry tomatoes, halved or quartered

75g pitted black olives, such as Kalamata, sliced

FOR THE DRESSING

2 tablespoons extra virgin rapeseed or olive oil

1 teaspoon balsamic vinegar (ideally apple balsamic)

1 teaspoon English mustard

A scrap of garlic (about ¼ clove), crushed or finely grated

Sea salt and freshly ground black pepper

Put the lentils into a saucepan and cover with cold water. Add the bay leaf and garlic clove, if using. Bring to the boil, turn down to a simmer and cook for up to 20 minutes, until the lentils are al dente – tender but with a little nutty resistance. Keep an eye on them, and taste after about 12 minutes, as they can go from al dente to soft very quickly. Top up with more boiling water if necessary during cooking.

Drain the lentils, discarding the bay and garlic. Toss with 1 tablespoon olive or rapeseed oil and a little salt and pepper and set aside to cool completely.

Bring a saucepan of water to the boil. Drop in the beans, time 3 minutes, then drain them in a colander. Run them immediately under cold water to stop the cooking and help fix their bright green colour. Set aside to drain thoroughly.

Combine the lentils, beans, cherry tomatoes and olives in a large bowl.

Put the dressing ingredients in a jar, adding a pinch of salt and a grinding of pepper, and shake to emulsify. Pour over the salad and toss well. Leave to stand for 10 minutes or so, then toss again.

Serve the salad from the bowl or divide between individual plates, making sure the different elements are well distributed across each portion.

Roast parsnip and apple salad

Apples and parsnips are excellent partners, particularly when they're tenderised and caramelised by roasting. A garlicky, lemony dressing adds a piquant contrast to their earthy sweetness. If you don't fancy hazelnuts, pecans or walnuts are really good in this dish too.

Serves 4

4 medium parsnips (about 500g in total)

1 tablespoon rapeseed or sunflower oil

4 eating apples (about 500g in total), peeled if you like, cut into eighths, cores removed

4 generous handfuls of salad leaves

50g hazelnuts (or walnuts or pecans), lightly toasted

FOR THE DRESSING

2 tablespoons rapeseed or sunflower oil

1 tablespoon lemon juice

½ garlic clove, crushed to a paste with a little salt, or finely grated

1 teaspoon English mustard

2 teaspoons runny honey

Sea salt and freshly ground black pepper

Preheat the oven to 190°C/Gas 5. Peel the parsnips and quarter them lengthways. Chop the parsnips into roughly 2cm pieces and put them in a large roasting tray (they should not be crowded). Sprinkle with some salt and pepper, trickle over the oil and toss well. Roast for 20 minutes, then give them a stir, add the apple pieces and return to the oven for another 10–12 minutes or until the apples are lightly coloured and tender.

Meanwhile, make the dressing by whisking all the ingredients together, adding salt and pepper to taste.

When the parsnip and apples are cooked, transfer them to a bowl and toss them in the dressing. Arrange the salad leaves on a large platter or individual plates, top with the still-warm dressed parsnip and apple, then finish off with the toasted nuts. Serve straight away.

VARIATION

Roast carrot salad with plums In late summer or very early autumn, during the plum season, and when carrots are getting chunky, try swapping carrots for the parsnips, roasting them for a little longer to get them tender – give them 30–40 minutes. Add 200g raw plums, stoned and sliced, to the finished carrots along with the dressing – to which you can add a little pinch of ground cinnamon or Chinese five-spice to enhance the fruit.

Brown rice salad

I couldn't resist the austerity of this title, but really the brown rice is a tasty, nutty element alongside super-crisp and crunchy mangetout, juicy cucumber, and an intense prune and tamari dressing. It's a great example of how to whip some simple, wholesome ingredients into irresistible shape.

Serves 2–3, or 4–5 as a starter

100g brown rice, such as wholegrain basmati

1 small cucumber (about 300g) or ½ large one

75–100g mangetout (raw or lightly blanched)

A bunch of spring onions (about 175g), finely sliced

A few mint leaves, shredded (optional)

FOR THE DRESSING

50g pitted prunes, thinly sliced

25ml tamari

1 tablespoon runny honey

2 teaspoons sesame seeds

2 teaspoons toasted sesame oil

A pinch of dried chilli flakes

Rinse the rice in a sieve, then tip it into a pan and add plenty of cold water. Bring to the boil, reduce to a simmer and cook until tender – about 25 minutes should do it. Drain and allow to cool completely (rice should not be left sitting about at room temperature for any length of time, so try and make the salad as soon as the rice is cool).

While the rice is cooling, mix the dressing ingredients together in a bowl with a whisk, adding 2 tablespoons water, and allow to sit for at least 10–15 minutes. This will allow the flavours to develop and the prunes to soften a little.

Quarter the cucumber lengthways and scoop out the seeds with a teaspoon. Halve each quarter again, lengthways, then cut each length into short batons. Combine the cucumber, mangetout, spring onions and mint, if using, with the cooled rice. Add the dressing and mix gently. Spoon on to plates and serve straight away.

Eat **Fish**

feel fab!

WHEN TIME IS at a premium, fish is your friend. You've pretty much got to cook it quickly – that's how you get the best out of it. So it's a surefire winner for busy cooks.

I want to help you keep fish fun as well as fast. I do love very simply cooked fish – pan fried fillets or roast whole fish, with just a pinch of seasoning and herbs. Served with a heap of fresh garden veg, it's very hard to beat. But I also like fish dishes that jump for joy around a fab set of flavours, or where a piece of fish nuzzles up to some surprising companions.

Pairing fish and shellfish with powerful partners is rarely a problem. They give up their own flavours and take on others even more generously than meat. So in the following pages I'm matching my fish with aromatic seasonings and bright colours, breaking out the sassy spices and pungent herbs to create fish dishes as lovely to look at as they are to eat.

The concept of fish curry gets three different outings (on pages 216–220). Just check out the pics and you'll see how deliciously different they are. More surprisingly perhaps, I'm also combining my fish with tart, tangy fruit. If you've never had mackerel with gooseberries (page 209) or crab with apple (as on page 189) then you have a treat in store.

A spirit of gung-ho experimentation runs right through this chapter. Mixing simple white fish fillets with the same spices I use to make chorizo (to create my 'fish-rizo' on page 201) turned out

to be a delight. And fish fingers, coated simply in beaten egg (page 225) rather than a fiddly breadcrumb coating, have proved such a big hit with my family that I've never gone back.

You can ensure your fish cookery feels good as well as tasting great by choosing sustainably caught species. This is an area where conscientious consumers are already having a huge positive impact. Supermarkets are increasingly stocking more sustainable fish in response to growing demand. It's a virtuous circle we can all take part in by continuing to make good choices.

There are some simple rules you can stick to: look for the Marine Stewardship Council logo as evidence of responsible sourcing, and check out the Marine Conservation Society's fishonline.org website for up-to-date info on which species to choose and which to avoid. And vary the fish you buy – ring the changes with different species and you will be lessening the pressure on hard-pressed species such as cod, salmon and prawns.

I avoid farmed fish, unless it's organic (which means reared less intensively and fed on sustainably sourced feed). The exception is farmed mussels and oysters, which are good sustainable choices as there are no problematic inputs, and the growing bivalves actually provide a haven for juvenile fish of other species. That should make the spicy mussel dish on page 195 a particularly tempting choice.

Mackerel and fennel escabeche

An escabeche is fish cooked in a highly seasoned, sweet-sour liquor and served warm or at room temperature with all its aromatic juices. With the subtle crunch of fennel, this is a beautifully light, clean-tasting version. I like to serve it with hunks of seedy rye soda bread (page 65) or with a lightly dressed potato salad.

Serves 2, or 4 as a starter

1 large or 2 medium fennel bulbs, trimmed and finely sliced

1 small onion, finely sliced

2 medium mackerel, filleted (i.e. 4 fillets)

Freshly ground black pepper

1 tablespoon chopped dill, to finish

FOR THE MARINADE

1 tablespoon coriander seeds

1 tablespoon fennel seeds

3 bay leaves

2 teaspoons soft light brown sugar

1 teaspoon fine salt

150ml cider vinegar

To make the marinade, put all the ingredients into a large, shallow pan with 150ml cold water, bring to a simmer and cook for 1–2 minutes.

Meanwhile, lay the sliced fennel and onion out on a large platter, deep enough to hold the fish and all the marinade.

Turn the heat down under the marinade so it is simmering very gently and add the mackerel. Cook for a couple of minutes, basting the fish with the hot liquid as you go, until the fillets are just cooked through.

Carefully transfer the mackerel fillets from the hot liquid to the serving platter, nestling them into the fennel and onion. Pour the hot, spicy marinade from the pan over the fish and vegetables. Leave to cool for at least 20 minutes, during which time the veg will soften slightly.

Finish the dish off with the chopped dill. Eat warm or at room temperature. You can keep this in the fridge for a couple of days, bringing it up to room temperature for an hour or so before serving.

Crab with sprouts

This is a fabulous thing to do with a fresh, ready-dressed crab, which you can get from any decent fishmonger. You can use the white meat alone, or a mixture of the white and slightly stronger-flavoured brown, as you choose. A small-medium dressed crab, around 200g, will easily give you enough meat for two.

Serves 2, or 4 as a starter

1 medium eating apple

1 small avocado

4 very fresh Brussels sprouts

About 100g fresh crab meat

50g skinned hazelnuts, lightly toasted

A pinch of dried chilli flakes

FOR THE DRESSING

2 tablespoons extra virgin rapeseed or olive oil, plus extra to finish

1 tablespoon lemon juice

½ teaspoon runny honey

Sea salt and freshly ground black pepper

Put the dressing ingredients in a jar, adding a pinch of salt and a grinding of pepper, and shake to emulsify.

Quarter and core the apple, peel it if you like, then slice it fairly thinly into a bowl. Add the dressing and toss the apple in it. Peel and quarter the avocado, discarding the stone. Cut into chunks and add to the bowl with the apple. Toss gently together, taking care you don't mash the avocado too much.

Trim the sprouts and remove any tough or damaged outer leaves. Slice the sprouts thinly and add them to the apple and avocado, breaking up the discs a little with your fingers as you go. Add the crab meat too and toss the whole lot very gently together.

Transfer the salad to a wide serving bowl or divide between individual bowls. Very roughly chop the hazelnuts and scatter them over, sprinkle on a pinch of chilli flakes, give the whole thing a final trickle of extra virgin oil, and serve.

VARIATIONS

Sprout swap Other well-flavoured greens can replace the sprouts: thinly sliced Savoy cabbage and kale work well, so do slightly bitter leaves like frisée and radicchio.

Raw fish with tomatoes and basil

This is based on the classic ceviche technique, where citrus juice is used to 'cook' raw fish. However, here I'm relying on the acidity in tomato juice and a touch of cider vinegar to do the job. With some aromatic basil and a splash of extra virgin oil, the result is a beautifully delicate raw fish salad.

Serves 4, or 6 as a starter

400–500g fillets of very fresh black bream, sea bass or pollack, skinned

750g ripe, mixed tomatoes (ideally a variety of shapes and colours)

1 medium red onion or 2 shallots, thinly sliced

½ small garlic clove, crushed

3 tablespoons extra virgin rapeseed or olive oil

1 tablespoon cider vinegar

A large handful of basil leaves, coarsely shredded

Sea salt and freshly ground black pepper

Place the fish on a board and check for pin bones, prising out any you find with tweezers. Working across the fillet with your knife at an angle, cut it into thin (3–5mm) slices. Place in a large bowl.

Cut the tomatoes into bite-sized chunks and add them to the fish with the onion, garlic, oil, vinegar, basil, a good pinch of salt and a couple of grinds of pepper. Use your hands or salad tongs to turn everything together very carefully without breaking up the fish.

Cover and leave in a cool place or the fridge for the flavours to mingle and the acidic juices to start gently 'cooking' the fish. You can serve this as little as 15 minutes after making it but it's better if you can leave it for at least an hour, and optimum after about 3 hours – ideally you should turn the ingredients over gently once or twice during that time. If refrigerated, remove half an hour before serving – it's better served at cool room temperature rather than fridge cold.

Serve just as it comes, as a starter or a light main course.

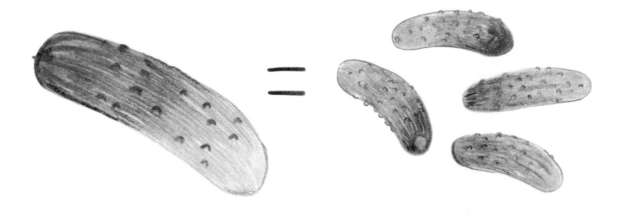

Smoked mackerel tartare

This is a very quick and easy, dairy-free alternative to smoked mackerel pâté. And I prefer it. Spread it on rye crispbreads for a fast but deeply satisfying lunch, or pack it up in a lunchbox.

Serves 3–4

2 smoked mackerel fillets

2 hard-boiled eggs, peeled and halved

4 cornichons (or 1 large gherkin)

4 tablespoons mayonnaise

About 1 tablespoon roughly chopped dill or parsley

A squeeze of lemon juice

Freshly ground black pepper

Oatcakes, crispbreads or Little Gem lettuce, to serve

Flake the mackerel off the skin and put it into a bowl or on to a board. Add the eggs and cornichons, the mayonnaise, most of the dill or parsley and some black pepper. Chop the ingredients together and mix well but without breaking them up too much. I simply use the blade of my chopping knife to lift, combine and chop the ingredients fairly coarsely on a board, for a nice chunky texture.

Taste the tartare and add lemon juice and a little more black pepper if you like. (The smoked mackerel usually contributes enough salt.)

Transfer to a serving dish, sprinkle with the remaining dill or parsley and a little more black pepper and serve, with crispbreads or oatcakes. Or for a lighter version that makes a great canapé, serve piled on to crisp Little Gem lettuce leaves.

Hot, sweet and sour mussels

I'm always looking for new ways to make one of my favourite – and one of the most sustainable – shellfish even more delicious. Here, the apple juice base with all the aromatics gives the mussels an appealing Asian tang, and leaves a delicious broth to sip when they are eaten. These days, mussels are sold pretty clean, so giving them a quick once-over shouldn't take too long.

Serves 2, or 4 as a starter

1kg mussels

1 tablespoon rapeseed or sunflower oil

2 garlic cloves, thinly sliced

3cm piece of ginger, peeled and sliced into matchsticks

½–1 medium-hot red chilli, to taste, thinly sliced

200ml cloudy apple juice (i.e. not from concentrate)

2 tablespoons tamari

2 teaspoons cider vinegar, or to taste

Scrub the mussels in a colander under a cold tap and use a small sharp knife to help remove any wiry little 'beards' that are attached to the shells. Discard any open mussels that don't close when given a sharp tap.

Put the oil into a large, wide, heavy-based saucepan (that has a tight-fitting lid) over a medium-low heat. Add the garlic, ginger and chilli (use just half the chilli if you don't like too much heat) and sizzle for a minute or two, making sure the garlic doesn't burn.

Pour in the apple juice, tamari and cider vinegar, increase the heat and bring to a brisk simmer. Tip in the mussels and put the lid on the pan. After 3 minutes, lift the lid, give the mussels a good stir, pop the lid back on and cook for another minute. They should almost all be open, but if quite a few aren't, just give them another stir and another minute. Discard any that refuse to open.

Turn off the heat, taste the mussely juices and adjust the sour and salty flavours by adding a little more vinegar or tamari if necessary. Serve the mussels and all their lovely liquor either on their own (with a spoon for the broth) or, to make a main course of them, over a pile of cooked noodles or rice.

Spicy sprats

Sprats are fantastic little fish – inexpensive, easy to prepare, full of healthy omega-3 oils, and quite delicious. Some lively seasoning and a brief spell under a hot grill turn them into one of my favourite finger foods. I like to eat them with an ice-cold beer.

Serves 2

300g sprats

¼ teaspoon cayenne pepper

Finely grated zest of 1 lemon, plus some of the juice

¼ teaspoon fine sea salt

A grinding of black pepper

1–2 teaspoons rapeseed or sunflower oil, plus a little extra for oiling

Lemon wedges, to serve

Preheat your grill to high and lightly oil a rack over a grill tray. Alternatively, if you want to bake the sprats in the oven, preheat it to 220°C/Gas 7 and lightly oil a rack over an oven dish.

To prepare the sprats, first hold one in your left hand (or right, if you are left-handed) and use a stout pair of kitchen scissors in the other hand to cut away a strip about 5mm wide all along the belly, from just below the tail to the gills. Pull this away then hold the fish, head down, under a running cold tap. Use your thumb to push out the gut, rinsing as you go. Put the sprats to dry on a plate lined with kitchen paper. Pat them all over with kitchen paper so they are fairly dry.

Combine the cayenne, lemon zest, salt, pepper and oil in a large bowl. Add the sprats to the bowl and use your hands to massage the lemony spice mix all over them, working it into the cavities and all over the skin.

Put the seasoned fish on the grill rack and grill for about 2 minutes each side until the skin is blistered and crispy and the juices bubbling. Alternatively, bake the sprats in the top of the hot oven for 8–10 minutes. Either way, give the hot sprats a good squeeze of lemon juice, transfer them to a serving dish and add a couple of lemon wedges.

Eat straight away, picking up the little fish with your fingers and nibbling the spicy flesh off the bones. A green salad and some rye soda bread make a meal of it – and you could add a dollop of mayonnaise if you want to push the boat out.

Red mullet with sesame root salad

This tangy, savoury, sesame-infused salad is a great way to bring together raw carrots and radishes with fish. Red mullet seems to match the veg particularly well for colour as well as flavour, but you can also use fillets of sea bass, mackerel, mullet or bream.

Serves 4

4 red mullet fillets

Rapeseed or sunflower oil, for frying

1 garlic clove, sliced

A small-finger-sized piece of ginger (about 20g), peeled and cut into matchsticks

Sea salt and freshly ground black pepper

FOR THE SALAD

1 tablespoon sesame seeds

5–6 young carrots (about 150g in total)

12 red or white radishes (about 125g in total), plus leaves if in good condition

1 tablespoon rice vinegar

½ teaspoon toasted sesame oil

2 tablespoons tamari

For the salad, lightly toast the sesame seeds if you have time – in a dry frying pan over a medium heat. This isn't essential but it does enhance their nutty flavour. Leave to cool.

Peel the carrots, then using the peeler again, shave them from top to bottom into ribbons. Place these in a bowl. Slice the radishes into thin rounds and add them to the carrots. Add the vinegar, sesame oil and seeds and tamari, turn together and set aside.

Check the fish for pin bones, prising out any you find with tweezers. Place a large frying pan over a medium heat and add a trickle of oil. Season the fish with salt and pepper and add to the pan, skin side down. Cook for 3–4 minutes, then flip the fillets over, add the garlic and ginger to the pan, give the whole pan a little shake to distribute the aromatics, and turn off the heat.

Allow the fish to finish cooking through in the heat of the pan for 1–2 minutes, stirring the garlic about a few times so it doesn't burn.

Place the red mullet on warmed plates and scatter over the dressed veg (and radish leaves, if you have them). Spoon on the remaining dressing from the carrot and radish bowl, along with any juices from the frying pan, and serve. Rice or rice noodles are lovely with this.

Fish-rizo with broad beans

This is so-called because it takes the classic seasonings of a chorizo sausage and mingles them with fresh fish to create a gloriously red, richly flavoured dish.

Serves 4

700g white fish fillets, such as pollack, coley, whiting or sustainably caught haddock, skinned and boned

1 tablespoon unsmoked paprika

1 teaspoon sweet smoked paprika

A small pinch of cayenne pepper

2 teaspoons fennel seeds

2 garlic cloves, sliced

2 tablespoons rapeseed or sunflower oil, plus a little extra for cooking

150g cooked broad beans, skinned if they are large

Juice of ½ lemon

Sea salt

A little roughly shredded mint, to finish (optional)

Check the fish for pin bones, prising out any you find with tweezer, then cut into roughly 2cm chunks. Put it into a bowl with the spices, garlic and oil. Add a pinch of salt. Turn together and, if you have time, leave it for up to half an hour in the fridge.

Heat a large frying pan or wok over a medium-high heat. Add a trickle more oil, then the fish, and cook, tossing often, for 4–5 minutes, until cooked through. Stir in the broad beans and cook for another minute. Squeeze over the lemon juice and remove from the heat. Taste and add more salt if needed.

Divide between bowls and serve, with some fresh mint sprinkled over if you like. For me, the combination of salty-spicy fish and bittersweet broad beans is delicious, and complete. But you can certainly serve this with rice, flatbreads (such as the cornmeal tortillas on page 72), or potatoes if you want a heartier supper.

VARIATIONS

Bean swaps The broad bean element can be swapped out with other veg and pulses of substance: a tin of chickpeas is a great standby alternative – drain, rinse and toss with the fish for the last couple of minutes. Peas work well too, as will nutty Puy lentils. And a combination of peas and lentils is particularly good. In all cases you can also toss a few little new potatoes – just cooked and still hot – into the mix.

Grilled sardines with marinated courgettes

The courgettes here are raw, but softened in a lemony, herby marinade – an excellent idea from River Cottage apprentice chef Sam Lomas and the perfect foil to crisp, smoky, grilled sardines. It's great with mackerel too. Of course you can barbecue the fish instead of grilling it.

Serves 4

8 large or 12 small sardines, gutted and cleaned

A little extra virgin rapeseed or olive oil

FOR THE MARINATED COURGETTES

2 tablespoons extra virgin rapeseed or olive oil

½ garlic clove, grated or crushed

A pinch of dried chilli flakes (optional)

Finely grated zest of 1 lemon, plus some of its juice

500g small, young courgettes

2–3 tablespoons shredded basil

2–3 tablespoons chopped parsley

Sea salt and freshly ground black pepper

Start with the courgettes. Put the oil, garlic, chilli flakes, lemon zest and a good squeeze of lemon juice into a bowl. Add some salt and pepper and mix well. Top and tail the courgettes, then use a veg peeler to slice them into long, thin ribbons. Drop these into the marinade, along with the chopped herbs, and stir well.

Cover and leave in a cool place (but not the fridge) for an hour or so until the courgettes are 'relaxed' and juicy. Then stir the mixture again, taste and add more lemon, salt and pepper as needed.

Shortly before you want to eat, preheat your grill to high. Rub the sardines all over with a little oil, then season them well inside and out with salt and pepper. Place them on a lightly oiled rack over a grill pan and grill for 2–3 minutes each side, depending on their size, until the flesh is cooked through and the skin nicely browned and blistered.

Divide the courgettes and juices between warmed plates and serve the sardines beside or on top of them. If you want something starchy alongside, boiled baby new potatoes are perfect.

White fish with quick cucumber pickle

I don't think we eat cold fish in a salad often enough. This inexpensive dish is clean, fresh and light, yet it's full of flavour.

Serves 4

1 medium cucumber (about 375g)

2 teaspoons fine sea salt

4 tablespoons cider vinegar

4 teaspoons caster sugar

2 teaspoons coriander seeds, lightly toasted if possible

500g white fish fillets, such as pollack, coley, whiting or sustainably caught haddock

6 bay leaves, torn (optional)

1 tablespoon chopped dill

3–4 spring onions, sliced

½ green chilli, deseeded and thinly sliced (optional)

Freshly ground black pepper

Peel the cucumber and cut it into roughly 2mm slices. Put these in a large bowl, add the salt and toss together, then tip into a sieve and leave, set over a bowl to catch any drips, for 15–20 minutes.

Rinse the cucumber under a gently flowing cold tap to remove the salt, turning the pieces as you go. Drain well.

In a large bowl, stir together the vinegar, sugar, coriander seeds and a good grinding of black pepper. Add the drained cucumber, mix well and set aside.

Check the fish for pin bones, prising out any you find with tweezers, then season very lightly with a pinch of salt. Cook, skin on, gently and simply in whatever way you like: in a steamer for 5–6 minutes, or a lightly oiled frying pan turning once, or baked in an oven dish with a little water, at 180°C/Gas 4 for about 10 minutes. A bay leaf or two tucked under the fish as it cooks will impart flavour.

In all cases test the fish by inserting the tip of a sharp knife into the thickest part: the flesh should flake apart easily. Leave the fish to cool completely. Discard the bay leaves.

When the fish is cold, peel off the skin and break the flesh into large flakes. Add these to the lightly pickled cucumber and its juices, along with most of the dill, the spring onions, and the chilli if using. Turn very carefully to combine all the ingredients. Leave for 10 minutes or so and combine again before serving, sprinkled with the rest of the dill. Eat with seedy rye bread (page 65) or crispbreads (page 80).

Poached smoked haddock with soft polenta

This speedy fish supper is comforting and soothing. The polenta is cooked with the fish poaching liquid so a gentle smoky savour pervades the whole dish. Look out for MSC certified smoked haddock.

Serves 4

400ml unsweetened almond milk (bought or home-made, see page 30), or oat milk

A small bunch of flat-leaf parsley, leaves chopped, stalks reserved

2 bay leaves

500g smoked haddock or pollack fillet

2 tablespoons extra virgin rapeseed or olive oil, plus extra to finish

125g quick-cook polenta

Sea salt and freshly ground black pepper

Wholegrain mustard, to serve (optional)

Put the dairy-free milk and 400ml water in a saucepan with the parsley stalks and bay leaves. Bring to a simmer. Check the fish for pin bones, then add to the pan and simmer gently for 2 minutes or until the fish is just cooked through. Carefully remove the fish, set aside and keep warm. Don't worry if the liquor starts to look curdled at this point, it will come together when combined with the polenta. Discard the parsley stalks and bay.

Put the fishy milk back over a gentle heat and add the oil. Pour the polenta into the hot milk in a steady stream, whisk until smooth and let the mixture return to a simmer. Stir gently as the polenta cooks and thickens. The quick-cook type should take barely a minute to reach a thick purée consistency. When this happens, take the pan off the heat.

Add the chopped parsley, along with a good few twists of black pepper, then taste and add salt as needed (the smoked fish will have added some salt).

Flake the smoked fish off its skin. Spoon the smoky polenta on to warmed plates and add the chunks of flaked fish. Grind over some black pepper, add a trickle of extra virgin oil and serve, with a good dollop of wholegrain mustard on the side, if you like.

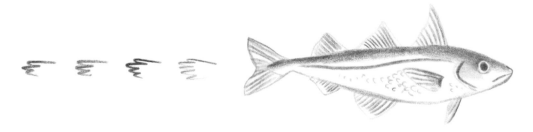

Mackerel baked on fennel and gooseberries

This is a great three-way combination – oily fish, aromatic fennel and tart gooseberries. Taste the berries first: if they are very tart when raw then add the sugar as suggested in the recipe. Great with sardines as well as mackerel, this dish also works with less oily, more robust fish, such as bream, red or grey mullet, or line-caught sea bass.

Serves 2

2 plump fennel bulbs

1 lemon

A couple of bay leaves

2 tablespoons rapeseed or sunflower oil

100g gooseberries, topped and tailed

2–3 teaspoons caster sugar (optional)

2–3 mackerel, gutted and cleaned

Sea salt and freshly ground black pepper

Preheat the oven to 180°C/Gas 4.

Trim the fennel and remove the tough outer layer. Cut each bulb into 8 wedges. Put into a shallow roasting tin. Use a veg peeler to pare about 6 strips of zest from the lemon, trying to get as little of the white pith as possible. Add these to the fennel with the bay leaves. Trickle over the oil, add some salt and pepper and toss together. Roast for about 20 minutes, stirring once, until the fennel is tender.

Add the gooseberries to the roasting tin, scattering them evenly over the fennel. Sprinkle over the sugar, if using (see above). Season the mackerel well, inside and out, then place on top of the fennel and gooseberries. Turn up the oven to 200°C/Gas 6 and return the dish to the oven for about 15 minutes, or until the fish is cooked through, the fennel is golden brown and the gooseberries are soft and bursting.

Serve with the lemon, cut into wedges for squeezing, and some waxy little potatoes.

VARIATION

With fillets I find this a great way to cook whole mackerel or sardines, but you can make a tidier, easier to eat version, using fish fillets instead of whole fish. Cook in the same way, but with a shorter cooking time – just 8–10 minutes once the fillets have been laid over the fennel and gooseberries.

Moroccan baked fish

The flavours here are distinctly North African: bittersweet and seriously spicy. They work brilliantly with robust, full-flavoured fish like bass, bream, grey mullet or gurnard. If you go for wild and line-caught or day-boat caught, these are all good sustainable choices too.

Serves 4

A little extra virgin rapeseed or olive oil

4 large (150–200g) or 8 small (80–120g) white fish fillets, such as sea bass, grey mullet, sea bream or gurnard

1–2 teaspoons harissa paste

About 2 tablespoons finely chopped preserved lemon rind

20 cherry or other small tomatoes, halved

Sea salt and freshly ground black pepper

Preheat the oven to 190°C/Gas 5. Take four pieces of strong kitchen foil, roughly 25cm square, and brush each with a little oil.

Check the fish for pin bones, prising out any you find with tweezers. Place 1 or 2 fillets, skin side down, in the centre of each piece of foil. Spread a little harissa over each fillet – as much heat as you think you can take. Scatter each with chopped preserved lemon rind and divide the tomatoes between each piece of foil, dotting them around the fish. Trickle the fish with a little more oil and season well with salt and pepper.

Bring up the sides of the foil up around the fish and crimp the edges together to form a well-sealed but baggy parcel with enough room inside for air to circulate.

Place the parcels on a baking tray and bake in the oven for 15–20 minutes (a little less if you are using small fillets) or until the fish is cooked through and the tomatoes hot and juicy.

Place each parcel on a warmed plate and take to the table so that people can open them up and enjoy the aromas as they are released. Serve with waxy potatoes and a green salad, or some simply cooked quinoa – well seasoned with a little extra virgin rapeseed or olive oil and freshly chopped parsley, mint or coriander.

HOME-MADE HARISSA

As an alternative to bought, ready-made harissa, you can whip up your own quick spicy paste: crush 2 garlic cloves with a pinch of salt, then stir with 1 teaspoon hot smoked paprika, ½ teaspoon cayenne or chilli flakes, 1 teaspoon ground cumin, 2 tablespoons tomato purée, 1 tablespoon rapeseed or olive oil and a grinding of black pepper. Keep in a sealed jar in the fridge and it will last for a month.

Foil-baked fish with celery and anchovies

Quick and easy, light but satisfying, this fantastic fish supper is bursting with tempting, salty-savoury flavours.

Serves 2

300–350g white fish fillets, such as bass, bream, gurnard, pollack, coley or sustainably caught haddock

6–8 tender inner celery stalks, thinly sliced, plus any leaves

6 anchovy fillets, torn into small pieces

4 teaspoons baby capers, rinsed (or regular capers, roughly chopped)

1 garlic clove, thinly sliced

1 or 2 pinches of dried chilli flakes (optional)

2 tablespoons extra virgin rapeseed or olive oil, plus a little extra for oiling

Sea salt and freshly ground black pepper

Preheat the oven to 190°C/Gas 5. Check the fish for pin bones, prising out any you find with tweezers. If you have two large fillets, cut each in half.

Put the sliced celery in a large bowl. Add the anchovies, capers, garlic, chilli flakes if using, and the oil. Season with a little pepper (the anchovies and capers are already pretty salty) and mix well.

Put the pieces of fish into the bowl with the celery mixture and mix with your hands so everything is well combined.

Take two pieces of strong kitchen foil, roughly 25cm square, and brush each with a little oil. Divide the fish fillets and all the flavourings between them. Bring up the sides of the foil around the fish and crimp the edges together to form a well-sealed but baggy parcel with enough room inside for air to circulate.

Place the parcels on a baking tray and bake in the oven for 15–20 minutes or until the fish is cooked through. Bring to the table straight away and serve – with boiled new potatoes or mashed old ones.

Trout with chermoula

Chermoula is a traditional North African concoction of herbs and spices, often served with fish. It lends itself well to the foil-parcel baking technique – a favourite of mine (see also pages 210 and 212). The foil encloses the fish in a steamy pocket, giving the fabulous flavours of the chermoula a chance to penetrate deeply. It also works with other whole plate-sized fish, such as mackerel and small bream.

Serves 2

2 small organic trout (350–400g each), gutted and cleaned, but heads left on

1–2 tablespoons white wine

30g flaked almonds (optional)

FOR THE CHERMOULA

2 tablespoons roughly chopped flat-leaf parsley

2 tablespoons roughly chopped coriander, stems included

½ small onion or 1 shallot, roughly chopped

½ garlic clove

½ teaspoon fine salt

1 teaspoon ground cumin

1 teaspoon ground coriander

½ teaspoon turmeric

½ teaspoon dried chilli flakes, or to taste

About 2 tablespoons extra virgin rapeseed or olive oil

1 tablespoon lemon juice

Preheat the oven to 200°C/Gas 6.

To make the chermoula, put all the ingredients except the oil and lemon into a food processor and process for a minute or so. Then, with the motor running, slowly trickle in enough oil to make a loose paste. Finally, stir in the lemon juice. (Or you could prepare the chermoula the traditional way, pounding the ingredients together using a pestle and mortar.)

With a sharp knife, slash the fish 4 or 5 times down both sides, going about 1cm deep but trying not to cut right through to the bone. Rub the chermoula all over the fish, working it into the cuts and the cavity.

Place the fish on a large sheet of strong kitchen foil, close together but not quite touching. Bring up the foil around the sides of the fish. Pour the white wine into the parcel (not over the fish) and scrunch the edges of the foil together tightly to seal the fish into a baggy parcel. Place the parcel on an oven tray and bake for 18 minutes.

Remove the fish from the oven, open the foil and sprinkle on the almonds, if using. Return the fish to the oven, with the foil open, for another 8 minutes or so until the fish is cooked through and the almonds are lightly toasted. Serve with potatoes or rice.

Fish with coconutty curried leeks

When I was in Sri Lanka a few years ago, I came across a wonderful dish of leeks cooked in lightly spiced coconut milk. It's a winning and adaptable combination and I have found that it works very well with fish. I like to keep the fish plain and to serve unadorned basmati rice alongside – that pared-back simplicity is just right with the rich and spicy veg.

Serves 4

4 white fish fillets, such as pollack, coley, whiting or sustainably caught haddock (150–200g each)

1 heaped tablespoon raw coconut oil

3 medium-large leeks

1 tablespoon of your favourite curry paste or powder

4 tablespoons coconut milk

Sea salt and freshly ground black pepper

Coriander leaves, roughly torn, to finish (optional)

Check the fish for pin bones, prising out any you find with tweezers. Melt the coconut oil in a large saucepan over a medium-low heat. With a pastry brush, brush the fish very lightly on both sides with a little of the melted oil. Season with a little salt and pepper, place on a grill tray and set aside. (You can fry or bake the fillets if you prefer.)

Trim and rinse the leeks and slice them into roughly 5mm discs. Add them to the remaining coconut oil in the saucepan with a pinch of salt. As soon as they are sizzling, turn the heat down low and cover the pan. Sweat, stirring occasionally, for 6–8 minutes, then stir in the curry paste or powder and cook for a further 5 minutes or until the leeks are silky and tender, stirring from time to time. Preheat the grill to medium.

Add the coconut milk to the tender leeks and stir well. Cook very gently for another few minutes, to give you a thick, saucy mixture. Taste it and add a little more salt if needed.

Meanwhile, get the fish under the grill and cook for 6–8 minutes, depending on the thickness of the fillets, until just done. To check, insert a knife into the thickest part – it should be opaque and flake easily from the skin.

Heap the coconutty leeks over portions of plain basmati rice in warmed bowls and top with the fish. Finish with a scattering of coriander, if you like, and serve.

Quick Thai squid curry

This is surprisingly speedy to rustle up, even if you make your own curry paste (see below), and it can be made with any green veg you fancy.

Serves 4

A little rapeseed or sunflower oil

1 small onion or large banana shallot, finely sliced

2 tablespoons ready-made Thai green curry paste (or a home-made paste, see below)

300ml fish, light chicken or vegetable stock

150ml coconut cream

Juice of ½–1 lime

1–2 teaspoons soft light brown sugar

400g cleaned squid tubes and tentacles

2 heads of pak choi or other green veg, such as spinach or chard (about 250g)

Fish sauce, to taste

A small bunch of coriander, leaves roughly chopped (save stalks for the paste)

Heat a wide, shallow saucepan or large deep frying pan over a medium heat. Add a dash of oil and fry the onion until soft and slightly coloured on the edges. Add the curry paste and turn down the heat to medium-low. Cook, stirring, for a further 3 minutes.

Add the stock and coconut cream, the juice of ½ lime and 1 teaspoon sugar. Stir, turn up the heat a little and bring to a gentle simmer. Simmer for 5–10 minutes to allow the sugar to dissolve, the flavours to combine and the sauce to thicken slightly.

Meanwhile, slice the squid into rings and cut the tentacles into 2 or 3 pieces. Quarter the pak choi lengthways (or cut other veg into small pieces). Stir the squid into the curry and tuck in the pak choi, then cover the pan and cook for a further 4 minutes.

Turn off the heat and taste the curry. Adjust the levels of sourness (with more lime) and sweetness (with more sugar, which will also tone down the heat if you find it too hot). Season with a little fish sauce (for saltiness) and then serve with the coriander leaves sprinkled over the top and lightly stirred through. Serve with rice.

HOME-MADE THAI GREEN CURRY PASTE

Gather the following: 3–4 medium-hot, medium-sized green chillies (according to your heat tolerance), a 5cm chunk of galangal or ginger (or both), peeled; 2 lemongrass stems, tough outer layers removed; 4 garlic cloves, peeled; 4 fresh kaffir lime leaves, finely chopped (or use the finely grated zest of 1 lime); a small bunch of coriander, including stalks; 2 tablespoons fish sauce. Roughly chop all the hard ingredients and put in a small food processor or blender with the fish sauce. Blitz together, adding a splash of water if necessary to help the paste come together. Don't worry if it isn't super-smooth – a slightly coarse paste is fine. You'll only need half this quantity of paste for this curry. The rest will keep in the fridge for a week, or you can freeze it.

Fish and tomato curry

Fish curry may sound like an undertaking, but it can be fast because the fish itself cooks through in a matter of minutes. All you need to do is create a flavoursome, spicy sauce first, which is easy, as this dish demonstrates.

Serves 3–4

2 tablespoons rapeseed or sunflower oil

1 large onion, sliced

2 teaspoons freshly grated ginger

3 garlic cloves, grated

1 tablespoon medium curry powder, or paste

1 cinnamon stick (optional)

300ml tomato passata

100ml coconut milk

½ teaspoon sugar

500g white fish fillets, such as pollack, coley or sustainably caught haddock, skinned

Juice of ½ large lime

Sea salt and freshly ground black pepper

TO FINISH

Coriander leaves

A few black onion (kalonji) seeds (optional)

Heat the oil in a large saucepan over a medium-low heat. Add the onion to the pan and cook, stirring regularly, for 8–10 minutes until soft.

Now add the ginger, garlic, curry powder or paste and cinnamon stick, if using, and fry for a minute or two. Add the passata and coconut milk, the sugar, a pinch of salt and some pepper. Stir well and simmer, stirring from time to time, for about 10 minutes until rich and well blended.

Meanwhile, check the fish for pin bones, prising out any you find with tweezers, then cut into large pieces, about 4cm square. Add these to the sauce, bring back to a very gentle simmer and cook for 4–6 minutes until the fish is just cooked through, stirring very carefully a couple of times (you don't want to break up the fish if you can help it). Remember it will continue to cook after you have taken it off the heat.

Stir in the lime juice, taste and add more salt or pepper if needed. Serve straight away with rice. Finish with a scattering of fresh coriander, and black onion seeds if you like.

Mustardy mackerel, spinach and spuds

Smoky fish with spuds and greens is always a winning combination. The baby spinach leaves in this hearty salad are barely cooked – just wilted in the heat from the potatoes.

Serves 4

About 800g new potatoes, cut into large-bite-sized chunks

150g baby leaf spinach

2 large or 3 medium smoked mackerel fillets

1 lemon

Sea salt and freshly ground black pepper

FOR THE DRESSING

3 tablespoons extra virgin rapeseed or olive oil

1 tablespoon cider vinegar

1 teaspoon English mustard

1 teaspoon grainy mustard

A scrap of garlic (about ¼ clove), crushed or grated

Put the potatoes in a saucepan, cover with water, add a little salt and bring to the boil. Reduce the heat and simmer for about 7–10 minutes, until just tender.

Put the dressing ingredients in a jar, add a pinch of salt and a grinding of pepper, and shake to emulsify.

When the potatoes are cooked, drain them well and return to the hot pan.

Flake the smoked mackerel off the skin, straight into the pan. Squeeze over the juice of half the lemon and add three-quarters of the spinach leaves. Toss well together again, so the leaves are gently wilted by the heat. Check and adjust the seasoning, adding more salt, pepper or lemon juice as needed.

Divide between bowls, scatter over the last of the spinach leaves, and serve.

VARIATION

Mustardy sardines and potatoes Replace the smoked mackerel with 2 tins of sardine fillets (or use tinned mackerel fillets), drained and broken into pieces. As well as the baby spinach, you can throw in a handful of chopped fennel or mint.

Eggy fish fingers with spring onion rice

Quicker, easier and much less messy than classic crumb-coated fish, egg-only fish fingers are a revelation. The egg cooks to a golden coating, somewhere between tender and crisp, which holds all the fish's succulent juices inside. These have become a firm family favourite, especially when served with this simple ricey side dish. Everyone likes it so much as it is that the ketchup stays in the cupboard.

Serves 4

500g white fish fillets, such as pollack, coley or sustainably caught haddock, skinned

3 large eggs

Rapeseed or sunflower oil, for frying

FOR THE SPRING ONION RICE

150g brown rice, such as wholegrain basmati

A bunch of spring onions (about 125g), trimmed and thinly sliced

Finely grated zest of 1 lemon, plus some of its juice

A little extra virgin rapeseed or olive oil

1–2 tablespoons chopped coriander or parsley (optional)

Sea salt and freshly ground black pepper

Rinse the rice in a sieve, then tip it into a pan and add plenty of cold water. Bring to the boil, reduce to a simmer and cook until tender – about 25 minutes should do it.

Drain the rice and return to the pan. Stir the sliced spring onions through, along with a squeeze of lemon juice, the lemon zest, a good trickle of extra virgin oil, some salt and pepper, and the chopped herbs, if using. Put the lid on the pan to keep it warm.

Now check the fish for pin bones, prising out any you find with tweezers, and cut the fillets into thick-finger-sized pieces or wedges (don't waste any fish trying to trim them into perfect shape). Break the eggs into a bowl, season with salt and pepper and whisk well.

Heat a thin layer of oil in a large frying pan over a medium-high heat. Working in batches, dip the pieces of fish into the seasoned egg, then place in the hot pan and fry for 1–2 minutes each side until golden and just cooked through. Transfer to a warmed plate, lined with kitchen paper, while you cook the rest of the fish.

Sprinkle the fish fingers, if you like, with a pinch more salt, then serve alongside the warm spring onion rice.

Storecupboard fishcakes

These tasty little fishcakes rely on the kind of ingredients I usually have to hand, including potatoes, tinned fish and capers.

Serves 2, or 4 as a starter

250g cold, cooked potato (about 2 baking potatoes' worth)

125g tin mackerel or sardine fillets in oil, drained

A bunch of spring onions (about 125g), finely sliced, or 1 medium onion, finely chopped

1 tablespoon capers, roughly chopped if large, whole if baby

1 medium egg

Rapeseed or sunflower oil, for cooking

4 tablespoons fine cornmeal

Sea salt and freshly ground black pepper

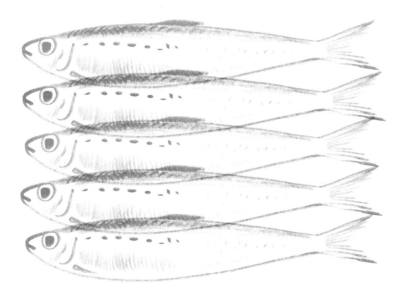

Mash the cooked potatoes roughly.

Put the tinned fish into a bowl and mash with a fork to break it up a little. Add the onion(s), capers, mashed potato and some black pepper. Lightly beat the egg and add this too. Stir the ingredients together.

Divide the mixture into four. Roll each portion into a ball, then squash lightly into a cake.

Heat a 1–2mm film of oil in the base of a non-stick frying pan over a medium heat.

Put the cornmeal in a bowl and season well with salt and pepper. Carefully (as they are quite fragile at this stage) transfer one of the fishcakes to the bowl of cornmeal and coat it all over, then gently place in the pan. Repeat with the rest. Cook for about 10 minutes, turning once or twice, until the cornmeal coating is crisp and brown and the cakes are piping hot through to the middle.

Serve straight away, with a simple leafy or tomato salad.

Meat
Less is more!

I USED TO EAT MEAT ALMOST every day, but now I'm as likely to have a meat-free day as a carnivorous one. And that's despite having a freezer full of home-grown pork, beef, lamb and chickens (along with a supply of rabbits and squirrels shot by my son). I've rethought my meat-eating partly for health reasons – my penchant for the crispy fatty bits wasn't doing my cholesterol any good – but mainly on principle.

I think it's hard to dispute that for most of us eating less meat is the right thing to do, in several senses. It's beneficial for our health, yes, but it's also good for the environment and, if eating less of it means we are able to afford better quality meat, from higher welfare farms, then it's good for our farm animals too. That's a lot of things to feel good about.

And that's why I wanted to put a *less is more* meat chapter in this book. Meat remains a fine ingredient – one I want to celebrate – and in moderation it provides excellent nutrition. It can also be a very quick and simple option. So I certainly don't think we have to give up meat altogether in order to eat more healthily and responsibly. I just think we need to rethink the way we use it a little.

I describe meat as an 'ingredient' deliberately. It doesn't always have to be the overbearing focal point of the dinner table. Good-quality meat, well used, is full of satisfying flavour, and a little can go a long way. If it's on a plate, it doesn't have to *own* the plate.

So there are plenty of recipes here where ingredients from the vegetable kingdom have just as much weight – or more – than the meaty ones. The lamb that features with cauliflower and chickpeas (page 249), finishes the dish nicely, but it would still be a dish without it. Similarly, in my parsnips, chorizo, kale and lentils (page 245) the chorizo is more a seasoning than a substantial meat portion. Dishes like these are the ones I turn to for quick, weekday meals.

There are also recipes in this chapter for meaty centrepieces – my aromatic nutty chicken (page 250) and fragrant Thai slow-cooked beef (page 253), for instance. These are the sort of dishes you might want to break out for a celebration or a weekend dinner. They are fairly speedy to prepare but then need time to do their thing in the oven or pot.

You'll find several recipes for leftovers towards the end of the chapter too. I find cooking with the remnants of previous meaty meals incredibly rewarding, not to mention convenient. And, of course, it's an excellent way to make good meat go further.

Whenever I'm going to roast, bake or barbecue a significant piece of flesh, I find I'm almost savouring the leftovers recipes before I start.

It's that reverence for what is surely the most precious of foods that encourages you to eke out your meat in the most satisfying and thrifty way possible. And that's good news all round.

Tamari steak tartare

This variation on the classic steak tartare takes the dish in an Eastern direction and it's a particularly delicious way to enjoy prime raw beef. Ask your butcher to cut you a nice, thick, lean steak, then trim and chop it yourself to make the dish.

Serves 4 as a starter

400–500g sirloin or rump steak, trimmed of any sinew and external fat

½–1 small, medium-hot red chilli, deseeded and finely chopped (optional)

½ teaspoon freshly grated garlic

½ teaspoon freshly grated ginger

1 tablespoon toasted sesame seeds, plus extra to finish

1 tablespoon tamari

½ teaspoon runny honey

2 teaspoons rice vinegar

Sea salt and freshly ground black pepper

TO FINISH

A small handful of coriander or parsley leaves

A few spring onions, very thinly sliced

If you're up for slicing the steak by hand (which gives a great texture) use a large, very sharp knife to slice the steak thinly. Now cut each slice lengthways into long ribbons, then cut across the ribbons to form small dice – ideally no more than 5mm.

Or you can cut the meat into rough cubes and pulse in a food processor – but make sure you stop while there's still some good texture – you don't want it blitzed into pâté.

Put the prepared steak into a large bowl with the remaining ingredients and combine gently and carefully, without mashing the meat. Taste and adjust the seasoning with more tamari, honey, vinegar, salt or pepper as required.

Divide the seasoned meat between four plates and sprinkle over the sesame seeds. Finish with the coriander or parsley and spring onions, then serve.

Spiced beef with bashed beans

This is fine comfort food – but definitely of the non-stodgy variety. For the best results, choose lean beef steak, ideally minced fairly coarsely.

Serves 2–3, or 4–6 as a starter or tapas

2 tablespoons rapeseed or sunflower oil

350g lean beef, coarsely minced

2 garlic cloves, finely chopped

2 teaspoons cumin seeds, lightly bashed

1 teaspoon coriander seeds, lightly bashed

½ teaspoon dried chilli flakes, or to taste

1 teaspoon smoked sweet paprika

2 Little Gem lettuces, separated into leaves

A good squeeze of lime (or lemon) juice

Leaves from a small bunch of coriander, or parsley

Sea salt and freshly ground black pepper

FOR THE BASHED BEANS

1 tablespoon rapeseed or olive oil

1 garlic clove, sliced

400g tin white beans, such as cannellini or butter beans, rinsed and drained

A small glass of vegetable stock or water (75ml)

TO SERVE

Lime or lemon wedges

Put a large frying pan over a medium-high heat. Add the oil and, when hot, crumble in the mince. Fry without turning for a couple of minutes to allow some good browning, then turn and stir and fry for about 5 minutes until all of the mince has lost its raw look.

Add the garlic, cumin and coriander seeds, chilli flakes and some salt and pepper. Cook for about 10 minutes more, stirring frequently to distribute the spices and brown the mince all over. If there is any excess fat, pour it off. Add the paprika, cook for a further 2 minutes, until the beef is beginning to get crispy, then take the pan off the heat.

Meanwhile, for the bashed beans, put the oil in a saucepan over a low heat. Add the sliced garlic and cook, stirring, for 1–2 minutes or until it is just starting to colour. Add the beans and a little salt and pepper. Cook for a couple of minutes, then add the stock or water and bring to a simmer. Simmer for a couple of minutes more then take off the heat. Give the beans a rough bashing in the pan with a potato masher to create a coarse-textured mash, with some whole beans retained. Add a little more liquid if it seems very dry. Taste and add more salt or pepper if needed.

Divide the lettuce leaves between serving plates or bowls, spoon over some warm bashed beans and top with the spicy beef. Add a good spritz of lime or lemon and a scattering of coriander or parsley and serve, with lime or lemon wedges.

VARIATION

With quick guacamole Make up a rough guacamole by mashing 2 ripe avocados in a bowl with a trickle of oil, a pinch of chilli flakes, some roughly chopped coriander if you have some, a little salt and pepper and a generous squeeze of lime. Serve the mince, beans and guacamole on, or with, a cornmeal tortilla (see page 72), with roughly shredded lettuce leaves if you like, and you've got yourself a proper little Mexican feast.

Spicy chicken livers on lemony cucumber

This is an easy, healthy and delicious way to eat chicken livers. The richness of the livers is cut nicely by coriander and the fresh crunch of lemon-dressed cucumber.

Serves 2

200g fresh, free-range chicken livers, trimmed of any sinew or greenish parts

1 teaspoon ground coriander

½ small red onion, thinly sliced

1 garlic clove, thinly sliced

Finely grated zest and juice of ½ lemon

1 tablespoon rapeseed or sunflower oil, plus a little extra for cooking

½ small cucumber (about 150g)

Extra virgin rapeseed or olive oil, to trickle

A pinch of sugar

Sea salt and freshly ground black pepper

Leaves from a small bunch of parsley, chopped, to finish (optional)

Cut the chicken livers into 2–3cm pieces, giving them a final trim as you go. Put them in a bowl with the coriander, onion, garlic, lemon zest, oil and some salt and pepper. Mix gently and set aside while you prepare the cucumber.

Thinly slice the cucumber and arrange the slices over two plates. Trickle with extra virgin oil and some lemon juice, and add a pinch of sugar and a twist of pepper.

Heat a large frying pan over a high heat. Add a dash of oil followed by the chicken livers and all their marinade ingredients. Cook the livers for 3–4 minutes, turning frequently, until well coloured all over. Remove from the heat, add a good squeeze of lemon juice and toss well.

Allow the livers to rest for 5 minutes in the pan before spooning them over the cucumber. Serve sprinkled with the chopped parsley if you like.

Pigeon with cabbage and star anise

The sweet pungency of star anise is terrific with red meats such as lean, subtly gamey pigeon. In this fragrant and very healthy dish, it also enhances raw cabbage, which is thinly shredded and ever so slightly wilted in the warm, anise-scented sauce.

Serves 2

½ pointed spring cabbage or ¼ Savoy (about 250g)

1 tablespoon rapeseed or sunflower oil

4 pigeon breasts

Sea salt and freshly ground black pepper

FOR THE SAUCE

½ star anise

1 medium-hot red chilli, deseeded and thinly sliced

A small-finger-sized piece of ginger (about 15g), peeled and finely chopped

100ml apple juice

2 tablespoons tamari

2 small or 1 large shallot, thinly sliced

2 garlic cloves, thinly sliced

Shred the cabbage thinly, discarding any thick stalks, and place in a bowl.

For the sauce, crush the star anise to a fairly fine powder, using a pestle and mortar. Combine with the remaining ingredients and set aside.

Put a heavy-based frying pan over a medium-high heat and add the oil. Season the pigeon breasts well with salt and pepper. When the pan is hot, add the pigeon breasts and sear them for 1 minute each side, if you like them very pink inside, or 2 minutes each side for a medium pink finish. Transfer to a warmed dish to rest.

Add the sauce to the pan and simmer for about 2 minutes, stirring well to scrape up any caramelised residues, until the shallot is just beginning to soften and the sauce has reduced a little. Add the raw cabbage to the pan and toss it briefly in the hot sauce (no more than a minute), then remove from the heat. Transfer to warm plates or dishes.

Slice the pigeon thickly, arrange over or beside the cabbage and serve, with rice or noodles if you like.

VARIATION

Steak swap This dish is also delicious made with sirloin steak in place of the pigeon. Cook it to your liking (see page 240), remove to rest, then add the sauce to the pan as above. As with the pigeon, serve thick slices of the steak over the cabbage.

Bloody Mary steak and avocado

The spicy, savoury flavours of a Bloody Mary are pretty special and needn't be confined to the famous cocktail. I've used them here to underpin a piquant, tomatoey dressing that makes a steak and avocado salad particularly tangy and appealing. If your diet is gluten-free, note that Worcestershire sauce may contain some gluten from barley.

Serves 2

1 large, ripe avocado

150g cherry tomatoes, quartered

Leaves from a small bunch of flat-leaf parsley, roughly chopped

A little rapeseed or sunflower oil, for frying

1 rump or sirloin steak, 3cm thick (about 300g), ideally at room temperature

Sea salt and freshly ground black pepper

FOR THE BLOODY MARY DRESSING

50ml tomato juice (home-juiced or from a carton)

2 tablespoons extra virgin rapeseed or olive oil

¼ teaspoon celery salt

5–10 drops of Tabasco sauce, to taste

1 teaspoon Worcestershire sauce

A good squeeze of lemon juice

Freshly ground black pepper

First make up the dressing by mixing all the ingredients together in a bowl with a fork or whisk until thoroughly combined. Adjust to your taste with more of any of the above seasonings. You'll find you can temper the heat by being generous with the lemon.

Halve, stone and peel the avocado, then cut into roughly 3cm chunks. Place in a bowl with the tomatoes and parsley, add about 1 tablespoon of the dressing and mix lightly.

Heat a heavy-based frying pan over a high heat. When hot, grease the pan with a trickle of oil, then add the steak. Do not touch it for 50–60 seconds, then flip it over, lightly season the browned side, cook for another minute or so and flip again. Continue cooking in this way, flipping and seasoning every minute or so. Cooked from room temperature, a 3cm thick steak will be rare after 3–4 minutes total cooking time, medium-rare after 5–6 and medium after 6–8. Transfer the steak to a warmed plate to rest for 3–5 minutes.

Arrange the avocado salad on two plates. Slice the steak thickly and lay the strips over or alongside the salad. Trickle over any meaty juices that have seeped from the steak while it was resting. Spoon over the remaining dressing and serve.

Lamb with green beans and mint

This dish makes the most of the rightly celebrated affinity between lamb and mint. It's fresh and light, with the added crunch of the beans. And it's very much quicker than a roast!

Serves 2

400g lamb leg steaks, about 2cm thick, trimmed of sinew and any excess fat

3 tablespoons rapeseed or sunflower oil

200g French beans, topped (no need to tail)

1 small garlic clove, chopped or grated

1 tablespoon cider vinegar or wine vinegar

2–3 tablespoons chopped or finely ribboned mint leaves

Sea salt and freshly ground black pepper

Put a large saucepan of salted water on to boil for the beans. While it's coming up to the boil, put a cast-iron grill pan or heavy frying pan over a high heat.

Rub the lamb steaks with 1 tablespoon of the oil, season with salt and pepper and lay them in the hot pan. Cook for about 7 minutes, turning the meat in the pan 2 or 3 times, which will give you lamb that is nicely caramelised on the outside and still pink in the middle. Transfer to a warm plate and allow to rest while you deal with the beans.

While the lamb is cooking, add the beans to the pan of boiling water and simmer for 3–4 minutes or until just cooked – and still a bit crunchy. Drain the beans.

Add the remaining 2 tablespoons oil to the lamb cooking pan and place over a medium heat. When hot, add the garlic, stirring to ensure it doesn't burn. Pour in the vinegar and then add the beans with the mint. Add any juices released by the lamb while it's been resting, along with some salt and pepper. Toss the beans in the minty juices for a minute, scraping up any meaty residues from the lamb, then take the pan off the heat.

Slice the lamb steaks thinly and serve on warm plates, with the beans alongside. If you'd like something a little starchy to round out this lovely meal, you can't do better than boiled new potatoes – by all means minted!

Parsnips, chorizo, kale and lentils

This is an earthy and pretty substantial take on the stir-fry, perfect for a chilly autumn evening. Check the chorizo if you're avoiding dairy – some brands contain milk powder.

Serves 2

3 medium parsnips (about 350g in total)

2 tablespoons rapeseed or sunflower oil

Leaves from 2 sprigs of rosemary, chopped

150g chorizo sausage, sliced into 5mm rounds

About 100g cooked Puy or green lentils (see page 289 for cooking your own, or use pre-packed)

A handful of young kale leaves, stripped off the stalk, shredded

Sea salt and freshly ground black pepper

Peel the parsnips and cut into roughly 3mm slices.

Place a large frying pan over a medium heat. When it is hot add the oil, followed by the parsnips and rosemary. Fry the parsnips for about 5–6 minutes, tossing occasionally, until they are beginning to soften and take on a little colour.

Add the chorizo, turn up the heat slightly and cook, stirring often, for a further 5–6 minutes or until the sausage is cooked and beginning to crisp. By now the parsnips should be tender, nicely browned and taking on some spicy colour from the chorizo.

Finally, add the lentils and kale to the pan and toss well so they also get the full benefit of the chorizo flavours. Cook for a couple more minutes so the kale is wilted down but still bright. Then serve straight away in warm bowls. This is a complete meal in a bowl, but it's nice to have a crunchy green salad on the side.

Pork chops, fennel and olives

The work involved in this dish is minimal, but it's worthy of a special occasion. The best free-range and organic pork chops are from slower grown animals and tend to have a decent layer of fat on them. This is great for flavour, and I'd be inclined to leave it on for cooking – but you don't have to eat it.

Serves 2

2 medium fennel bulbs

1 garlic clove, sliced

2 tablespoons rapeseed or sunflower oil

2 outdoor-reared pork chops, trimmed of fat if you like

75g black olives, pitted if preferred

50ml white wine or water

Sea salt and freshly ground black pepper

Preheat the oven to 190°C/Gas 5.

Trim the fennel and remove the tough outer layer. Slice the fennel fairly thinly and put into a roasting dish with the garlic – you need a smallish roasting dish so the fennel overlaps considerably rather than sitting in a single layer. Trickle over 1 tablespoon oil and season with salt and pepper. Mix well, then cover with foil and place in the oven for 10 minutes.

About 5 minutes before the fennel cooking time is up, heat a frying pan over a high heat and add 1 tablespoon oil. Season the pork chops well on both sides and add to the hot pan. Brown them for 3–4 minutes, turning once or twice, until well coloured.

Take the fennel out of the oven and add the pork chops, nestling them down into the fennel. Scatter over the olives. Pour the wine or water into the hot pork frying pan and let it bubble and boil briefly, scraping the base of the pan to lift any nice brown residues from the pork. Pour this pan liquor over the fennel in the dish.

Return the dish to the oven and bake uncovered for 15–20 minutes, depending on the thickness of the chops, until they are cooked through and the fennel is beautifully tender.

Serve on warm plates, and accompany with potatoes – I like this with some waxy salad or new potatoes, boiled until tender then roughly crushed with a lick of extra virgin rapeseed or olive oil, a little grated lemon zest and some salt and pepper.

VARIATION

Veal version This is a good way to cook veal chops too. Choose higher welfare British rose veal. You may need to cook the chops for less time than the pork, depending on the thickness of the meat and how rare you like your veal.

Lamb with cauliflower and chickpeas

This lovely lamb dish starts with the sort of ingredients you might expect to find in a slow-cooked stew – meat, pulses, carrots – but turns them around very quickly into something lighter and fresher.

Serves 2–3

2 tablespoons rapeseed or sunflower oil

350–400g lamb leg steak, cut into 3–4cm cubes

½ medium cauliflower, trimmed and cut into small florets

½ teaspoon cumin seeds

1 garlic clove, chopped

1 tablespoon sesame seeds

400g tin chickpeas, drained and rinsed

A generous squeeze of lemon juice

A squeeze of orange juice (optional)

1 smallish carrot (about 75g), peeled and coarsely grated (or cut into matchsticks)

Sea salt and freshly ground black pepper

A little torn mint, to finish (optional)

Heat the oil in a large frying pan over a high heat. Add the lamb pieces, stir-fry for a minute or two until starting to colour nicely, then add the cauliflower and cumin. Cook over a medium-high heat for about 8 minutes, stirring or tossing from time to time, until the lamb and cauliflower are both lightly browned, and the cauliflower is softened a little but still nicely al dente.

Throw in the garlic and sesame seeds, cook for a minute more, then add the chickpeas, a good squeeze of lemon juice, a pinch of salt and a grinding of pepper. Stir-fry for a couple of minutes to heat the chickpeas through, then take off the heat.

Heap the mixture into warm serving bowls. Scatter over the carrot, then give the whole thing a squeeze of orange juice (or just more lemon juice if you prefer). Scatter with mint if you've got it. Leave for a few minutes to allow the lamb time to rest, then serve.

Aromatic nutty chicken

The flavourings for this fragrant roast chicken are based on the peanut sauce that usually accompanies Malaysian satay. An aromatic, nutty paste is pressed under the skin and bastes the bird as it cooks, rendering it extra moist and full of great flavours.

Serves 4, with leftovers

1 medium-large, free-range chicken (1.75–2kg)

2 tablespoons crunchy almond or peanut butter

2 tablespoons tamari

1–2 medium-hot red chillies, to taste, deseeded and finely chopped

2–3 garlic cloves, grated or crushed

1 teaspoon freshly grated ginger

Finely grated zest and juice of 1 large lime

1 tablespoon rapeseed or sunflower oil

Leaves from a bunch of coriander, roughly chopped

Sea salt and freshly ground black pepper

Remove the chicken from the fridge about an hour before cooking so that it comes up to room temperature. Preheat the oven to 210°C/Gas 6–7.

Combine the nut butter with the tamari, chilli, garlic, ginger and lime zest.

Untruss the bird and put it into a medium-small roasting tin. Separate the skin from the breast by lifting the flap of skin at the neck end of the bird, and carefully edging your fingers between the skin and the meat. You are aiming to create a pocket over the breast meat where the flavouring paste can go. Try not to tear the skin but don't panic if you do.

Use a teaspoon or your fingers to ease the spicy nut butter mix under the skin of the breast, pushing it as far down the breast as possible. Massaging the skin of the breast will help it spread. Level out the mixture with your fingers. Any leftover paste can be put into the cavity. Brush the bird with the oil and season the skin well with salt and pepper.

Put into the hot oven for 20 minutes, then remove and baste the bird with its own juices. Turn the oven setting down to 180°C/Gas 4. Add 200ml water to the roasting tin (but do not pour it over the bird or you'll wash off the seasonings and prevent the skin crisping). Roast for a further 40–60 minutes. To check that the bird is cooked, pull at one leg. It should come away from the body with relative ease and the juices between the leg and breast should be clear. If the leg is reluctant and the juices still pink, give it another 10 minutes and test again. When the bird is done, squeeze the lime juice over it and scatter with chopped coriander, then leave to rest in a warm place for 10–15 minutes.

Tip up the bird so any juices inside run out into the roasting tin. Transfer the bird to a warmed plate and carve. Serve the meat, with the fragrant juices from the roasting tin spooned over, with a green salad or sautéed peppery greens, and plain rice or noodles.

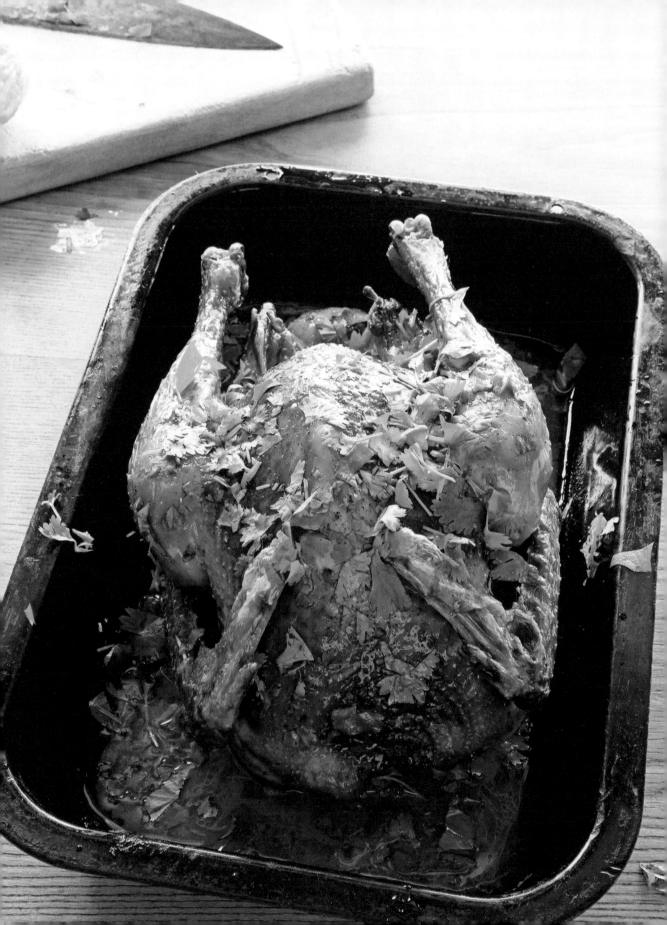

Thai slow-cooked beef

This simple stew has all the richness that comes with slow-cooked shin of beef, but is lifted by Thai-inspired aromatic flavours.

Serves 4–6

1.2kg shin of beef, off the bone

2 lemongrass stems, bashed

1 large red chilli, deseeded and sliced

4 garlic cloves, sliced

25g chunk of ginger, peeled and thinly sliced

2–3 lime kaffir leaves, fresh or dried (optional)

2 tablespoons Thai fish sauce

2 tablespoons rice vinegar

1 tablespoon sugar

2 medium leeks, sliced about 1cm thick (optional)

Juice of 1 large lime

3–4 tablespoons roughly chopped coriander

Sea salt and freshly ground black pepper

Preheat the oven to 220°C/Gas 7.

Cut the meat into large chunks and put into a roasting tin, into which it will fit fairly snugly. Add a little salt and pepper and toss well (you don't need any oil). Cook in the oven for 20 minutes, until the meat is nicely browned and has released lots of juice. Take the meat out and lower the oven setting to 150°C/Gas 2.

Add the lemongrass, chilli, garlic, ginger and lime leaves to the meat in the roasting tin. Combine the fish sauce, vinegar, 300ml water and the sugar and pour this over the meat. Give everything a good stir, cover with foil and return to the oven for 2–2½ hours or until very tender, giving the meat a stir once during cooking. If you'd like to add the leeks, stir them in about 1 hour before you take the beef out. When the beef is cooked, squeeze over the lime juice and scatter over the coriander.

Serve the beef and its richly flavoured liquor with rice or rice noodles, and a steamed or stir-fried green vegetable such as broccoli, spinach or bok choi.

Spring chicken

This one-pot dish is generous and filling, but still feels light. The chicken and veg poach gently in the oven, creating their own savoury broth. The spuds need to be sliced quite thinly to make sure they cook through properly.

Serves 4–6

1 tablespoon rapeseed or sunflower oil

1 medium, free-range chicken (about 1.75kg), jointed into 6–8 pieces (or 6–8 skin-on, bone-in chicken thighs)

200g carrots, peeled and sliced on the diagonal, about 5mm thick

3–4 celery stalks, sliced on the diagonal, about 1cm thick

1 large onion, thinly sliced

1 garlic bulb, halved horizontally

2–3 bay leaves

150ml white wine

300g new potatoes, sliced 8–10mm thick

About 200g spring onions or baby leeks, washed and trimmed

About 4 tablespoons roughly chopped herbs, such as chives, mint, flat-leaf parsley and/or tarragon

Sea salt and freshly ground black pepper

A little extra virgin rapeseed or olive oil, to serve (optional)

Preheat the oven to 180°C/Gas 4.

Heat the oil in a large frying pan and brown the chicken pieces, in two batches, turning the meat from time to time and seasoning with salt and pepper as it sizzles. Transfer, skin side up, to a roasting dish large enough to fit in all the chicken and veg fairly snugly. Put the carrots, celery, onion, garlic and bay leaves around the chicken.

Pour the wine into the browning pan and let it simmer for 2–3 minutes, scraping up any caramelised bits from the base. Add this liquid to the roasting dish. Boil the kettle and add 600–750ml hot water to the dish – you want the veg to be covered so they can cook, but the chicken skin to still be a little proud of the liquid, so it can continue to brown in the oven. Cover the dish with foil and put in the oven for 30 minutes.

Remove the foil and add the potatoes, making sure they're submerged in the cooking liquor. Return to the oven, uncovered, for 15 minutes, then lay the spring onions or baby leeks on top of the meat and veg and put back in the oven for a final 15 minutes. Check that the chicken is cooked right through, and that the veg are just tender.

Sprinkle generously with herbs and serve in warmed bowls, topped with a trickle of extra virgin oil, if you like.

Lamb and cashew curry

This 'traybake' lamb curry is very easy to put together. At the end of cooking, I stir in some cashew cream in place of the more usual yoghurt, which gives a wonderful, creamy richness.

Serves 6

1kg lean lamb shoulder, cut into 4–5cm pieces

2 tablespoons rapeseed sunflower oil

2–3 tablespoons ready-made curry paste (or a home-made paste, see below)

1 onion, thinly sliced

10 cardamom pods, lightly bashed

400g tin whole plum tomatoes, in juice

200g unsweetened cashew cream (page 394)

Sea salt and freshly ground black pepper

TO SERVE

Coriander leaves (optional)

Lime wedges (optional)

Preheat the oven to 220°C/Gas 7.

Put the pieces of lamb in a large roasting tin, trickle with the oil and season with a little salt and pepper. Roast the lamb, uncovered, for 20 minutes. If this isn't enough time to colour the meat, give it a little longer. When the lamb is nicely browned, take it out of the oven and lower the setting to 170°C/Gas 3.

Stir the curry paste into the browned lamb, then add the sliced onion and cardamom pods. Crush the tinned tomatoes in your hands and add these to the roasting tin, along with their juice (removing any stalky bits). Combine well, then cover tightly with foil and return to the oven for 1¼ hours.

Remove the lamb from the oven. Stir in the cashew cream, along with 3–4 tablespoons water if it appears to need loosening – the sauce should have a nice coating consistency. Return to the oven, uncovered, for a further 10 minutes or until heated through, then taste and add a little more salt if necessary. Serve scattered with coriander leaves, with lime on the side for squeezing if you like. Rice is the ideal accompaniment.

HOME-MADE CURRY PASTE
Finely grate 50g peeled fresh ginger, 4 large or 6 medium peeled garlic cloves and 1 small or ½ medium onion, then mix with 1 tablespoon curry powder, 1 tablespoon rapeseed or sunflower oil and a pinch of salt. Alternatively, put all these ingredients into a small blender with 2 tablespoons water and pulse to a purée.

VARIATION
Coconutty version Replace the cashew cream with coconut milk.

Chicken with lentils and rosemary

An easy one-pot supper for a cold night, this is started off on the hob, then transferred to the oven to bake. A sturdy casserole, or any good pan that's both flameproof and ovenproof, is the ideal vessel.

Serves 4

2 tablespoons rapeseed or olive oil

1 large onion, sliced

4 garlic cloves, chopped

Leaves from 2 sprigs of rosemary

200g red lentils, well rinsed

500ml chicken or veg stock

8 skin-on, bone-in, free-range chicken thighs, or 1 medium chicken (about 1.75kg), jointed into 6–8 pieces

Sea salt and freshly ground black pepper

Flat-leaf parsley, chopped, to finish

Preheat the oven to 180°C/Gas 4. Choose a flameproof casserole dish or a wide, ovenproof pan that will hold all the chicken pieces snugly but comfortably.

Put the casserole on a medium-low heat. Add the oil, then the onion and cook, stirring regularly, for 6–8 minutes until it begins to soften. Add the garlic, rosemary and some salt and pepper. Cook gently for a further 5 minutes, then stir in the lentils and stock.

Season the chicken thighs and place skin side up in the casserole. You want most of the chicken skin to remain exposed above the liquid in the dish so it can brown in the oven. Bring to a simmer on the hob, then transfer to the oven and bake, uncovered, for 1 hour. Check that the chicken is cooked right through and the lentils are soft. If not, return to the oven for 10–15 minutes and test again. Skim off any excess fat from the surface.

Taste the lentilly liquor and add more salt or pepper if needed. Serve, scattered with chopped parsley, just as it is or with steamed broccoli or spring greens on the side.

VARIATION

Rabbit casserole Wild rabbit is a delicious lean meat, and a young specimen, skinned and jointed (just ask your butcher) works very well in this recipe in place of the chicken. A couple of rashers of streaky bacon, cut into thick matchsticks, can be sweated with the onions and will help to keep the rabbit tender.

Leftover lamb with minty mushy peas

Scraps of leftover lamb are irresistible when torn into small pieces and fried 'hard', i.e. until crisp and well coloured. Caramelised and super-savoury, these meaty shards are fantastic on top of soups, in hearty salads or, as here, with a well-seasoned vegetable purée.

Serves 4

2 tablespoons rapeseed or olive oil

250–300g cooked lamb

A squeeze of lemon juice

Salt and freshly ground black pepper

FOR THE MUSHY PEAS

2 tablespoons extra virgin rapeseed or olive oil

3 shallots or 1 medium onion, chopped

3–4 garlic cloves, finely chopped

500g fresh or frozen peas or petits pois

2 tablespoons finely chopped mint, plus an extra sprig

TO SERVE (OPTIONAL)

Extra virgin rapeseed or olive oil, to trickle

Cornmeal tortillas (see page 72)

For the minty mushy peas, heat the oil in a saucepan over a low heat. Add the shallots or onion and sauté, stirring from time to time for about 15 minutes, until very soft. Add the garlic and sauté for a couple more minutes, then set aside.

Meanwhile, cook the peas with a sprig of mint in lightly salted boiling water until tender. Drain, saving some of the cooking water (discard the mint sprig). Put the peas into a food processor or blender with the sweated shallots or onion, garlic and chopped mint. Add a twist of pepper and blitz, adding just a little of the pea cooking water, to a coarse purée. Taste and add more salt and pepper if needed. Keep the mushy peas warm.

Heat the oil in a large frying pan over a medium-high heat (if you have a smaller pan, cook the lamb in two batches). Tear the cooked lamb into small-bite-sized pieces – you can cut it with a knife if you prefer but tearing gives a rougher edge and maximises crispness. Add to the hot pan and fry for 3–4 minutes, shaking or stirring it from time to time and keeping the heat quite high, so that the lamb quickly takes on plenty of colour. Add salt and pepper as it cooks.

When the lamb is brown, crispy and enticing, take it off the heat and add just a squeeze of lemon juice. You can now either spoon the warm pea purée into tortillas, add some lamb and wrap them up, or just serve the mushy peas and lamb on warm plates with a trickle of extra virgin oil and a green salad on the side.

VARIATIONS

Crispy pork and rooty purées You can use leftover cooked pork in place of the lamb. And other vegetable purées make a great foil to crispy, fried meat: try a soft mash of butternut squash, spiked with finely chopped sage, or a blitzed-up purée of carrots, or celeriac with chopped onion and parsley.

Cold chicken, anchovies and eggs

This is a great way of using up leftover chicken. So much so that I've been known to roast two birds to make sure I've got enough leftovers to rustle this up later in the week.

Serves 2

200–300g cold, cooked chicken, torn into pieces

12 anchovies in oil, drained

A squeeze of lemon juice

4 medium eggs, at room temperature

2 tablespoons baby capers, rinsed

1–2 tablespoons chopped parsley

Sea salt and freshly ground black pepper

Pick over the cold chicken and tear it up into small pieces. Place in a bowl and toss with a trickle of oil from the anchovy tin (or olive oil if you prefer), a squeeze of lemon, and a twist of salt and pepper.

Bring a pan of water to the boil, add the eggs and cook for 6½ minutes. Take off the heat and run the eggs under cold water briefly, to stop the cooking and render them just cool enough to handle.

Peel and halve the eggs and add to the chicken. Tear up the anchovies and add them too, along with the capers and parsley. Season everything with black pepper – the anchovies and capers contribute enough salt. Combine gently and serve straight away.

VARIATION

Chicken niçoise You can build this up to a more salady main course, with niçoise overtones, by adding some or all of the following: cooked French beans; lettuce; cooked new (or waxy) potatoes; black olives, whole or coarsely chopped.

Cold pork with plums and five-spice

The aromatic dressing really makes this salad, which is ideal for a lunchbox. It's a good one for early autumn, when our native plums are at their juicy best.

Serves 2

2–3 good handfuls of salad leaves

3–4 medium plums or greengages, stoned and cut into 6–8 slices each

About 150g cold, cooked pork, shredded or cut into bite-sized pieces

A few sprigs of coriander (optional)

FOR THE DRESSING

1 teaspoon tamari

1 teaspoon honey

A small scrap of garlic (about ¼ clove), grated or crushed

2 teaspoons rice wine vinegar, cider vinegar or white wine vinegar

2 tablespoons rapeseed or sunflower oil

A pinch of ground Chinese five-spice

For the dressing, shake all the ingredients together vigorously in a jar to combine.

If you're taking this in a lunchbox and you're able to transport the dressing separately in its jar and add it at the last minute, so much the better – just put the leaves, plums and pork in your plastic lunchbox and dress before eating.

Alternatively, arrange the leaves on serving plates, scatter over the plums and pork, then trickle over the dressing. Top, if you like, with a few coriander leaves and serve.

VARIATIONS

Ricey version This is a great light lunch, but if you want to make it more substantial, add a handful of cooked nutty brown rice.

Meat swaps This combo works very well with other leftover meats, particularly duck or chicken. Chunks of cold sausage (wheat-free) go down a treat too.

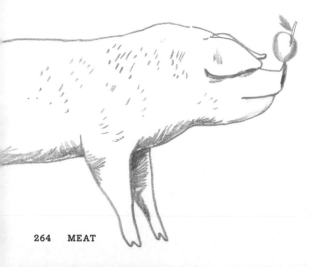

Veg RULES!

RAW, ROASTED, STEAMED OR sautéed, vegetables – ideally in abundance – bring colour, texture and a host of wonderful flavours to the table. For me, no meal is complete without at least one generous helping of something that surfaced in the veg patch. And those which are replete with two, three or four different vegetables keep me inspired, nourished and full of energy.

Quick ways to bring the best out of your veg abound. Quickest perhaps is not to cook them at all. Raw and crunchy, their vibrant colour undimmed, taste and nutrients are firing on all cylinders. You'll find plenty of examples of that approach in the salad and soup chapters but raw and nearly raw veg feature in this chapter too, in a noodly salad (page 286), zesty salsas (pages 313–4) and even in my tempura dish (page 272), where the veg stays full of snap and bite beneath its crunchy batter coating. Arm yourself with a sharp knife, a good grater and, if you like, an inexpensive mandoline, and you have the means to milk the raw veg resource for all it's worth.

At the other end of the scale in terms of cooked-ness, is roasting. Since many cooks only ever roast potatoes and parsnips, it's easy to assume that roasting other vegetables – carrots, shallots, cauliflower, broccoli, Brussels sprouts, beetroot to name some of those I roast a lot – is somehow a cheffy or tricky thing to do.

But it's dead quick and dead easy. Which is why (even if I am a sort of chef) this is the technique I turn to all the time.

All you have to do is peel your veg (sometimes not even that) and chop it roughly (if at all) before adding a lick of oil, a dusting of salt and pepper and entrusting it to the alchemy of the oven.

Once roasted – golden, caramelised and tender – your veg is ready to eat right away. But you can then rustle it into something super special with just a modicum of effort and a minute or two: purée it to make an intensely flavoured soup (see pages 122–8), trickle it with a tangy dressing, add an egg, rice, fruit, nuts, seeds, pulses, leaves. It's hard to go wrong: the sheer depth of flavour created by roasting makes for especially satisfying veg-based meals.

Another way to make sure you don't miss the meat when dishing up the veg is to partner your veg, whether it's raw, roasted, fried or braised, with piquant ingredients that season and define it. Think olives, capers, chillies, garlic, vinegar, citrus juice and zest. Keep a stock of these fail-safe veg-enhancers close to hand and any delivery of vegetables – whether it's your weekly organic box, a bag from the supermarket or an earthy offering from your own garden – is only a very short distance away from outright deliciousness.

Smashed roast Jerusalem artichokes

Nutty artichokes are roasted alongside red peppers, then bashed up with sweet garlic and smooth tahini into a chunky-creamy amalgamation. The silky roasted pepper finishes it off nicely.

Serves 4 as a starter or dip

500g Jerusalem artichokes

1 garlic bulb, halved horizontally

2 teaspoons ground cumin

2 tablespoons extra virgin rapeseed or olive oil

1 large red pepper

2 tablespoons tahini

A squeeze of lemon juice

Sea salt and freshly ground black pepper

TO FINISH

Extra virgin hempseed or rapeseed oil, to trickle

2 tablespoons toasted sunflower seeds

Chopped parsley (optional)

Preheat the oven to 180°C/Gas 4.

Peel the artichokes and cut them into roughly 2cm chunks. Place in a roasting tin with the garlic and sprinkle with the cumin. Trickle over the oil, season with salt and pepper and stir well. Add the whole red pepper to the tin too. Roast for 45–50 minutes, turning everything halfway through, until the artichokes are tender and the pepper has softened and the skin is wrinkled all over.

Remove the tin from the oven, place the pepper in a small bowl and cover with cling film or a plate that fits snugly – this will trap in the steam and help the skin to come off easily.

Squeeze the roasted garlic cloves from their skins back into the tin with the artichokes (or pop them out with the tip of a sharp knife). Add the tahini and 2 tablespoons water, then use a potato masher to bash and mash the artichokes together with the garlic to a rough purée. Add a dash more water if needed. Add lemon juice, salt and pepper to taste. Keep warm in the dish.

Peel the skin from the pepper, then tear it open (pouring any juices from inside on to the smashed artichokes and stirring them in). Discard the seeds and roughly chop or tear the pepper flesh.

Pile the artichokes into a bowl or serving dish and top with the roasted pepper. Give the whole thing a sprinkling more salt, pepper and lemon juice and a trickle of extra virgin oil. Finish with a scattering of sunflower seeds and chopped parsley, if you like.

Serve warm – either as a starter with some salad leaves, or as a dip with crispbreads (such as those on page 80) or a piece of freshly cooked socca (page 74).

Tempura spring veg with sesame dipping sauce

This is one sure-fire way to make a plate of vegetables irresistible. Fine white rice flour makes a light and crunchy batter – especially if you mix it with well-chilled fizzy water – and the tangy, aromatic dipping sauce will have everyone asking for more.

Serves 2–4

A selection of vegetables, such as asparagus, small radishes, baby carrots and spring onions

Sprigs of flat-leaf parsley

Sunflower or groundnut oil, for frying

Fine sea salt

FOR THE BATTER

100g white rice flour

160ml chilled sparkling water

FOR THE DIPPING SAUCE

½ teaspoon freshly grated ginger

½ garlic clove, grated

1 tablespoon tamari

1 tablespoon lime juice

1 teaspoon runny honey

2 teaspoons sesame seeds

For the sauce, mix all the ingredients together in a small bowl.

Now prepare the vegetables. If they are to be nice and tender, they need to be in slender enough pieces to cook through quickly. Cut asparagus spears and spring onions in half lengthways if thick. Cut carrots lengthways in half, or into quarters if they are quite chunky – the thickest part should be no thicker than the tip of your little finger. I'll make an exception for young veg picked straight from the garden, such as whole baby radishes or carrots, and pert asparagus spears. They're so vibrant and crunchy I like them naked and almost raw beneath their veil of toothsome batter.

Pour a 5cm depth of oil into a deep, heavy-based saucepan and heat to about 180°C.

Meanwhile, make the batter by mixing the flour and fizzy water together.

Use a cook's thermometer to check the temperature of the oil, or drop in ½ teaspoonful of batter – it should fizz enthusiastically and just start to colour in about 1 minute.

Dip the vegetables, a few at a time, into the batter, dunking them down to the bottom of the bowl so they get a good coating. Then lift them out, briefly letting the excess batter drip back into the bowl, and swiftly drop them into the hot oil. Fry for about 2 minutes until crisp and very lightly golden. Don't let the vegetables clump together in the oil or the batter won't cook properly – it helps to drop them in one at a time.

Transfer the cooked veg to a plate lined with kitchen paper and, while still sizzling hot, sprinkle with a little salt. Serve as soon as they are all cooked, with the dipping sauce.

Three perky pestos

A pungently herby pesto transforms the simplest of ingredients into a satisfying meal. I love to tinker with the pesto concept and I've come up with a trio of new ones here (all cheese-free). Classically, of course, pesto is partnered with pasta but it works brilliantly too with polenta, with fresh veg, and with pulses. It's also a great finisher for soups and risottos and can even be added to savoury pancake batters (see page 74). Although I've given the following three pestos individual serving suggestions, they all work deliciously in any potential pesto scenario.

Nasturtium, apple and almond

The nasturtium is a beautiful annual plant with flamingly bright flowers and is easy to grow. It contains some of the same aromatic compounds as mustard, horseradish and wasabi, and has a similarly hot, peppery punch. This pesto condenses a colander-ful of leaves and flowers into a few spoonfuls of feisty flavour.

Serves 4

75g blanched almonds

100g nasturtium leaves and a handful of flowers

1 small eating apple, peeled, cored and chopped

1 garlic clove, chopped

100ml extra virgin olive oil

100ml extra virgin rapeseed or sunflower oil

Lemon juice, to taste

Salt

If you want to toast the almonds, which will deepen the nutty flavour, preheat the oven to 180°C/Gas 4. Spread the almonds on a baking tray and toast them lightly in the oven for about 5 minutes, until just coloured. Tip on to a plate and leave to cool completely.

Put the almonds, nasturtiums, apple and garlic into a food processor and pulse to chop finely. Combine the oils and, with the motor running, trickle in slowly until you have a loose, green purée. You may not need all the oil, or you may need a bit more. Add salt and a squeeze or two of lemon juice. The pesto will keep in a jar in the fridge for a few days.

HOW TO EAT
This is excellent spooned over hot polenta made by cooking 125g quick-cook polenta in 400ml each almond milk and water. Bring the liquid to a simmer, add 2 tablespoons rapeseed or olive oil and ¼ teaspoon salt, then stir in the polenta. Cook for just a minute or two until smooth.

VARIATION
Fennel and apple pesto If you have some fennel herb, use it in place of the nasturtiums for a seriously aniseedy flavour – delicious, as you might expect, with fish.

Parsley, anchovy and walnut pesto

Rich with the salty tang of anchovies – which are nicely balanced by the delicately bitter walnuts – this is a properly punchy pesto.

Serves 4

50g parsley leaves (from a roughly 100g bunch)

50g walnuts, ideally lightly toasted

1 garlic clove, chopped

50g tin anchovies in oil

Finely grated zest and juice of ½ lemon

About 100ml extra virgin rapeseed or olive oil

Freshly ground black pepper

Put the parsley leaves, walnuts, garlic, the anchovies and their oil, lemon zest and juice into a food processor. Blitz until finely chopped, then keep the motor running and trickle in enough oil to form a thick paste – about 100ml, possibly a splash more. Taste the pesto and add pepper, as well as more lemon juice if you think it is needed (it shouldn't require any salt). This will keep in a jar in the fridge for a few days.

HOW TO EAT

This is particularly good tossed through warm or cold cannellini beans and served on crisp Cos lettuce leaves.

Caper and olive pesto

This intense pesto is based on the classic basil version, but without the Parmesan. Instead, olives and capers provide the shot of 'umami' flavour.

Serves 4

50g pine nuts, lightly toasted

Leaves from a 30g bunch of basil and a 30g bunch of flat-leaf parsley (or use all basil or all parsley if you prefer)

1 garlic clove, chopped

1 tablespoon baby capers, rinsed and drained

50g pitted green olives

Finely grated zest of ½ lemon, plus a couple of squeezes of the juice

About 150ml extra virgin rapeseed or olive oil

To make the pesto, put the toasted pine nuts into a food processor, along with the basil and/or parsley, garlic, capers, olives and lemon zest. Blitz to a paste. Then, with the motor running, slowly pour in the oil until you have a thick, sloppy purée. Scrape the pesto into a bowl and season with pepper and a good squeeze of lemon juice (you may not need salt – capers and olives are already pretty salty). It will keep in a jar in the fridge for a few days.

HOW TO EAT

I love to serve this tossed with freshly boiled new potatoes – and sometimes I throw in some other summer veg too, such as broad beans, peas or blanched courgette batons.

Rice, eggs and creamed watercress

I get huge pleasure from dishes that are as simple and pared down as this: plain, fluffy rice, a perfect boiled egg with its molten yolk, and the spicy kick of blitzed watercress. You can taste every ingredient and it looks stunning too.

Serves 4

200g white basmati rice, rinsed

1 tablespoon extra virgin rapeseed or olive oil, plus extra to finish

1 onion, chopped

2 garlic cloves, chopped

250g watercress, tougher stalks removed, plus extra to finish (optional)

4–6 medium eggs, at room temperature

Sea salt and freshly ground black pepper

Bring a pan of lightly salted water to the boil, add the rice and simmer gently until the grains are tender, about 10–12 minutes. Drain thoroughly and keep warm. (Or by all means use a rice cooker, or your preferred method of cooking rice.)

Meanwhile, in a large saucepan, heat the oil over a medium-low heat. Add the onion and sweat for about 8 minutes, until soft, then add the garlic and cook for another couple of minutes. Now add the watercress to the pan, cramming it all in, along with 100ml water. Cook, covered, for about 5 minutes, stirring from time to time, until the watercress leaves are completely wilted.

Tip the contents of the pan into a blender, add salt and pepper and blitz to a thick, bright green purée. Taste and add more salt and pepper as needed. Put the lid back on the blender to keep the purée warm.

Bring another pan of water to the boil, add the eggs and cook for 6½ minutes. Take off the heat and run the eggs under cold water briefly, to stop the cooking and render them just cool enough to handle. Peel the eggs.

Divide the rice between four warmed dishes. Halve the eggs and arrange over the rice, then spoon over the watercress purée. Finish with a few more sprigs of watercress, if you have them. Give everything a final shake of salt and pepper and a trickle of extra virgin oil, and serve.

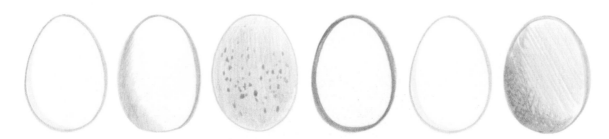

Beetroot burgers

Packed with veg, pulses and oats, as well as the earthy tang of beetroot, these are as good as a veggie burger gets. And there are lots of fun and tasty ways to serve them (see below).

Serves 4

200g raw beetroot, peeled and chopped

1 medium carrot (100–125g), peeled and chopped

½ medium onion, chopped

1 large or 2 small garlic cloves, grated or crushed

100g drained tinned chickpeas (about ½ tin)

1 teaspoon tamari

75g porridge oats

1 medium egg

1 teaspoon ground cumin

1 teaspoon ground coriander

Rapeseed or sunflower oil, for cooking

Sea salt and freshly ground black pepper

Put the beetroot, carrot, onion, garlic, chickpeas and tamari in a food processor and blitz to a fine texture, stopping to scrape down the sides with a spatula once or twice. Add the oats, egg, cumin, coriander, a good pinch of salt and a grind of black pepper. Blitz again to ensure everything is well blended. You should end up with a thick, coarse paste. Don't worry if it seems slightly wet – it is much softer than a meaty burger mix.

Heat a non-stick frying pan over a medium heat and add enough oil to cover the base in a thin film.

Use your hands or a large spoon to drop a quarter of the mix into the pan and pat it into a burger, about 10cm across and 2cm deep. Repeat with the remaining mix. Gently fry the burgers for about 10 minutes, turning them carefully once or twice or until lightly charred on the outside and hot all the way through.

You can either eat the burgers straight away, hot from the pan, or (my preference) let them cool until warm or at room temperature, when they will have firmed up a little.

WAYS TO SERVE YOUR BURGER
» With any of the salsas on pages 313–4
» Falafel style – topped with a dollop of hummus, shredded cabbage and chilli sauce
» Topped with a poached egg (cooked as suggested on page 110)
» With mayonnaise and lots of crisp lettuce
» With a squirt of ketchup, chutney or mustard (or all three!)
» In all of the above cases, wrapped in a wheat-free flatbread, such as my rye chapatis or cornmeal tortillas (both on page 72)

Braised new potatoes and lettuce

I like to cook waxy little new potatoes in a good stock with lettuce and some sweet summer vegetables – baby carrots, just-picked peas, broad beans. You get something fresh and light, but hearty – more substantial than a soup. Here's a pared down version using lettuce and spring onions, more than good enough to enjoy on its own, to which you could happily add any of the suggestions listed below.

Serves 2, or 4 as a side

350g small new potatoes, cleaned and quartered, or cut into 2–3cm pieces

About 400ml hot veg stock

½ large head of Romaine or 2 Little Gem lettuces, coarsely shredded

3–4 spring onions, cut into 2cm slices

Sea salt and freshly ground black pepper

TO FINISH

Extra virgin rapeseed or olive oil

Chopped flat-leaf parsley or lovage (optional)

Put the potatoes in a large frying pan, add about 250ml hot stock, bring to a simmer and cook, half-covered, for 15–20 minutes, stirring occasionally, until the potatoes are tender. Add a little more stock if you need to, but the idea is to end up with reasonably well-reduced juices, so don't go mad.

Add the shredded lettuce and spring onions, cover again and cook for a further 3–5 minutes until the lettuce is wilted. Add salt and pepper to taste.

Serve straight away, trickled with a little extra virgin oil and scattered with parsley or a little lovage if you like.

VARIATIONS

Veg it up A few handfuls of infant summer veg make this dish particularly special. Choose any or all of the following and add to the pan along with the lettuce: baby peas (up to 50g), baby broad beans (up to 50g), baby carrots (a small bunch, whole if tiny, or sliced lengthways), a couple of dozen mangetout or a couple of dozen broad bean tops or pea shoots.

Buckwheat noodles with wakame and ginger

This is an easy and tasty way to enjoy the mineral-rich goodness of seaweed. It's a dish that can be prepared in advance and travels well – so it makes a great lunchbox. Despite its name, buckwheat is not a form of wheat and is gluten-free. However, do check the packet when you buy buckwheat noodles (aka soba noodles) as some brands contain wheat flour too.

Serves 2, or 4 as a side

15g dried wakame seaweed (either strips or flakes)

150g buckwheat (soba) noodles

1 large or 2 medium carrots (about 150g)

1 large or 2 small courgettes (about 100g)

10g toasted sesame seeds

FOR THE DRESSING

2cm knob of ginger (about 15g), peeled and grated

2 tablespoons mirin (or 1 tablespoon each sweet sherry and water)

1½ tablespoons tamari

½ tablespoon Japanese rice vinegar

1 tablespoon toasted sesame oil

Put the dried wakame seaweed in a bowl of cold water to rehydrate. Follow the packet instructions: it may take anywhere from 2–15 minutes.

Meanwhile, cook the noodles according to the packet instructions until tender but with a slight bite (usually in boiling water for 5–6 minutes). Drain and immediately run them under cold water to cool down. Drain thoroughly, then tip the noodles into a large bowl.

Peel the carrots and slice into 'spaghetti' or thin matchsticks on a mandoline, or use a food processor, or coarsely grate. Do the same with the (unpeeled) courgettes. Add to the noodles.

When the seaweed has plumped up and become fleshy, drain it well and squeeze out excess water with your hands. Pick through it, discarding any tough stalks if necessary. Chop the seaweed roughly (unless it is in flakes) and add to the noodles and veg.

For the dressing, mix together the ginger, mirin, tamari, vinegar and sesame oil. Pour this over the noodles and toss so that everything is coated and the ingredients are evenly distributed. Taste and adjust the flavours as necessary – you may need a little extra vinegar or a touch more mirin.

You can serve this at once, or keep it cool for a few hours – in which case toss once more before serving – with toasted sesame seeds sprinkled over.

Puy lentils with roast Brussels sprouts

Roasting sprouts renders them nutty and sweet, which in turn makes them delicious tossed with earthy Puy lentils and a delicately garlicky balsamic vinaigrette. This is a great winter side dish for a simple roast chicken or pheasant. But it's also, especially with the walnut addition, lovely to eat as a vegetable main course.

Serves 4

250g Brussels sprouts

1 tablespoon extra virgin rapeseed or olive oil

200g Puy lentils, rinsed

1 bay leaf (optional)

½ onion (optional)

A squeeze of lemon juice

75g walnuts, roughly broken up or chopped (optional)

Sea salt and freshly ground black pepper

FOR THE VINAIGRETTE

4 tablespoons extra virgin rapeseed or olive oil

1 tablespoon balsamic vinegar (ideally apple balsamic)

½ teaspoon English mustard

½ small garlic clove, grated or crushed

Preheat the oven to 190°C/Gas 5. Quarter large sprouts, halve smaller ones, peeling off damaged or discoloured outer leaves as you go. Put into a small roasting dish with the oil and some salt and pepper. Toss well, then roast for about 15 minutes until the sprouts are tender, and browned in places. Set aside.

Meanwhile, put the lentils in a pan and cover with plenty of cold water. Add a bay leaf if you have one and an onion half if you like. Bring to the boil, reduce the heat and simmer for about 12–15 minutes, until the lentils are tender but still al dente.

While the lentils are cooking, put all the vinaigrette ingredients in a jar, including some salt and pepper, and shake well to emulsify.

As soon as the lentils are done, drain well and toss them with the dressing. Stir in the sprouts. Taste and add salt, pepper and lemon juice as needed. Serve warm or at room temperature, topped if you like with roughly broken-up walnuts.

Roast squash, chicory and blackberries

There's a glorious medley of autumn flavours and colours in this dish.
Have it as a light meal or starter, or serve with a little air-dried
ham or a heap of Puy lentils (see page 289).

Serves 2

½ butternut, onion or small
Crown Prince squash
(about 500g)

2 tablespoons extra virgin
rapeseed or olive oil

2 garlic cloves, sliced

Several sprigs of thyme

2 small or 1 large red or
white chicory bulb

A few handfuls of
blackberries (about 100g)

Sea salt and freshly ground
black pepper

FOR THE DRESSING

Juice of 1 small lemon

1 teaspoon runny honey

3 tablespoons extra virgin
rapeseed or olive oil

½ teaspoon thyme leaves

Preheat the oven to 180°C/Gas 4.

Cut the squash into wedges about 2cm wide at the outside edge. Scoop out the seeds
and place the squash (skin still on) in a roasting tin. Trickle over the oil, scatter over
the garlic and thyme and season well with salt and pepper.

Roast for 45–60 minutes, turning the pieces over about halfway through, until the
squash is tender and starting to caramelise. Remove from the oven and allow to cool
until just warm, or at room temperature.

Cut the base from the chicory and separate the leaves. Add these to the cooled squash
in the roasting tin along with the blackberries.

Whisk the dressing ingredients together, adding salt and pepper to taste, then pour this
over the fruit and veg. Carefully 'muddle' everything together in the dish, scraping up
any sticky, sweet garlicky bits as you go. Taste and add more salt or pepper if needed,
then divide between plates and serve.

Roast beetroot and potatoes with anchovies

This is a lovely way to make the most of new season's beetroot and sweet little summer potatoes. The salty, savoury anchovies, which almost dissolve during the cooking, give the dish depth so you need very little with it except perhaps some super-fresh salad leaves.

Serves 4, or 6 as a side dish

About 500g new potatoes, scrubbed

About 500g young beetroot, scrubbed and trimmed

2 tablespoons extra virgin rapeseed or olive oil, plus extra to finish

1 whole garlic bulb, halved horizontally

8–12 anchovy fillets, to taste

A squeeze of lemon juice

Sea salt and freshly ground black pepper

A crisp lettuce or a handful of flat-leaf parsley, to serve (optional)

Preheat the oven to 180°C/Gas 4.

If the potatoes aren't really small, cut them into bite-sized (3–4cm) pieces. Halve or quarter the beetroot so they are in similar-sized pieces to the potatoes.

Put all the veg into a roasting tray. Trickle over the oil, add some black pepper (the anchovies are already quite salty) and toss together well. Nestle the two halves of the garlic bulb in among the veg and lay the anchovies on top of the veg (you don't want them to touch the base of the tray or they'll get over-cooked).

Cover the veg with foil and roast for 1 hour. Check that the beetroot is completely tender by poking a few pieces with the tip of a sharp knife. Give it another 10–20 minutes if it needs it (older beetroot can take quite a bit of roasting). Then leave to cool completely, still covered with the foil, to keep the juices in.

When the veg is cool, transfer it to a large bowl. Squeeze the soft garlic cloves out of their skins back into the veg then tumble the whole lot together, so the juices are well distributed and the anchovies, which will be almost dissolved by now, break down into the juices and coat the veg. Taste and give it a squeeze of lemon juice and more black pepper, plus a little salt if it's needed.

You can toss a handful of flat-parsley leaves through, or serve with, or over, a crisp green salad if you like.

New potatoes, asparagus and eggs

New potatoes and asparagus both roast really well and, as long as you take account of asparagus's shorter cooking time, you can happily throw them in the oven together. Add some eggs and you've got a satisfying supper dish – a sort of deconstructed frittata-without-palaver.

Serves 4

600–700g new potatoes, cleaned and cut into small chunks

5–6 garlic cloves, bashed

3 tablespoons extra virgin rapeseed or olive oil

About 400g asparagus

4 eggs

Sea salt and freshly ground black pepper

Preheat the oven to 190°C/Gas 5.

Put the potato chunks into a roasting dish with the garlic. Trickle over the oil and plenty of salt and pepper and toss well. Roast for 30 minutes, or until the potatoes are tender.

Meanwhile, snap the woody ends off the asparagus. Add the spears to the potatoes, toss together and roast for another 15 minutes, until the asparagus is tender and a little charred and the potatoes are becoming pleasingly crisp.

Now create four little spaces among the veg. You want to contain the egg as much as you can (though some egg-scaping is inevitable) so shuffle the potato and asparagus pieces into a reasonably snug surround for the egg-spaces. Working quickly, so everything stays hot, break an egg into each space. Return the dish to the oven for 4–5 minutes, until the whites are set but the yolks still runny.

Sprinkle some salt and pepper over the eggs and serve straight away (the eggs will continue to cook in the dish so don't delay).

Baked onions with savoury porridge

(V) My friend and colleague Gill Meller created this fun and tasty dish, which manages to be warming and satisfying while remaining healthy and pleasingly thrifty too. It might sound a little unusual, but a savoury porridge is really very similar to a classic risotto – it has the same comforting, soothing quality. Sweet, silky roasted onions complement the savoury oats, and toasted hazels add a welcome crunch.

Serves 4

2 tablespoons rapeseed or sunflower oil

6–8 thyme sprigs

4 large onions

6–8 bay leaves

2–3 garlic cloves, sliced

750ml chicken or vegetable stock

150g porridge oats

50g hazelnuts, toasted

Sea salt and freshly ground black pepper

Chopped parsley, to finish (optional)

Preheat the oven to 200°C/Gas 6.

Choose a flameproof roasting dish (it will need to go on the hob later), big enough to hold the onions, when halved, in a snug single layer. Trickle in the oil, then lay the thyme sprigs over the bottom of the dish and add a sprinkling of salt and pepper.

Take a slim slice off the base and top of each onion to help the heat penetrate, but leave the skins on. Cut them in half around their circumference and place on top of the oil and seasonings, with the larger cut surface (i.e. the middle of the onion) downwards.

Bake for 25–35 minutes until the onions have taken on some colour and their bases are slightly caramelised. Take the dish from the oven, throw in the bay leaves and garlic, then cover with foil. Turn the oven setting down to 120°C/Gas ½ and bake for a further 40–50 minutes, until the onions are nice and tender. Use a spatula to carefully remove them to a warm plate and re-cover with the foil.

Leaving all the herbs and garlic in the roasting dish, add the stock and place over a low heat. Bring to a gentle simmer. Add the porridge oats and cook, stirring, for 5–10 minutes, until the mixture has thickened (just as if you were making porridge). Taste and season with salt and pepper as needed. Add a little more stock if necessary.

Spoon the porridge into warm bowls and top each portion with two onion halves (leave them in their skins for now and scoop out the tender onion flesh as you eat). Lightly bash the hazelnuts to break them up a little and sprinkle over the onions. Finish with a scattering of parsley if you like.

Roast aubergines with sweet and sour tomatoes

This is a take on the classic Middle Eastern recipe *imam biyaldi* which translates as 'the Imam swooned' (because it was so delicious). This simpler version uses much less oil and borrows some *agrodolce* (sweet/sour) seasonings from the Sicilian aubergine dish, caponata.

Serves 4

2 largeish aubergines (about 750g in total)

3 tablespoons extra virgin rapeseed or olive oil

3 garlic cloves, sliced

1 large onion, thinly sliced

1 tablespoon balsamic vinegar (ideally apple balsamic)

1 teaspoon sugar

1 tablespoon tomato purée

50g sultanas or raisins

250g cherry tomatoes, halved (or larger tomatoes, cut into bite-sized pieces)

50g pine nuts, lightly toasted

Sea salt and freshly ground black pepper

Chopped flat-leaf parsley or mint, to finish (optional)

Preheat the oven to 190°C/Gas 5.

Halve each aubergine down the middle, stalk to base. Use a sharp knife to make diagonal cuts deep into the cut side of the flesh, going almost through to the skin but not quite, about 1.5cm apart. Repeat the other way, to create a diamond pattern.

Measure out 2 tablespoons of the oil, and brush it all over the cut aubergine flesh, using a pastry brush to work it into the cuts. Now stuff the slices of garlic into the cuts so that each aubergine half has a good garlicky share. Season the flesh well with salt and pepper. Put the aubergine halves in a large roasting dish and bake for 30 minutes.

Combine the onion, balsamic vinegar, sugar, tomato purée, sultanas or raisins and remaining 1 tablespoon oil in a large bowl. Mix well, then stir in the tomatoes.

After their first 30 minutes, the aubergines should be looking nice and tender. Add the onion and tomato mixture to the roasting dish, pushing it around the aubergine halves so they are snugly surrounded but not covered. Trickle 100ml water over the tomatoes and onions (not the aubergines) and return the whole lot to the oven for 30 minutes.

As soon as the dish comes out of the oven, spoon the soft onions and tomatoes and all their juices on top of the aubergines, so each one has a nice covering. Leave to settle for 10 minutes or so, then serve, scattered with the pine nuts, and parsley or mint, if using. Serve with a green salad and/or rice.

Oven-baked shallot and mushroom risotto

A risotto made without butter or cheese can still be hearty and comforting. This one is finished off with a splash of chilli oil, which rounds out the dish nicely (if you haven't time to make your own, use a good ready-made oil). As with any risotto, the quality of the stock is important. By all means make up your stock from a cube or granules, but taste it before you use it. If the flavour isn't deep enough, doctor it with a good pinch of celery salt and/or a splash of Worcestershire sauce (though the latter is not for vegans or coeliacs). If it seems too salty, dilute it a little – you can always add more salt later.

Serves 4

2 tablespoons extra virgin rapeseed or olive oil

300g shallots, peeled and quartered lengthways

A few good sprigs of thyme

1 garlic clove, finely chopped

300g chestnut mushrooms, destalked and cut into large chunks

1 tablespoon balsamic vinegar (ideally apple balsamic)

250g risotto rice

1 litre hot chicken or vegetable stock

Sea salt and freshly ground black pepper

Chilli oil (bought or home-made, see below), to finish

Preheat the oven to 180°C/Gas 4. Put the oil, shallots, thyme and some salt and pepper in a large roasting tin and toss together well. Roast for 30 minutes, then add the garlic, mushrooms and balsamic vinegar. Stir well and return to the oven for 15 minutes.

Tip the risotto rice into the tin and stir to coat lightly with the oils and flavourings, then add the hot stock and stir again. Return to the oven for 30 minutes, giving it a good stir halfway through.

Let the risotto settle for 5 minutes, then taste and add salt and pepper as needed. Spoon into warm dishes, removing the thyme stalks as you go. Serve, trickled with the chilli oil.

TO MAKE A GOOD CHILLI OIL

Put 100ml extra virgin rapeseed or olive oil in a pan with 1 teaspoon dried chilli flakes, 2 finely chopped garlic cloves and, if you like, the leaves from a small sprig of rosemary. Heat gently, just until the garlic is fizzing. Cook for a minute or so, to take the raw edge off the garlic without allowing it to colour, then set aside to infuse and cool. When it is completely cold, pour into a jar or, through a funnel, into a small bottle – with all the bits. You can use it immediately, but it improves after keeping for a bit. Store it in the fridge for up to 2 weeks.

Squash, red onion and butter bean roast

This is a very satisfying all-in-one dish: warming, filling and easy to throw together. The roasted beans take on a toasty crispness that complements the silky squash and sweet onions.

Serves 4

1 large or 2 small squash, such as butternut, Crown Prince or onion (about 1kg in total)

4 red onions

1 garlic bulb

4 tablespoons extra virgin rapeseed or olive oil

400g tin butter beans (or cannellini or borlotti beans), drained and rinsed

2 tablespoons chopped sage

Sea salt and freshly ground black pepper

Preheat the oven to 190°C/Gas 5.

Halve the squash. Peel it and scoop out the seeds, then cut the flesh into 3–4cm chunks. Put these in a large roasting tin.

Peel the onions. Leaving the root intact so that the layers stay together, slice them top-to-toe into slim wedges, about 2cm thick at the outer edge. Add to the squash.

Peel all the garlic cloves and add these too (or, if you're in a hurry, just separate the cloves and give them a quick bash with the flat of a knife).

Add salt and pepper and the oil to the veg and mix well together. Cover the tin with foil and roast for 45 minutes. Remove the foil, add the butter beans and stir to mix with the veg. Return the tin to the oven, uncovered this time, for a further 10–15 minutes or until all the veg start to take on some golden brown colour.

Add the chopped sage to the hot veg and stir well. Serve with some steamed greens or a leafy green salad on the side.

VARIATIONS

Potato, parsnip, apple and bean roast In place of the squash, use a 50:50 mixture of potatoes and parsnips or celeriac, peeled and cut into roughly 3cm chunks. After their initial 45 minutes' cooking with the onions and garlic, add 2 cored and roughly chunked-up eating apples and 1 tablespoon chopped rosemary, along with the beans before the final 10–15 minutes' roasting. Finish with a scattering of toasted hazelnuts if you like.

Soup Any significant leftovers (of either roast) can be whizzed up with a little stock to make a hearty soup (squeeze unpeeled garlic cloves out of their skins before puréeing).

Roast PSB and beans

Purple sprouting broccoli is a great spring treat. I never tire of finding new ways to serve it. Here, it's lightly roasted – which gives it a gorgeous, slightly caramelised flavour. The addition of creamy beans and a mustardy dressing make a meal of it. I like to enrich the dressing with an egg yolk to make it extra creamy but you can leave it out if you prefer.

Serves 4

About 400g purple sprouting broccoli

2 tablespoons rapeseed or sunflower oil

400g tin white beans, such as cannellini, drained and rinsed

About 20g sunflower seeds

Sea salt and freshly ground black pepper

FOR THE DRESSING

A scrap of finely grated or crushed garlic (¼ clove max)

½ teaspoon English mustard

A pinch of sugar

1 teaspoon cider vinegar

3 tablespoons rapeseed oil

1 large egg yolk (optional)

Preheat the oven to 180°C/Gas 4.

Snap off any tough ends from the broccoli – like asparagus, the stems should break at the point where they become tender. You can strip off and use any good leaves from the discarded ends. Cut the broccoli into 4–5cm lengths. Any stems thicker than 1cm should be split lengthways. Put the broccoli and saved leaves in a roasting tray, trickle over the oil, season with salt and pepper and toss well to coat the broccoli.

Roast the broccoli for about 8 minutes, until the stems are just tender and the leaves are turning dark and crisp. Add the beans and sunflower seeds, stir gently into the broccoli and return to the oven for 2 minutes or so. Leave to cool slightly in the tin.

Thoroughly combine all the dressing ingredients – including a good pinch of salt and a few twists of pepper – by either whisking them in a small bowl or shaking them in a jar. Taste and adjust the seasoning, including mustard, sugar and vinegar, as you like.

Arrange the broccoli, beans and seeds on individual plates, spoon on the dressing and serve warm or at room temperature.

VARIATION

Scale down for a starter or side Leave out the beans, and the dressed broccoli and seeds alone make for a handsome starter or side dish – particularly good with fish.

Sesame roast carrots

Whacking chunks of carrot into a hot oven intensifies their sweet, rooty, earthy taste. Add raisins, nuts, seeds and a little fresh parsley and you've got a well-balanced veg dish – great as a simple supper, or as part of a vegetable mezze spread.

Serves 2, or 4 as a side

1kg carrots

3 tablespoons extra virgin rapeseed or olive oil

2 tablespoons sesame seeds

Finely grated zest of 1 orange and the juice of ½ the fruit

1 teaspoon runny honey

100g raisins

A generous handful of flat-leaf parsley leaves, coarsely chopped

Sea salt and freshly ground black pepper

1 tablespoon toasted almond flakes, to finish (optional)

Preheat the oven to 180°C/Gas 4.

Peel and trim the carrots. Slice them about 2cm thick (I like to cut them on the diagonal) and put them in a large roasting dish – not too crowded or piled up, so they caramelise nicely, rather than steam in their own juices.

Add the oil, some salt and pepper and the sesame seeds and toss well. Roast the carrots, giving them a good stir once or twice, for 40–50 minutes, or until tender and starting to colour and caramelise.

Meanwhile, put the orange zest and juice and the honey in a small saucepan and bring to a simmer. Add the raisins and turn off the heat. Leave them to soak and plump up while the carrots roast – 20 minutes should do it, but longer is better.

Add the plumped-up raisins and their orangey liquor to the carrots, along with the parsley leaves, and combine. Finish with a scattering of toasted flaked almonds if you like. Taste and add more salt or pepper if needed, then serve.

Nutty green beans with orange

This is the kind of side dish that can really steal the show alongside a grilled fillet of fish or a piece of barbecued chicken. Alternatively, add one or two more ingredients (see the variation below) and this is a main course in its own right.

Serves 4 as a side

200g French beans, topped (no need to tail)

100g blanched hazelnuts or almonds

4 tablespoons extra virgin rapeseed or olive oil

1 fat garlic clove, sliced

Finely grated zest of ½ large orange, plus a squeeze of orange juice

Sea salt and freshly ground black pepper

Bring a medium pan of salted water to the boil. Drop in the French beans and cook for 3–4 minutes, until just tender.

Meanwhile, using a pestle and mortar, crush the nuts very roughly – you want some of them to be just broken in two, others to be quite bashed-up. (If you don't have a pestle and mortar, roughly chop the nuts.)

Tip the beans into a colander to drain. Return the saucepan to a medium heat. Add the oil, then the garlic and bashed-up nuts. Cook, stirring often, for about 3 minutes, until the nuts are getting toasty and the garlic is just starting to turn golden.

Take off the heat, stir in the orange zest, a good pinch of salt and a grind of pepper, then return the beans to the pan and toss them in the nutty, garlicky oil. Finish with just the subtlest spritz of fresh orange juice. Serve right away.

VARIATION
Main additions Add some chopped black olives and a couple of roughly chopped hard-boiled eggs to make this a delicious light main course for two.

Dry-fried broccoli with toasted almonds and chilli

This broccoli is thrown into a hot pan with no oil at all, which gives it a pleasing smoky flavour and keeps the texture crisp and crunchy. It's a fine side dish for something a little bit saucy, such as the lamb and cashew curry on page 256. Or serve it as a starter – either on its own or with one of the creamy dressings suggested below.

Serves 4 as a side, or starter

25g flaked almonds

1 large head of broccoli or 2 small heads (about 500g in total), trimmed and cut into small florets

1 medium-sized, medium-hot red chilli, sliced

Sea salt

Heat a large, heavy-based frying pan over a medium heat. Toast the almonds in the frying pan for a couple of minutes, tossing them often so they don't burn, until they are golden brown. Tip the almonds into a bowl.

Return the frying pan to a medium heat. Add the broccoli and season with a generous pinch or two of salt. Leave to cook for 4–5 minutes, without stirring, until it starts to take on the bright and shiny green of cooked broccoli, with a few charred patches here and there. Give the broccoli a stir and continue to cook for 6–8 minutes, shaking and stirring now and again, until there are charred areas on all the pieces. By now the stalks should also be getting tender, but still al dente.

Add the chilli to the pan, seeds and all if you think you can take the heat, and cook over a medium heat for another 2 minutes or until the chilli is softening. Add more salt if needed then serve, with the toasted almonds sprinkled over.

VARIATION

With a creamy dressing This makes a great stand-alone starter served with either the luscious tahini-based dressing on page 166, or the mustardy dressing on page 304.

Four feisty salsas
These super-simple assemblies of fresh, crisp, juicy and aromatic ingredients can transform a simple meal – they'll make your burgers brilliant and your fish funky. They can all be served as soon as they're made but benefit from at least 10 minutes' standing, just to let their flavours mingle and merge.

Radish, mint and spring onion

Crisp, crunchy and pretty, this colourful little side is delicious with chicken or fish. Try it with smoky grilled sardines (page 202) or alongside smoked mackerel fillets for a quick and peppy lunch.

Serves 4–6

150g radishes

5–6 spring onions, trimmed and sliced

2 tablespoons chopped mint

2 tablespoons extra virgin rapeseed or olive oil

Sea salt and freshly ground black pepper

Trim the radishes, roughly chop them and put in a bowl. Add the remaining ingredients, leave for 10–15 minutes if possible, then toss well and serve.

Black bean and blueberry

Dark and devilishly well flavoured, this is hot, sharp, sweet and smoky all at the same time. Dish it up with a sliced avocado and some cornmeal tortillas (see page 72), with burgers (it's fab with the beetroot burger on page 283), or anything from the barbecue.

Serves 6

400g tin black beans, drained and rinsed

200g blueberries

1 small red onion, chopped

2 medium-hot red chillies, deseeded and chopped

1 garlic clove, chopped

Finely grated zest and juice of 1 lime

1 teaspoon sweet smoked paprika

1 teaspoon sugar

2 teaspoons cider vinegar

1 tablespoon extra virgin rapeseed or olive oil

Sea salt and freshly ground black pepper

Toss all the ingredients together. If possible, let stand for half an hour or so before eating.

Tinned tomato salsa

I was sceptical about tomato salsa based on uncooked, tinned toms, until Gill rustled up this recipe – which I really like. It goes a treat with my storecupboard fishcakes (page 227) or eggy fishfingers (page 225). It's also good with baked or roast spuds, and creamy polenta (as prepared, for example, on page 275).

Serves 3–4

400g tin whole plum tomatoes, in juice

½ small red onion, chopped

1 tablespoon extra virgin rapeseed or olive oil

1 teaspoon red wine vinegar or cider vinegar

2 tablespoons roughly chopped coriander, basil or parsley

Sea salt and freshly ground black pepper

Open the tin of tomatoes and tip them into a sieve. Drain off the juice (save it for a soup, sauce or curry). On a board, chop the tomatoes, removing any skin or whitish stalky ends, so you have a coarse, chunky mixture.

Add to a bowl with all the remaining ingredients and mix well.

Fresh tomato, avocado and red onion

A classic combo this, and such a good one – creamy avocado combined with sweet tomatoes and sharp onion and lemon. It goes brilliantly with burgers and fish, but I also like this on its own, for lunch, piled on to a rye crispbread.

Serves 4–6

2 large, ripe (but not over-ripe) avocados

200g cherry tomatoes, quartered (or larger tomatoes, cut into small pieces)

1 small red onion, very finely chopped

A good handful of coriander, chives or flat-leaf parsley leaves, roughly chopped

1 tablespoon extra virgin rapeseed or olive oil

Juice of ½ lemon or 1 lime

Sea salt and freshly ground black pepper

Quarter the avocados and remove their stones and skin, then roughly chop the flesh and put it into a bowl. Add all the other ingredients and turn together gently, being careful not to mash the avocado. Taste and add more salt and pepper as needed. Leave to stand for 10 minutes, then stir gently again and serve.

Fruit *is our friend*

FRUIT IS NATURE'S TREAT, an offering of such unmitigated, juicy, sweet loveliness that it's almost too good to be true. I would genuinely rather eat a bowl of sun-warmed raspberries or a ripe mango than a bar of chocolate (though, if those last two were combined, as in the recipe on page 326, I wouldn't complain).

That something which is so good for you should also be so tempting and so instantly gratifying may be proof that there is a higher intelligence. Or at least that apples are smarter than we think.

Why even bother with recipes, you may ask, when a sweet banana, a bowl of scented strawberries or a ripe pear offer the quickest of fruity fixes with so little effort? Well, I certainly think we should all enjoy regular helpings of unashamedly naked fruit. But I'm not such a purist that I think fruit can't be made even more alluring with just a little intervention from the cook.

So my aim in this chapter has been to do as little as possible to the fruit itself in order to produce dishes of unrivalled, fresh, vibrant gorgeousness.

If it's at the point of perfect ripeness, I often like to leave fruit raw and simply chop or slice it before serving it with a surprising seasoning or a pinch of something good – brown sugar, lime juice and spice, perhaps (as with the dressed pineapple on page 323), or just-picked elderflowers (which do wonders for strawberries, as you'll see on page 324).

Really ripe raw fruits such as pears and peaches can be puréed to a velvety consistency for fools or ices. Indeed, there are almost no fruits that you can't enjoy raw in some form – even rhubarb and gooseberries, as long as they are sliced thinly and dressed cleverly.

But cooking fruit opens a different spectrum of flavours and textures that I wouldn't want to miss out on. Baked pears (page 351), stewed apples (page 347) and simmered gooseberries (page 348) have an intensity and a tenderness all their own, while a fruit crumble (like the one on page 355) remains an eternally desirable prospect, as far as I'm concerned. Cooking fruit should be a quick and simple process. It often brings the best out of less than perfectly ripe specimens, and means fresh fruit can be kept for longer – so it's a thrifty option too.

I don't have any qualms about sweetening fruit if I think it needs it. It doesn't take very much to perfectly balance fruit's natural acidity. Both sugar and honey have a seasoning effect too: they enhance fruity flavours. But I'd encourage you to experiment with keeping even the most natural and unrefined sweeteners to an ever-decreasing minimum.

Your palate has a remarkable knack of adjusting to be quite content with even a tiny amount of sugar. You might be surprised at how much you end up enjoying the inherent tartness in your favourite fruits. You'll also find that other ingredients – notably lime juice and vanilla – enhance the sweetness of sharp fruits, raw and cooked.

Tricks like these and the repertoire of recipes that follow will ensure that your fast fruit quota is never a sliver less than lovely.

Raspberry, date and lime salad

This sounds unexpected, but is very simple and rather special. The flavours – sharp lime, tangy-sweet raspberries and fudgy dates – nicely span the sour-sweet spectrum. I love the fleshy, juicy, sticky and chewy textures too.

Serves 2

250g raspberries

1 teaspoon runny honey

2 limes

4 fat Medjool dates (or similar), pitted and sliced into thick strips

Put 100g of the raspberries into a bowl with the honey and the juice of ½ lime. Mix them together, crushing the raspberries with a fork or spoon to release the juices. Leave to macerate for 10–15 minutes to draw the juices out of the fruit, then rub the mixture through a sieve, so you have a tangy-sweet raspberry coulis.

Put the remaining whole raspberries in a bowl with the sliced dates.

Take a little slice off the top and base of the whole lime. Stand it on a board and use a sharp knife to cut away the peel and pith, leaving you with a skinless fruit. Working over the bowl of raspberries, slice out the little lime segments from between their membranes and drop them over the salad.

Add the red raspberry coulis, stir gently and serve.

VARIATION

Orange swap This salad is also delicious, and a little sweeter, if you substitute 1 large juicy orange for the 2 limes.

Pineapple with muscovado sugar and allspice

I love the Caribbean feel of this simple fruit salad, which is sweetened with dark, treacly muscovado sugar, spiked with lime and seasoned with peppery allspice. A fresh pineapple that you've sliced yourself will give you the edge on flavour – and it takes only a moment – but you could use one of those little pots of prepared fresh pineapple pieces.

Serves 2

250g peeled and cored pineapple flesh (about ½ medium pineapple)

Juice of 1 lime

4 teaspoons dark muscovado sugar

A pinch of ground allspice

Cut the pineapple into fairly even 4–5mm slices (if it isn't already) and arrange over two plates. Squeeze the juice of the lime over both plates. Sprinkle the sugar over the pineapple, then dust each plate with a pinch of allspice and it's ready to serve.

VARIATIONS

Boozy/peppery pineapple For a slightly more grown-up and even more Caribbean taste, replace the lime juice with 1 tablespoon dark rum. You could also use a grinding of black pepper instead of, or as well as, the allspice.

Elderflower strawberries

This dish combines two of my very favourite summer ingredients in the easiest possible way. It looks beautiful and tastes heavenly. Fresh, young elderflower heads (those with just a few flowers still unopened are the most deliciously perfumed) can usually be harvested from mid-May to late June – the variation below gives you a later season option.

Serves 6–8

1kg strawberries

25g caster sugar

Juice of ½ lemon

8–10 large, just-picked heads of elderflower

Hull the strawberries then slice them thickly – 3 or 4 slices per berry – working from top to bottom. Put them in a bowl with the sugar and lemon juice, turn very gently together and leave in a cool place to macerate for about half an hour.

Lay out the now-juicy berries on a large platter in a more or less single layer, making sure you pour over any juice left in the bowl. Put the elderflower heads, flowers down, on top of the berries, agitating them very gently as you do, to help them release their fragrant pollen into the berries.

Leave to stand for another hour, giving the elderflowers a twiddle and a push into the strawberries every now and again. The contact between the upturned flowers and the juicy strawberries will be enough to transmit their heady muscat aroma into the fruit.

Bring the dish to the table with the elderflowers on – they look so pretty – then remove them and dish up the strawbs.

VARIATION

Cordial version Later in the summer, when the elderflower blooms are gone, you can prepare a version of this dish by adding 1 tablespoon elderflower cordial to the macerating strawberries.

Mango with lime and chocolate

This easy fruity treat looks dramatic and tastes decadent. Perfectly ripe, fragrant mangoes are essential.

Serves 4

50g dark chocolate (at least 70% cocoa solids)

15g coconut oil (raw or odourless)

Finely grated zest and juice of ½ lime

2 large mangoes

Break up the chocolate into small pieces and put into a small heatproof bowl with the coconut oil and lime zest (not the juice). Set over a small pan of gently simmering water, making sure the base of the bowl does not touch the water, and leave to melt, stirring once or twice until smooth. (Or you can heat the ingredients directly in a small pan over a low heat if you're very careful!).

Peel the mangoes using a veg peeler or a small paring knife. Slice the flesh away from the stones in large pieces, then cut into slices. Arrange on four plates. Spritz over the juice of the lime, then trickle over the still-warm chocolate sauce in lavish ribbons. Tuck in straight away.

VARIATION

Mangochocococo Add a few curls of fresh coconut flesh to the mango slices before pouring over the chocolate sauce. (To prepare your own coconut by quickly baking in the oven, see page 154.)

Apple with basil and pine nuts

I've borrowed from the flavours of a classic pesto here (minus the garlic and cheese of course!). The subtle aniseed flavour of basil makes it a fantastic herb to use with fruit and sweet little toasted pine nuts add a satisfying crunch. This makes a nice breakfast salad and can also be served with or after a cheese course.

Serves 2

2 medium eating apples, such as Cox's or Ashmead's Kernel

A pinch of caster sugar

Finely grated zest and juice of ½ lemon

About 12 large basil leaves, shredded or torn

25g pine nuts, lightly toasted

A trickle of extra virgin rapeseed or olive oil, to finish (optional)

Peeling the apples is optional (I don't), but quarter them, remove their cores, then slice them fairly thinly into a bowl. Add the sugar, lemon zest and juice and most of the basil. Toss together.

Arrange the apple and basil mixture over two plates. Scatter with the pine nuts and the remaining basil. I like to finish this with a trickle of extra virgin oil, for a touch of pepperiness. Eat straight away.

VARIATIONS

Nut and herb swaps Try swapping in some roughly chopped almonds or walnuts in place of the pine nuts. Mint also works well instead of the basil. And, if you don't have any herbs or nuts to hand, a simple salad of sliced apple dressed with lemon zest and juice and a trickle of honey is pretty good too.

Carroty dried fruit salad

When mingled with citrus juice and zest, dried fruits become plump, succulent and tangy. Coarsely grated carrot adds texture and its own subtle sweetness to the mix. This sustaining fruity combo is great as a between-meals snack and will also perk up a lunchbox.

Serves 4

200g mixed dried fruit (any combination of coarsely chopped prunes, dates, apricots and apples; whole cherries or cranberries; sultanas, raisins or currants)

100g raw carrot, grated

Finely grated zest of 1 and juice of 2 medium oranges

Finely grated zest and juice of 1 lemon

½ teaspoon ground cinnamon (optional)

Broken pecans or toasted, slivered almonds (optional)

In a bowl, thoroughly mix together the dried fruit, carrot, citrus zests and juice, and cinnamon, if using. Cover and leave in a cool place for 4–5 hours until the fruit starts to plump up.

You can eat this straight away, or refrigerate it for up to 3 days, and decant portions into a watertight plastic tub for packed lunches or picnics. Either way, you might like to scatter a few pecans or almonds over the top shortly before eating.

VARIATIONS

Go nutty You can build this from a sweet treat into a nourishing snack lunch by adding raw nuts (such as cashews, pecans or walnuts) and/or seeds (pumpkin or sunflower, for example). Add them with the carrots and dried fruit at the start, with an extra squeeze of lemon juice, as they will also plump up and become tender (like my soaked nuts on page 25).

Pear, ginger and cashew fool

Spiked with ginger and laced with honey, a velvety, raw pear purée makes the basis for a light and fresh fruit fool. Choose pears that are nicely ripe (though not over-ripe) and they will be soft enough to purée easily.

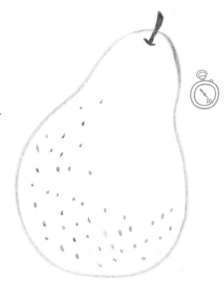

Serves 4

4 large, ripe pears

2–3 tablespoons runny honey

1 large-thumb-sized piece of ginger (25–30g)

4–6 tablespoons sweetened cashew cream (page 394)

Toasted almond flakes, to finish (optional)

Peel, quarter and core the pears and put them in a blender with 2 tablespoons honey.

Peel the ginger and grate it finely, scoop up the grated pulp into your hand and squeeze the juice into the blender; discard the pulp. Blend to a purée, then taste and add a little more honey if needed.

Spoon the pear purée into glasses, and top with a dollop of cashew cream. You can build up a few layers, or swirl the purée with the cream, or simply serve the cream over the purée and let the eaters do the fooling around. Scatter with a few toasted almond flakes if you like.

VARIATION

Pear and ginger fumble Top the fool with a generous topping of my wheat-free crumble (see page 355) and… it's a fumble!

Melon and pineapple in coconut milk

 This refreshing yet luxurious dessert is based on a south Indian *rasayana* – a kind of deconstructed lassi where fruit pulp is mixed with curd or yogurt, and sometimes spices. Here the coconut stands in for the dairy element. It's every bit as delicious.

Serves 4

200g tin coconut milk

1–2 teaspoons icing sugar

Finely grated zest of 1 lime, plus a little of the juice

½ ripe, fragrant small melon, such as a Charentais or Galia (about 400g), chilled

About ½ ripe, small pineapple (about 400g flesh), chilled

If your coconut milk has separated in the tin into a solid top layer and watery under-layer, tip into a pan and heat gently, stirring, until smooth, then leave to cool.

In a small bowl, whisk the coconut milk with a little icing sugar, half the lime zest and a few drops of lime juice, until smooth and lightly sweetened. Chill in the fridge. (You may need to whisk it again after chilling.)

Slice the chilled melon into wedges, remove the seeds, then slice the flesh off the skin. Cut into small bite-sized pieces.

Cut the skin from the pineapple, slice the flesh thickly and remove the core. Cut the flesh into similar-sized pieces to the melon.

Pile two-thirds of the fruit into chilled dishes or glasses and spoon over the blended coconut milk. Add the rest of the fruit and top each portion with a pinch more lime zest to serve.

Plum, honey and star anise granita

This is the first of a trio of light, refreshing frozen puds – and an ideal way to use a glut of Victorias, or other reasonably sweet plums or gages. Tart cooking plums, such as Czars, work well too but may require more sweetening.

Serves 4
1kg plums
4 star anise, lightly bashed
75–100g honey

Slash a few of the plums and put these first into a large saucepan with just a scrap of water – this will help the juices run more quickly. Add the rest of the plums, the star anise and 50g of the honey. Heat very gently, then, as the plum juices start to flow, increase the heat a little and bring to a merry simmer. Cook, stirring often to prevent sticking, until the fruit has completely collapsed and reduced to a rich compote. This can take anything from 10–25 minutes, depending on the plums. Turn off the heat and leave to cool down a bit.

Once it is no longer scalding, push the compote through a sieve (it shouldn't be too fine) to remove the stones, skins and star anise.

Taste this sieved purée and, while it is still warm, whisk in a little more honey if you want to sweeten it more. The purée should be nicely sweet at this stage as it will seem a little less so when frozen.

Pour into a shallow freezer container and freeze until solid – give it at least 6 hours. Remove about 30 minutes before you want to serve it, so it softens just a little. Scratch it into soft crystals with a fork, pile into serving glasses and serve.

VARIATIONS

Spice swaps Replace the star anise with 2 cinnamon sticks or a split vanilla pod. Or leave the spices out altogether for a simple plum and honey taste.

Plum lollies Alternatively – and even more easily – you can freeze the spiced or plain plum purée in lolly moulds for a gorgeous frozen treat.

Rhubarb and rose sorbet

I have rhubarb growing next to roses in my herbaceous border, so I couldn't resist bringing the two together. Cooking real rose petals with the rhubarb didn't quite do it (they became bitter), but when I turned to the bottle of rose water in the larder the fragrance of roses and tartness of rhubarb came together beautifully. Orange flower water works perfectly too, if you prefer that flavour (or that's what you have in your cupboard).

Serves 4–6

750g rhubarb

75ml fresh orange juice or cloudy apple juice

100g caster sugar

Up to 50g icing sugar

Up to 2 teaspoons rose water (or orange flower water)

Trim the rhubarb and cut into 3–4cm lengths, then put into a large saucepan with the orange or apple juice and caster sugar. Bring to a simmer and cook gently for about 15 minutes until the rhubarb is completely soft. Purée the rhubarb in the pan, using a stick blender, until smooth (or use a free-standing blender). Leave to cool completely. Taste, and whisk in a little icing sugar if you think it needs it.

Stir the rose water into the cooled rhubarb purée. I start by adding just a ¼ teaspoon or so, then gradually stirring in more until I have the intensity of flavour I want. Different brands of rose water can vary considerably in strength and it pays to be cautious.

Transfer the purée to a jug and chill until cold, then churn in an ice-cream machine until soft-set, before transferring to a freezer container and freezing until solid.

If you don't have an ice-cream machine, pour the purée into a plastic freezer container and freeze for about an hour until the sides start to get solid, then mash up the mixture with a fork or whisk, mixing the frozen sides into the liquid centre. Put it back in the freezer straight away for another hour. Repeat this at hourly intervals until the sorbet is soft-set, then let it freeze solid.

Remove from the freezer about half an hour before serving to soften slightly.

VARIATION

Rhubarb and rose lollies You can also simply freeze the rhubarb purée in lolly moulds to create luscious pink fruit lollies.

Peach and orange sorbet

There is undeniably something very sexy about ripe peaches. This sorbet captures and intensifies their gorgeous colour and fragrant flavour – sharpened with a citrusy note – and, if you fancy pushing the boat out a little, it can be turned into a decadent frozen bellini (see below).

Serves 4

1kg ripe, fragrant peaches or nectarines

Finely grated zest and juice of 1 medium orange

Finely grated zest and juice of 1 lemon

50–75g icing sugar, sifted

Halve, peel and stone the peaches, then cut each half in two. Put the peach quarters in a blender with the citrus juice and zest and 50g icing sugar and whiz to a purée. Taste and add more icing sugar if you like – the purée should be tart but sweet.

Transfer the purée to a jug and chill until cold, then churn in an ice-cream machine until soft-set, before transferring to a freezer container and freezing until solid.

If you don't have an ice-cream machine, pour the purée into a plastic freezer container and freeze for about an hour until the sides start to get solid, then mash up the mixture with a fork, mixing the frozen sides into the liquid centre. Put it back in the freezer straight away for another hour. Repeat this at hourly intervals until the sorbet is soft-set, then let it freeze solid.

Remove from the freezer about half an hour before serving to soften slightly.

VARIATIONS

Frozen bellini Put a scoop of peach sorbet in a glass, pour over a generous glug of very cold Champagne or other sparkling wine, sit back and enjoy a taste of pure, summery, Bellini-esque decadence.

Granita version You can certainly do a freeze-solid-and-scrape-with-a-fork version of this ice. Just freeze the sweetened purée in a tray for at least 6 hours. Before serving, soften a little, for 30 minutes or so, then scratch into soft shards with a fork.

Peach and orange lollies As with all the ices in this book, the purée can also be frozen in lolly moulds for a super-easy frozen fruit fix.

Strawberry cashew ice cream

This dairy-free ice has a lovely creamy texture and the base can be used to create lots of other fruity ice creams – see below. In order to purée well, the cashews need to be soaked in cold water first.

Serves 4–6

75g cashew nuts

1 large or 2 small ripe bananas (about 200g)

125g runny honey

400g ripe strawberries, hulled and roughly chopped

Juice of ½ lemon

TO SERVE (OPTIONAL)

Extra strawberries

A little sugar

A squeeze of lemon juice

First soak the cashews in cold water to cover for 6–8 hours, or overnight, then drain.

Peel the banana, break it into chunks and put it in a blender with the cashews, honey and 100ml water. Blitz thoroughly until you have a thick, creamy-looking purée. Add the strawberries and lemon juice. Give the whole lot a final blitz, just until smooth. Transfer to a jug and chill until cold.

Now churn the mixture in an ice-cream machine until soft-set, before transferring to a freezer container and freezing until solid.

If you don't have an ice-cream machine, pour the mixture into a plastic freezer container and freeze for about an hour until the sides start to get solid, then mash up the mixture with a fork, mixing the frozen sides into the liquid centre. Put it back in the freezer straight away for another hour. Repeat this at hourly intervals until the ice cream is soft-set, then let it freeze solid.

About 30 minutes before serving, remove the ice cream to soften slightly. Serve with sliced strawberries, macerated with a little sugar and a squeeze of lemon, if you like.

VARIATIONS

Fruit swaps The soaked cashew/honey base can be used to make a whole range of non-dairy, but distinctly creamy, ice creams. Instead of the strawberry flesh, try the same weight of raspberries; or skinned ripe kiwi fruit; or mango – they all work. You can also make a banana ice cream by leaving out the other fruit and doubling the amount of ripe banana you put in (don't forget the lemon juice).

Ice cream lollies For an even easier way to enjoy any version of this fruity, creamy ice, freeze in lolly moulds.

Banoffee split

Home-made banana ice cream, fresh bananas and a delectable, dairy-free toffee sauce make a tempting trio – not exactly virtuous, perhaps, but not unfeasibly naughty either. Do use raw, extra virgin coconut oil in the toffee sauce – the subtle coconut flavour it imparts is a delight.

Serves 4

4 medium-sized, medium-ripe bananas

4 scoops of cashew banana ice cream (see page 343), or your favourite dairy-free ice cream

FOR THE TOFFEE SAUCE

100g soft light brown sugar or coconut sugar

25g raw coconut oil

A pinch of salt (optional)

Start with the toffee sauce as it needs time to cool a little. Put the sugar and coconut oil in a small, heavy-based pan and add 100ml water, and a pinch of salt if you like. Heat the mixture gently, stirring, until the sugar has dissolved, then bring to a rolling boil. Boil it hard for 4–5 minutes, then turn off the heat and leave it to cool a little in the pan.

If you can see as it cools that it hasn't quite emulsified (i.e. there is still some separation between the oil and the syrup) boil for a bit longer. If you're a sugar-thermometer kind of person, 109°C will do the trick. You want to end up with a thick, dark brown syrup.

Leave the syrup to cool until just warm. If you let it cool right down and it becomes very thick, or if it separates, you can reheat it very gently to bring it back to pourability.

Peel the bananas, slice in two lengthways and arrange on plates. Add a generous scoop of ice cream, then trickle the warm toffee sauce over everything (any leftover sauce can be saved for pancakes or other ice creamy treats). Tuck in straight away.

VARIATION
Go nutty A scattering of toasted flaked almonds, or roughly bashed toasted hazelnuts or almonds, make this even more special.

Apple and prune compote

The prunes bring plenty of sweetness to this tart but satisfying compote so you don't need much sugar. The vanilla contributes its own sweetness and aroma too.

Serves 4

3 large or 4 medium cooking apples, such as Bramleys (about 800g in total)

125g pitted prunes, halved

½ vanilla pod

1 tablespoon caster sugar

Peel, quarter and core the apples, then slice them into a saucepan. Add the prunes. Split open the vanilla pod and scrape out the seeds with the tip of a small, sharp knife. Add these and the scraped-out pod to the pan. Scatter over the sugar and add 150ml water.

Put the saucepan over a medium-low heat and bring to a simmer. Cook gently for about 20 minutes, stirring now and then, until the apples are tender and mostly broken down and you have a thick compote. Add an extra splash of water if the apples look like they may start to stick. Take off the heat and leave to cool.

Eat warm or lightly chilled, with perhaps a scoop of lightly sweetened cashew cream (page 394). Remove the vanilla pod before serving.

VARIATIONS

Apple and prune crumble/fumble This compote is a prime candidate for a topping of the independent crumble on page 355. Just sprinkle it generously over the finished compote – either hot or cold. Alternatively, swirl a couple of spoons of the chilled compote with a spoon of my cashew cream (page 394), pile into a glass, then top with the crumble and you have yourself a luscious, dairy- and wheat-free, fumble.

Gooseberries with rosemary

Herbs can often make winning partners for fruit. Here the aromatic, resinous tones of rosemary complement the sorrelly sharpness of gooseberries deliciously.

Serves 3–4

500g gooseberries (fresh or frozen and defrosted), topped and tailed

A couple of generous sprigs of rosemary

50g caster sugar

Put the gooseberries into a saucepan with the rosemary, sugar and 4 tablespoons water. Bring slowly to a gentle simmer, stirring often to help the sugar dissolve, then cook gently for 5–10 minutes, stirring now and again, or until the gooseberries are soft and partly collapsed. Add a little more water if necessary to keep the compote nicely juicy but not swimming. Leave to cool.

Remove the rosemary, then serve the gooseberry compote at room temperature or lightly chilled, on its own or with a rye-gestive (page 87). It's also very good with a scattering of my pre-cooked crumble (page 355).

VARIATION

Gooseberry, strawberry and rosemary compote Replace a third to a half of the gooseberries with thickly sliced strawberries. You can cook these with the gooseberries or, if you have some really luscious, ripe and sweet strawberries, just stir them in once the gooseberries are cooked and cooled.

Baked pears with almonds and apricots

Here's an easy, luscious pud that's a great alternative to the traditional baked apple, and quicker too. It works best with pears that are nicely ripe – though definitely not squishy over-ripe ones, as they may fall apart.

Serves 4

2 very large, ripe pears, or 4 smaller ones

50g whole almonds, roughly chopped

8 unsulphured dried apricots, chopped

Finely grated zest and juice of 1 lemon

2 tablespoons cloudy apple juice

1 tablespoon runny honey

Preheat the oven to 180°C/Gas 4. Line a baking dish with baking parchment.

Peel the pears and slice them in half lengthways. Scoop out the cores with a melon baller or teaspoon to create a cavity about 4cm in diameter. Take a little slice off the underside of each pear so they will sit steady, and put them, cut side up, in the baking dish.

Mix together the chopped almonds, dried apricots and lemon zest. Distribute the almond mixture between the pears – it will fill the cavities and overflow on to the cut surface of the pears too. Sprinkle the lemon juice over the pears, spoon on the apple juice, then trickle over the honey.

Cover the dish with foil and bake for 20 minutes, until the pears are tender, then uncover and return to the oven for 7–10 minutes or so to lightly toast the almonds.

Serve hot, with any juices spooned over. This is particularly good with a spoonful of sweetened cashew cream (page 394) dolloped over, or a scoop of peach and orange sorbet (page 340) alongside.

VARIATIONS

Chop and change You can of course vary the nutty, fruity filling: try walnut and prune, or hazelnut and raisin.

Boozy pears For something a shade more indulgent and adult, replace some or all of the apple juice with a shot of Calvados or Poire William.

Rhubarb, apple and ginger pie

The gluten-free pastry on this fragrant pie is a revelation: amazingly light and crisp. You could, of course, use it on top of all kinds of fruity fillings, but this tart and aromatic combination is particularly winning. A scoop of lightly sweetened cashew cream (page 394) is very good on the side.

Serves 6–8

FOR THE PASTRY

75g white rice flour, plus extra to dust

50g gram (chickpea) flour

A pinch of salt

50g ground almonds

50g caster sugar

50g coconut oil (raw or odourless), plus extra for greasing

1 large egg, beaten

FOR THE FILLING

400g rhubarb, trimmed and cut into 2.5cm pieces

2 medium Bramley apples (400g in total), peeled, cored and roughly chopped

100g caster sugar

30g piece of ginger, peeled

Beaten egg, to glaze

TO FINISH

30g flaked almonds

To make the pastry, sift the flours, salt and ground almonds into a large bowl (the last of the almonds will probably be stubborn – push them through with a spoon, or just tip straight in from the sieve). Stir in the sugar. Add the coconut oil and roughly cut it into the dry ingredients using a table knife, then rub it in with your fingertips until the mix resembles fine breadcrumbs. Stir in the egg, then knead the pastry into a smooth dough. Shape into a disc, 2–3cm thick, wrap in cling film and rest in the fridge for 30 minutes.

Meanwhile, preheat the oven to 190°C/Gas 5. For the filling, mix together the rhubarb, apples and sugar. Finely grate the ginger into the fruit and mix well. Transfer to a 23cm ceramic flan dish, 3–4cm deep.

Take the pastry from the fridge. Dust a large sheet of baking parchment with rice flour and place the unwrapped dough on it. Sprinkle with more rice flour then put a second large sheet of baking parchment on top. Roll out the pastry carefully between the sheets to a thickness of about 3mm. The paper will help the pastry roll out evenly without sticking. (If the pastry is very cold, it may crumble – in which case give it a few minutes at room temperature. Any small breaks or cracks can be patched together.)

Carefully peel back the top layer of paper, dust the pastry with a little rice flour, replace the paper and flip the pastry over so the other piece of baking parchment is now on top. Peel this back, dust the pastry with a little more rice flour, then roll the pastry carefully over the rolling pin. Unroll the pastry over the flan dish, tamp it down around the edge of the dish and trim away the excess.

Brush the pastry with beaten egg and scatter over the flaked almonds. Bake for about 35 minutes, until the pastry is golden brown and the filling is bubbling. Leave to settle for 10–15 minutes, then serve, with cashew cream (page 394) if you like.

Peach crumble

I'm a great fan of 'independent crumble' – a crispy, crumbly topping mixture that can be baked separately and added to fruit at a moment's notice. You can use it to top a crumble and give it a second baking (as here), or just scatter it over fresh or cooked fruit, no further cooking required (just bake it initially to a toastier finish). This is my favourite wheat- and dairy-free version. It's crisper and lighter than a conventional crumble and it keeps well in an airtight container. The quantities here make enough to top two smallish crumbles – double them up and you'll have a good stash on stand by.

Serves 4

4 large or 6 small, just-ripe/slightly under-ripe peaches or nectarines (700g in total)

Juice of 1 small-medium lemon

1 teaspoon vanilla extract

1 tablespoon runny honey, or soft light brown sugar

FOR THE CRUMBLE TOPPING

50–75g coconut oil (raw or odourless)

100g fine oatmeal or oat flour

100g porridge oats

A pinch of salt

25g ground almonds

50g soft brown sugar

TO FINISH (OPTIONAL)

A handful of flaked almonds

To make the crumble topping, preheat the oven to 170°C/Gas 3 and line a baking tray with baking parchment. Melt the coconut oil gently in a large saucepan – use 50g oil if you are using fine oatmeal in the topping, and 75g if you are using oat flour, which will absorb more. Take off the heat, add all the other ingredients and mix thoroughly until well combined. Spread this oaty mixture over the prepared tray. Bake for 25–30 minutes, giving it a good stir halfway through and keeping a close eye on it, until golden but not brown, so that it can take a bit more cooking later on. Leave to cool completely.

When you're ready to make the pudding, preheat the oven to 180°C/Gas 4. Halve and stone the peaches or nectarines and cut each half into 7 or 8 wedges. Put them into an oven dish (I use one 20cm square) and squeeze over the lemon juice. Stir the vanilla into the honey and trickle it reasonably evenly over the fruit. (Alternatively, if you're using sugar, just toss it into the fruit along with the lemon juice and vanilla.)

Spoon roughly half the crumble topping over the fruit – enough to get a thin, fairly even layer (keep the rest for another pud). It's nice to have some fruit poking through. Sprinkle with flaked almonds if you like and bake for 25–30 minutes until the fruit is bubbling and the topping nicely browned. Leave to settle for 10–15 minutes before serving. For an extra treat, pair with cashew cream (page 394) or a scoop of peach sorbet (page 340).

VARIATIONS

Fruit swaps This is also lovely with just-ripe pears. Peel, quarter and core the pears, then cut each quarter into two. Layer in the dish and proceed as above. Halved plums are very good too – if the plums are tart, add a little more honey.

Pear and chocolate cobbler

The natural sweetness of pears balances beautifully with bittersweet dark chocolate and a crusty, cobblery topping in this baked pud. It's luxurious without being heavy.

Serves 6

4 large or 5 ripe, medium pears (about 800g in total)

100ml apple or pear juice

1 tablespoon runny honey

50g dark chocolate (at least 70% cocoa solids)

FOR THE TOPPING

100g ground almonds

50g brown rice flour

2 teaspoons baking powder

50g light soft brown sugar

2 large eggs

1 tablespoon rapeseed oil

Preheat the oven to 180°C/Gas 4. Have ready an oven dish, about 1.5 litre capacity.

Peel the pears, quarter them and remove their cores. Cut each quarter into 3 or 4 slices, dropping them into the oven dish as you work. Spread them into a roughly equal layer. Trickle the apple or pear juice all over the pears, followed by the honey. Finally break the chocolate into small pieces and distribute evenly over the fruit.

Sift the ground almonds, rice flour, baking powder and sugar into a bowl (or mix thoroughly with a whisk to disperse any little lumps). Add the eggs and rapeseed oil and beat together thoroughly until you have a thick batter.

Drop the batter in 6 large dollops around the edge of the dish, partially covering the pears. Bake for 35–40 minutes or until the cobbler topping is firm and golden brown. You can poke a skewer into the topping to make sure it's cooked through – it should come out clean.

Leave the cobbler to settle for 10 minutes or so, then serve. (You may find the chocolate has gone a bit grainy where it's mixed with the hot pear juices, but this will in no way detract from the all-round deliciousness of the pud!)

WE ALL DESERVE A SWEET BOOST every now and again (and even if we don't, we're probably going to have one anyway). But these treaty recipes offer goodies with added goodness, so that you can feel virtuous, even while indulging.

When baking without wheat flour or dairy ingredients, I have found myself reaching for alternative fats and flours, and complementary ingredients, that contribute a definite nutritional fillip to the mix. So the treats that follow are full of good things: unrefined and natural fats and flours, whole fruits, ground nuts. They still pack a high-energy, calorific punch – so a degree of moderation is in order. But there's certainly no call for denial.

There is of course no butter, cream or milk in this collection. Instead, you'll find alternatives such as ripe avocado, which makes the silkiest of chocolate mousses (page 363), dairy-free 'milks' and 'creams' – check out the gorgeous almond rice pud on page 364 – and a healthy helping of coconut oil. This is a wonderful fat for baking since it behaves very much like butter, and is good for you to boot (see page 398). You can use the extra virgin oil, which will give a hint of subtly sweet coconuttiness to your recipe, or, if that's not for you, opt for the de-aromatised oil.

As well as fruit, a good smattering of vanilla and ingredients such as chestnut flour and ground almonds (which have their own gentle sweetness), I've used honey or sugar (often an unrefined soft brown sugar) to sweeten these lovely recipes. In all cases, my aim has been to add the minimum amount required – but to make sure the finished bake is tempting and delicious.

Cakes made without gluten-rich wheat flour, such as the citrus polenta cake on page 372 and brownies on page 379, are often more tender in texture than their conventional counterparts. They also 'steal' less from the tastes and texture of the other ingredients (whereas wheat flour is a terrible flavour thief). You may therefore, as I have, quickly come to think of these treats not as ascetic, high-minded alternatives to old favourites – but as delightful and delicious recipes that truly deserve to replace your old-school wheaty repertoire in your affections.

None of these treats are doughy or heavy. They may not rise as spectacularly as a wheat flour sponge, but you'll find that these easy bakes achieve a different kind of lightness – often combined, almost paradoxically, with a pleasing richness. One of the secrets to this is the simple technique of whipping eggs and sugar, or honey, for a few minutes to create a creamy mousse. If you've a free-standing mixer, or hand-held electric whisk, this is a doddle and provides a fluffy, slightly elastic, base into which you can mix your dry ingredients and oils.

Beyond that, these recipes require very little in the way of skill or finesse. Yet the results, with their subtle and delightful differences from the baking mainstream, will win you plaudits from all sides. So don't be shy or modest. Take a bow. And another slice…

Chocolate and avocado mousse with honeyed strawberries

Raw and dairy-free, this is one of the richest, glossiest, chocolatiest mousses you'll ever taste. Lightly macerated strawberries are wonderful with it. Cherries, raspberries, peaches or apricots are also great companions.

Serves 4

2 very ripe, large avocados

3 tablespoons cocoa powder

A good squeeze of lime juice, or more to taste

3–5 tablespoons runny honey (or use agave syrup)

FOR THE HONEYED STRAWBERRIES

200g strawberries, halved or thickly sliced

1 tablespoon runny honey

A good squeeze of lemon or lime juice

Combine the strawberries with the honey and lemon or lime juice. (Don't worry if the honey doesn't seem to combine too easily at first.) Cover and leave for 20–30 minutes then, once the juices are starting to seep out of the berries, stir again and set aside until ready to serve.

Meanwhile, to make the mousse, halve the avocados, remove the stones and peel, then put the flesh into a food processor. Add the cocoa powder, a good squeeze of lime juice and 3 tablespoons honey. Process to a velvety, thick purée, then taste and add more honey or lime juice as you like.

Scoop the mousse into small serving dishes, cover and chill for an hour or so. Serve with the honeyed strawberries and their juices spooned on top.

Almond rice pudding with lemon and bay

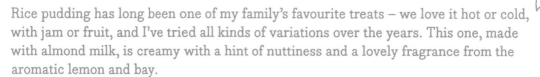

Rice pudding has long been one of my family's favourite treats – we love it hot or cold, with jam or fruit, and I've tried all kinds of variations over the years. This one, made with almond milk, is creamy with a hint of nuttiness and a lovely fragrance from the aromatic lemon and bay.

Serves 4–6

75g pudding rice

50g caster sugar

1–2 bay leaves, twisted or torn

6 strips of lemon zest (pared from 1 lemon)

800ml unsweetened almond milk (bought or home-made, page 30)

Preheat the oven to 150°C/Gas 2.

Put the rice in a sieve and rinse well under cold running water, then tip into an oven dish (about 1.5 litres capacity). Add the sugar, bay, lemon zest and almond milk and stir well.

Transfer the dish carefully to the oven. Bake for 1½–2 hours, until the rice is completely tender and the pudding thick and creamy, giving it a good stir every 30 minutes or so to ensure all the rice cooks evenly. You can stop baking when the pudding is still fairly loose textured, or give it a little longer if you prefer a firmer result. Either way, bear in mind that it will continue to thicken as it cools.

Let the pudding rest for at least 10 minutes. Serve it warm, at room temperature or chilled, straight up or partnered with some lightly fried apples or pears and a trickle of honey or syrup. Or of course, with your favourite jam!

VARIATION

Vanilla rice pud For a more traditional rice pud, replace the bay and lemon with a split vanilla pod. Scrape the vanilla seeds into the almond milk and stir well. Snip the scraped-out pod into shorter lengths and drop these into the mix too.

Castagnaccio

This chestnut flour cake, traditional in Liguria and other parts of northern Italy, is free of gluten, dairy products and eggs. It's dense and rich without being too sweet and the orange and rosemary give it a gorgeous aromatic quality.

Serves 10

75g sultanas or raisins

100ml extra virgin olive oil, plus extra to serve

400g chestnut flour

50g soft light brown sugar

A pinch of sea salt

Finely grated zest of 1 orange

25g pine nuts

Leaves from 1 rosemary sprig

Honey, to serve

Soak the sultanas in a little freshly boiled water (or hot tea) for about 10 minutes, so they plump up, while you prepare everything else.

Preheat the oven to 150°C/Gas 2. Brush a 22–23cm springform cake tin with some of the oil and line the base with baking parchment.

Drain the sultanas over a measuring jug to catch the soaking liquid, then make up the liquid to 400ml with cold water.

Sift the flour, sugar and salt into a large bowl. Add the orange zest, then gradually beat in the 400ml water until you have a smooth batter. Beat in the olive oil and sultanas.

Scrape the mixture into the prepared tin, then scatter over the pine nuts – patting them in slightly with your hand so they adhere – and rosemary. Bake for 45 minutes. The cake will look very similar to how it did when it went into the oven but the top should be dry and slightly cracked in places and a skewer inserted into the centre should come out clean.

Remove the side of the tin and leave the cake to cool on the base on a wire rack. Peel away the lining paper as you transfer the cake to a board to cut into slices.

Serve the cake just warm, or completely cooled, trickling each slice with honey and a little extra virgin oil.

Chocolate bean cake

It may seem strange to put beans in a cake, but the Japanese do it all the time, with lovely results. A tin of kidney beans makes this cake fudgily moist, while a healthy hit of cocoa renders it yummily chocolatey. It couldn't be easier to make – you just throw all the ingredients into a food processor and press 'go'. It's worth noting that, as well as being gluten- and dairy-free, this is also a nut-free cake – provided of course you check your rice flour and cocoa for the dreaded phrase 'may contain traces of nut'. Served with summer fruits and cashew cream (see below) it makes a delicious dessert (though of course it loses its nut-free status).

Serves 8–10

75ml sunflower oil or melted coconut oil (raw or odourless), plus extra for greasing

400g tin red kidney beans, drained and rinsed (or other tender tinned pulse, such as cannellini or butter beans)

100g rice flour

50g cocoa powder

1½ teaspoons baking powder

A pinch of salt

125g soft light brown sugar

3 large eggs

1 teaspoon vanilla extract

Preheat the oven to 180°C/Gas 4. Lightly oil a 20cm springform cake tin and line the base with baking parchment.

Now simply put all the ingredients into a food processor and blitz to a smooth batter, stopping once or twice to scrape down the sides.

Spoon the mixture into the prepared tin and spread out evenly. Bake for 20–25 minutes until it has risen and a skewer inserted into the middle comes out clean, or almost clean.

Leave the cake to cool slightly in the tin for about 10 minutes, then turn out and transfer to a wire rack to cool completely before cutting.

VARIATIONS

With cherries or berries For pud I love to serve this cake with cherries (fresh or lightly cooked with a little sugar), strawberries (macerated with honey and lemon if you like, as on page 363), or raspberries (including the spiced berry salad on page 20). You can go the whole hog and serve with a dollop of sweetened cashew cream (page 394) too.

Fruity cider loaf

Cider gives a rich autumnal mellowness to this very easy fruit bread, or you can use apple juice for a fresher, tangier version. Choose any dried fruits that take your fancy, but I particularly like this combination of fairly evenly distributed raisins and occasional plump, whole prune-bombs.

Makes 10–12 slices

150g raisins

150g pitted prunes

75g soft light brown sugar

150ml medium-dry cider or apple juice

A little rapeseed or sunflower oil, for oiling

1 large egg

100g ground almonds

100g brown rice flour

2 teaspoons baking powder

½ teaspoon ground mixed spice

Put the raisins and prunes in a bowl with the sugar and pour over the cider or apple juice. Mix well and leave for about 2 hours (longer if you like) to soak and plump up.

Preheat the oven to 170°C/Gas 3. Lightly grease a loaf tin (18 x 8cm approximate base measurement) and line the base with baking parchment.

Beat the egg lightly in a bowl, add it to the wet fruit and stir in. Combine the ground almonds, rice flour, baking powder and ground spice, add to the fruit mixture and beat until everything is well combined. Pour the mixture into the prepared tin and bake for 50–55 minutes or until a skewer inserted into the centre of the cake comes out clean.

Leave to cool for 15 minutes in the tin before turning out on to a rack to cool completely. This fruity loaf will keep well in an airtight tin for up to 5 days.

VARIATION

Smoky tea loaf For a different but delightful flavour, replace the cider/apple juice as the fruit soaking liquid with 150ml hot lapsang souchong tea. Make sure it's a strong brew that's had a good long stew.

St Clements polenta cake with blueberries

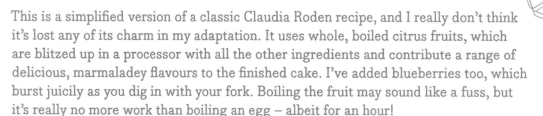

This is a simplified version of a classic Claudia Roden recipe, and I really don't think it's lost any of its charm in my adaptation. It uses whole, boiled citrus fruits, which are blitzed up in a processor with all the other ingredients and contribute a range of delicious, marmaladey flavours to the finished cake. I've added blueberries too, which burst juicily as you dig in with your fork. Boiling the fruit may sound like a fuss, but it's really no more work than boiling an egg – albeit for an hour!

Serves 10

2 unwaxed lemons

1 medium orange (unwaxed if possible, or scrubbed under warm water if not)

A little rapeseed or sunflower oil, for oiling

150g fine (not quick-cook) polenta or cornmeal

100g ground almonds

2 teaspoons baking powder

4 large eggs

250g caster sugar

200g blueberries

Put the lemons and orange in a saucepan and cover with boiling water from the kettle. Place a lid from a smaller pan, or a small heatproof plate or something similar on top of the fruit to stop them floating, then cover the pan. Bring to a simmer and cook for 1 hour until very soft, topping up the water if necessary. Remove the fruit from the water and leave to cool completely.

Preheat the oven to 170°C/Gas 3. Oil a 23cm springform cake tin and line the base with baking parchment.

Tear the boiled fruit apart and remove any pips, as well as the stem ends at the top of the fruit. Put the orange and lemon pieces in a food processor and add all the remaining ingredients except the blueberries. Blitz thoroughly, stopping to scrape down the sides once or twice, until you have a thick batter.

Scrape the batter into the tin. Add the blueberries and stir them in lightly, getting them fairly evenly distributed. Bake for 45–50 minutes or until a skewer inserted into the centre comes out clean.

Leave to cool completely in the tin on a wire rack, then run a knife around the sides to release the cake and remove from the tin. Serve in thick slices.

VARIATION

Greedy pud version Serve the cake warm from the oven, with a sauce made by warming a couple of tablespoons of good marmalade with a little cider, apple or orange juice. Add a sprinkling of toasted almonds if you like.

Hazelnut chocolate cake

Here's another treat to serve straight up at teatime or in a more indulgent and pud-like manner (see the variations below). If you can't find ready-ground hazelnuts, you can always grind whole nuts in a food processor – in fact, I like the slightly coarser texture you get when you prepare them this way. The cake also works well with ground almonds.

Serves 6–8

50ml rapeseed or sunflower oil, plus extra for oiling

150g ground hazelnuts (or almonds)

1 teaspoon baking powder

1 tablespoon cocoa powder

2 large eggs

50g caster sugar

1 tablespoon runny honey

Preheat the oven to 180°C/Gas 4. Line a 20cm springform cake tin with baking parchment and brush very lightly with oil.

Thoroughly combine the ground hazelnuts, baking powder and cocoa and set aside.

Put the eggs, sugar and honey into the bowl of a free-standing mixer (or use a hand-held electric whisk in a regular bowl) and whisk together for 4–5 minutes until very thick, pale and foamy and roughly tripled in volume. The mixture should hold a trail on the surface when you lift the beaters.

Add the hazelnut mix to the bowl and continue to whisk while you trickle in the oil. Keep whisking for 30–60 seconds until the mix is thoroughly combined.

Scrape the batter into the prepared tin and level it out. Bake for 20 minutes or until just firm to the touch in the centre (it will remain quite shallow). A skewer inserted in the middle of the cake should come out clean.

Leave to cool completely in the tin then remove and carefully peel away the lining paper. Serve in slices, just as it is or with one of the toppings suggested below.

VARIATIONS

Creamy choc-topped version Spread the cooled cake with sweetened cashew cream (page 394) and add a generous sprinkling of grated chocolate.

Nutty choc-topped version Scoop about 6 heaped tablespoons of my chocolate nut butter (page 392) into a small pan. Add 3 tablespoons water, almond milk or coconut milk and heat gently, stirring, until the spread has 'melted' into a loose, pourable consistency. Serve warm over the cake.

Chestnut marmalade muffins

This is another great recipe from Gill, and everyone I've served these to has wolfed them down in seconds. The combination of subtly sweet, earthy chestnut flour and a hidden pocket of tangy marmalade is just irresistible.

Makes 10
125g chestnut flour
A pinch of salt
2 teaspoons baking powder
125g marmalade
2 large eggs

75g runny honey
½ teaspoon vanilla extract
75g odourless coconut oil, melted and slightly cooled
Pumpkin seeds, to finish

Preheat the oven to 170°C/Gas 3 and put 10 large muffin cases in a muffin tray.

Combine the flour, salt and baking powder and set aside.

Put the marmalade in bowl and beat it to loosen it. Set aside.

Put the eggs, honey and vanilla into the bowl of a free-standing mixer (or use a large mixing bowl and a hand-held electric whisk). Whisk for 4–5 minutes until the mixture is very thick and moussey, roughly tripled in volume, and holds a trail on the surface when the beaters are lifted.

Sift the flour mixture over the egg mousse, then start whisking again and continue for another 2 minutes, trickling in the melted coconut oil and 1 tablespoon water as you go, to produce a glossy, loose batter. Fold in the marmalade.

Pour the batter into the muffin cases – they should be half to two-thirds full. Top each muffin with a few pumpkin seeds. Bake for 25 minutes until risen and golden brown. Allow the muffins to cool completely before you tuck in. These will keep well in an airtight container for a couple of days.

Ultra choc brownies

These wheat- and dairy-free treats are densely fudgy and very, very chocolatey. In fact around one-third of their body weight is good dark chocolate – perhaps not unlike my friend Nikki after devising this delightful recipe. She did get through a lot of brownies. It was worth the sacrifice – this recipe has now surpassed and supplanted all previous wheat-flour based brownies in my affections.

Makes 12

200g dark chocolate (at least 70% cocoa solids)

100g coconut oil (raw or odourless)

100g ground almonds

75g brown or white rice flour

A pinch of salt

1 teaspoon baking powder

2 large eggs

150g soft light brown sugar

1 teaspoon vanilla extract (optional)

75g walnuts, roughly chopped

Preheat the oven to 180°C/Gas 4. Line a brownie tin or baking tin, about 24 x 16cm or 20cm square, with baking parchment.

Break up the chocolate into small pieces and put into a heatproof bowl with the coconut oil. Set the bowl over a pan of just-simmering water and leave to melt slowly, stirring occasionally until smooth, then leave to cool until barely warm. You can do it in a heavy-based saucepan over a very low heat – but super carefully, removing from the heat when the chocolate is about half melted and stirring to finish the melting. Either way, the molten mix must not be hot when you add it to the other ingredients later.

Sift together the ground almonds, rice flour, salt and baking powder; set aside.

Whisk the eggs and sugar together, with the vanilla if using, until well blended and frothy. It doesn't have to be a thick mousse (as with the chocolate cake on page 374): a minute with an electric whisk will do it, a couple by hand with a rotary or balloon whisk.

Make a well in the centre of the dry ingredients. Pour in the egg and sugar mix, followed by the molten chocolate. Starting slowly, mix the whole lot together with a wooden spoon or whisk until all is combined in an even but thick batter. Stir in the walnuts.

Scrape the mixture into the prepared tin, spread it out with a spatula and bake for 20–25 minutes, or until the top looks firm and a skewer inserted into the centre comes out fairly clean but with a few moist crumbs sticking to it.

Let the brownie cool in the tin completely – leave for several hours or even overnight – then cut into squares or slices. These brownies are fairly gooey and a bit fragile – but very yummy indeed. If you put them in the fridge they'll get a bit fudgier and a bit firmer.

Chestnut and almond shortbread

Made with a pleasing blend of ground nuts and wholegrain buckwheat, this richly flavoured, not-too-sweet shortbread is perfect as a treat with a cup of tea. It also makes a winning companion to fresh strawberries, and fruity ices or compotes.

Makes 8–12 pieces

100g chestnut flour

100g buckwheat flour

1 teaspoon baking powder

A good pinch of salt

100g ground almonds

50g soft light brown sugar, plus a little extra to finish

125ml rapeseed or sunflower oil

Preheat the oven to 170°C/Gas 3. Line a loose-based 20cm sandwich tin with baking parchment, or use an 18cm square tin or rectangular tin with similar dimensions.

Sift the flours, baking powder, salt, ground almonds and sugar into a bowl. Any stubborn bits of almond left in the sieve can just be tipped into the bowl and any little nuggets of brown sugar crumbled with your fingers – just make sure the dry ingredients are well combined and any lumps got rid of.

Pour in the oil and mix thoroughly to create a soft, crumbly dough. Tip this into the lined tin and press it into an even layer, smoothing down the top with the back of a spoon. Prick the shortbread all over with a fork.

Bake for 30 minutes, until the shortbread is a rich brown colour. Take it out of the oven and immediately cut into 8 wedges, or 8–12 squares, in the tin. Scatter with a little more brown (or caster) sugar, if you like, then leave until cool enough to remove from the tin.

Transfer the pieces to a wire rack. When the shortbread is completely cool it will have the correct crumbly texture for serving, which it will retain if stored in an airtight container, for up to a week.

Coconut macaroons

A good old-fashioned teatime treat, these are golden and deliciously toasted on the outside, tender and chewy within – and incredibly easy to make. If you need any further excuse to give them a go, they're a great way to use up leftover egg whites.

Makes about 12
(or 30 mini macaroons)

A little rapeseed or sunflower oil, for oiling

150g caster sugar

200g unsweetened desiccated coconut

4 medium egg whites

Preheat the oven to 170°C/Gas 3. Line a large baking tray with baking parchment and grease it very lightly with oil (the macaroon mixture is very sticky).

Put the sugar, coconut and egg whites in a large bowl and mix together thoroughly until the egg white is evenly distributed and you have a mixture resembling wet sand (it doesn't need to froth up like a meringue mix).

Drop heaped dessertspoonfuls of the mixture on to the baking tray in little mounds, spacing them 1cm apart (you should get about 12 mounds). Alternatively you can make teaspoon-sized mounds (around 30), in which case you may need two baking trays.

Bake for 15–20 minutes (a little less for smaller ones), until pale golden brown. Transfer the macaroons, still on their paper, to a wire rack to cool.

Carefully peel the cooled macaroons off the paper. Store in an airtight tin and eat within 2–3 days.

VARIATIONS

Chocolate-topped macaroons Break 100g dark chocolate into pieces and melt in a heatproof bowl over a pan of gently simmering water, stirring from time to time, until liquid and glossy. Remove the bowl from the pan. Trickle the melted chocolate over the cooled macaroons, using a fork. Leave to cool and set before peeling the macaroons off the paper.

Almond macaroons Replace the coconut with ground almonds. Whip the egg whites first, until they hold soft peaks, then combine the ground almonds and sugar and fold them in. Stir in a few drops of almond extract too, if you'd like a strong marzipanny flavour. Dot on to lined baking trays in heaped teaspoonfuls and bake at 180°C/Gas 4 for about 20 minutes. You can trickle these with melted chocolate too, if you like.

Oaty, nutty, fruity cookies

I can't think of a nicer way to refuel mid-morning or teatime than with one (or two) of these. In texture they're somewhere between a soft, chewy cookie and a tender rock cake – a pretty good place to be.

Makes about 12

200g crunchy, no-sugar-added peanut butter

75g runny honey

1 large egg

¼ teaspoon bicarbonate of soda

75g raisins

50g porridge oats

Preheat the oven to 170°C/Gas 3. Line a baking tray with baking parchment.

Put the peanut butter in a mixing bowl. Add the honey and beat it in, then add the egg and beat that in thoroughly. Sprinkle the bicarbonate of soda over the surface and beat it in, then stir in the raisins and oats. You will end up with a very stiff, chunky dough.

Put heaped dessertspoonfuls of the mixture on to the prepared baking tray. If you like you can shape them gently into rough rounds with lightly oiled fingertips. Leave a little space between each because they will expand slightly in the oven.

Bake for 10 minutes, then transfer carefully to a wire rack to cool. These are best eaten within 2–3 days of baking.

Spiced date and almond cookies

These soft cookies – devised by my friend Anna Horsburgh – are delightfully spiked with ginger and Chinese five-spice. They're incredibly moreish and, since they contain no added fats or refined sugar, I don't feel too bad about giving in to temptation.

Makes 12–14

200g pitted dates

2cm knob of ginger (about 15g), peeled and roughly chopped

2 medium eggs

250g ground almonds

¼ teaspoon bicarbonate of soda

1½ teaspoons ground Chinese five-spice

A pinch of salt (optional)

Preheat the oven to 170°C/Gas 3. Line two baking sheets with baking parchment (or use one and bake in two batches).

Put the dates and ginger into a food processor and blitz to a thick, smooth paste. Add the eggs and blitz until completely incorporated. Add the remaining ingredients and blitz until well combined into a thick, sticky dough.

Lightly wet your hands – it'll help to stop the dough sticking to them – then take a heaped dessertspoon of the mixture and roll between your palms into a ball. Place on the baking tray, leaving a little space in between, and flatten with your fingers until you have a patty about 1cm thick. Repeat with the remaining mixture.

Bake for about 20 minutes or until firm around the edges, golden in colour and with a slight give in the middle. Remove to a wire rack and leave to cool before eating. These will keep for several days in an airtight container.

Nutty cherry choccy bites

Treats these undoubtedly are – but they are also full of nutty, fruity goodness. A couple make a boosting snack mid-morning or afternoon. Even more treaty – in an after-dinner kind of way – are the chocolate-dipped variation.

Makes 12

150g crunchy, no-sugar-added peanut butter

30g desiccated coconut

75g dried cherries (or cranberries, sultanas, chopped dried apricots etc.)

15g cocoa powder, sifted

Using a fork, work the peanut butter, coconut and dried fruit thoroughly together into a thick paste.

With lightly oiled hands, take heaped teaspoonfuls of the mixture and roll into balls. Drop into the cocoa powder in a small bowl, and turn with a pair of forks until coated.

Put the cocoa-dusted balls on a small tray or plate and chill in the fridge for at least 2 hours.

These are best stored in the fridge or a very cool place and will keep for up to a week.

VARIATION

Peanut, cherry and coconut chocs Make as above, but instead of dusting with cocoa powder, put the balls straight into the fridge on the tray to cool and set. Break 100g dark chocolate into small pieces and melt in a bowl over a pan of simmering water, stirring occasionally until smooth and flowing. Dip the chilled balls in the chocolate, using a couple of forks – or a pair of chopsticks if you're nifty with them – to turn and coat them, then place on a parchment-lined tray. Return to the fridge to set. They will keep in a cool place for a week.

Popcorn variations

We pop corn regularly at home and it never fails to go down a storm. Of course it's ripe for customisation: once you've popped your kernels you can flavour them with different sweet and savoury seasonings.

Serves 4

1 tablespoon rapeseed
or sunflower oil

100g popcorn maize

Put the oil and maize in a very large pan that has a well-fitting lid. The popcorn will increase many times in volume, and the lid is required to contain the flying puffs of popping corn – a stockpot-sized pan is ideal. Put the lid on the pan, place it over a medium heat and give it a shake after the first minute or so to coat the corn with oil. After 2–3 minutes, you should smell a delicious, toasted-corn aroma and start to hear pings and pops as the heated kernels explode, one by one, and hit the lid of the pan.

Turn down the heat a little and leave the pan, giving it a bit of a shake now and then, until all the popping has just about stopped, probably 3–4 minutes in all.

Tip the popped corn into a very large bowl and, while it is still warm, add your chosen flavourings (see below), stirring or shaking thoroughly to distribute them evenly. Serve the popcorn straight away.

FLAVOURINGS FOR YOUR POPCORN

Olive oil and salt Trickle 2–3 tablespoons good extra virgin olive oil over the warm popcorn, stirring as you go, and sprinkle on ¼–½ teaspoon fine sea salt. Shake well to distribute the flavours. My favoured method for doing this is to put a second large bowl, upside down, on top of the first, then shake the popcorn inside the two like a giant rattle.

...plus paprika After adding olive oil and salt, a light dusting of sweet smoked paprika (about 2 teaspoons) makes popcorn into something rather sophisticated. Add a pinch at a time, followed by a stir and a shake, for even distribution. A pinch of cayenne will give it extra kick.

Honey-corn Let the popcorn cool, then trickle about 3 tablespoons runny honey (or gently warmed set honey) over it. The easiest way to distribute this is to toss it with one hand while you stir with the other. I also like the salty-sweet-savoury effect off adding honey as well as salt and olive oil. Honey sometimes makes the popcorn lose a little of its crispness but the sheer yumminess is ample compensation. (This version is clearly not vegan.)

Chocolate nut butter

Ready-made chocolate nut spreads tend to contain a lot of refined sugar, as well as palm oil and dairy products – and often far fewer nuts than you would hope for. This easy home-made version knocks the socks off any of them: sweetened with honey and packed with nuts, coconut oil and cocoa, it's both deliciously nutty and divinely chocolatey. The texture is thicker and firmer than a shop-bought spread. I love it slathered generously on to oatcakes for breakfast and topped with a couple of slices of banana. It's also brilliant on pancakes. Toasting the nuts adds real depth of flavour to the spread – you can buy them ready-toasted to save time.

Makes 1 jar

200g blanched hazelnuts or almonds, ready-toasted if you like

100g runny honey

50g odourless coconut oil

3 tablespoons cocoa powder

1 teaspoon vanilla extract

A pinch of salt (optional)

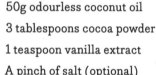
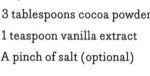

If your nuts aren't already toasted, preheat the oven to 180°C/Gas 4. Put the nuts on a baking tray and toast lightly for 5–10 minutes, until golden. Keep an eye on them so they don't burn. Leave to cool completely.

Put the toasted nuts in a food processor with all the other ingredients and 3 tablespoons water. Process to a thick, slightly grainy paste, stopping once or twice to scrape down the sides. Transfer to a jar and cover. The delicate nut oils will go off quickly if left at room temperature, so store in the fridge and use within a week.

Cashew cream

Cashews are tender, mildly flavoured nuts and can be blitzed into a thick, subtly sweet purée that stands in for dairy cream extremely well. You can use this nut 'cream' in its plain form in savoury dishes – try the fantastic lamb curry on page 256. Or sweeten it a little for use in puds such as the pear fool on page 332. It's also a great pouring accompaniment to puddingy treats such as rhubarb, apple and ginger pie (page 352).

Makes about 400g

250g plain cashew nuts

FOR THE SWEET VERSION

Seeds scraped from
½ vanilla pod or ½ teaspoon
vanilla extract

2 tablespoons runny honey
(or another sweetener such
as agave or maple syrup)

A tiny pinch of salt

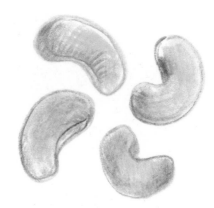

Put the cashew nuts in a bowl and cover with cold water. Leave to soak in the fridge for 6–8 hours, or overnight.

Drain the cashews, discarding the soaking water, and rinse well. Put them in a high-powered blender, or a food processor (a standard blender may struggle to break the nuts down fully). Add 80ml fresh water. If you're making the sweet version, add the vanilla, honey or syrup, and salt.

Purée the nuts, stopping to scrape down the sides of the jug or processor with a rubber spatula as needed, until you have a thick cream. Add more water as necessary – you may need to add up to 180ml total, depending on your particular batch of cashews, to reach a spoonable consistency, and more if you want it to be pourable. A powerful blender should give you a smooth cream, whereas a processor will give a slightly coarser result – both are delicious.

The cashew cream will keep in an airtight jar in the fridge for a week.

Ingredients

A well-stocked larder is a boon for any cook, of course – but all the more so if you are planning to go wheat- and dairy-free for a while. It pays to have a phalanx of 'alternative' good things to hand if you're experimenting with something new. Many of the following ingredients have become essentials in my kitchen. A good health food shop is my first call for most of them – but a good number can now be found in supermarkets and high-street grocers too. Failing that, they can all be sourced from online suppliers such as healthysupplies.co.uk or goodnessdirect.co.uk.

I've written this book from the perspective of making a positive choice to avoid wheat and dairy, in order to enhance good health, rather than out of necessity, in order to avoid illness. I'd be happy to eat oats that aren't guaranteed 100% gluten-free, for instance (see page 401), or dark chocolate made in a factory that handles milk. However, if you are intolerant of, or allergic to, wheat, gluten, milk or lactose (the sugar in dairy products) – or if you are catering for someone who is – you will of course need to make sure there's no trace of these in your cooking. Always read the packet carefully because these ingredients can sometimes crop up in unexpected places. If you're ever unsure, contact the manufacturer.

Coeliac UK (coeliac.org.uk) is an excellent resource for anyone who needs to avoid gluten. They publish a yearly food and drink directory that lists hundreds of gluten-free products. There are lots of other online resources if you are trying to avoid certain foods, including some great blogs about 'free-from' cooking.

AGAVE SYRUP

This sweetener, which is also called agave nectar, is derived from the spiky-leaved agave plant which grows in Mexico and other parts of the Americas. It's sweeter than sugar, with a lower glycaemic index and has been much-touted as a healthy alternative to refined sugars. However, it is not entirely unprocessed, and it is still very high in fructose and in calories – neither of which are good for us in excessive quantities. It is not an everyday ingredient for me, but in moderate amounts it remains a useful alternative to honey, especially if I'm cooking for vegans.

BAKING POWDER

A blend of raising agents, usually mostly sodium bicarbonate, this is an extremely handy ingredient for wheat-free baking, helping to give cake batters a nice lift. Some brands of baking powder contain wheat flour so double-check before you buy.

BEANS AND PULSES

I feel my cupboard is bare if there's not at least a few tins of beans and a packet of lentils in there. Tinned cannellini beans, butter beans and chickpeas are my favourites, and incredibly quick to use. I like the tinned British fava beans called Hodmedods too, though like all fava beans (aka broad beans) they have a slightly bitter note that might not be everyone's cup of tea. Puy lentils are a staple in my kitchen and I almost always cook them from scratch. It only takes about 20 minutes and you can store the cooked lentils in the fridge for a few days. However, the ready-to-eat Puy lentils you can now buy in sachets are a useful standby in an emergency.

BUCKWHEAT

Despite its name, this is not a form of wheat but a seed. It's ground to make a nutty-tasting flour – the basis for traditional French galette pancakes and for blinis – and also milled into flakes that can be used like porridge oats. Buckwheat is naturally gluten-free. However, it can sometimes be 'contaminated' with gluten because it may be grown or processed in the vicinity of wheat. If you want to avoid wheat and gluten completely, look for guaranteed gluten-free buckwheat. Be aware that some buckwheat noodles contain wheat flour too.

CACAO, COCOA POWDER AND DARK CHOCOLATE

These ingredients represent different stages on the journey from raw cacao bean to finished chocolate bar. The process begins when mature cacao pods are split open and the seeds and pulp inside are allowed to ferment and then dry out (fermentation begins to develop all those gorgeous chocolatey flavours). Once de-husked, the fermented beans are broken into little bits: these are cacao or cocoa 'nibs'. (The distinction between cacao and cocoa in this context is not a clear one – they are essentially the same thing.) They may be left raw (i.e. unroasted) and are completely unsweetened. With a distinct bitterness as well as a chocolatey flavour, they make a delicious addition to muesli or to biscuit doughs.

Most cacao beans, however, are not destined to become raw nibs. They are roasted before being de-husked and the nibs are then ground into a paste. When the cocoa fat or 'butter' is removed from this paste, you're left with cocoa powder – a mere spoonful of which adds a powerfully chocolatey punch to a mousse or biscuit. Some cocoa powders contain traces of milk or cereals, so do check this. A gluten- and dairy-free cacao powder or carob powder is a good alternative here (carob is a sweet, chocolatey-tasting tropical pod).

If, instead, the cocoa paste has further ingredients added to it, such as extra cocoa butter, sugar and vanilla, it turns into chocolate as we know it. Clearly milk chocolate contains milk. Dark chocolate is unlikely to include dairy or wheat as ingredients but many dark chocolates are produced in factories that also handle dairy or wheat products, so cannot be guaranteed dairy- and wheat-free. (My go-to dark cooking chocolate is an organic 73% bar in the Montezuma organic range. It's gluten-free but 'may contain traces of milk and nuts'.) High-end, single-estate brands are usually 'pure' – so there's an excuse to indulge if you need one. The Grenada Chocolate Company's bars are an excellent choice, and ethically produced. You could also try Marou, a Vietnamese single origin brand. Both are available at chococo.co.uk, and both are wheat- and dairy-free.

CHESTNUT FLOUR

This is a lovely ingredient, imparting a soft sweetness and a rich colour, and has long been used in traditional, wheat-free cakes such as the Italian castagnaccio (page 366). It combines very nicely with buckwheat or rice flours. This flour can go off rather quickly so refrigerate it after opening and use within a month.

CHICKPEA/GRAM FLOUR

Made from finely ground chickpeas, gram flour (aka besan flour) has a rich, beany flavour. It's often used in batters, and for pancakes such as socca (page 74) or my savoury pan scones (page 70). Gram flour batters do have a tendency to stick, so use a good non-stick pan and a dab of oil when cooking them.

COCONUT MILK, CREAM AND OIL

Delicately sweet and nutty, with a subtle coconut flavour that becomes barely discernible in some dishes, coconut milk brings richness and creaminess to a huge range of recipes. As well as being a fantastic base for curries and soups, coconut milk is a great partner to fruit, and works brilliantly in smoothies (pages 39–41), rice pudding and even porridge (page 32). It's richer than dairy milk and, in most cases, is best tempered with another liquid such as water or stock.

This 'milk' is made by adding water to pulverised coconut flesh and boiling it. (It's not to be confused with coconut water, which is the thin, clear fluid from the centre of the nut.) Often (almost always in my experience!), the milk separates in its tin, forming a thick, or even solid, layer on top and a watery one beneath. A vigorous shake of the tin before you open it may be all that's needed. Otherwise, to re-amalgamate the milk, scrape the lot into a pan and heat it gently, stirring until recombined.

Coconut cream is very similar to coconut milk but has a lower water content, so it's thicker and richer. Creamed coconut (slightly confusingly) is richer again – usually solid, it can be melted into dishes or dissolved in hot water to make coconut milk!

Coconut oil is a versatile cooking fat that you can use for frying, roasting or baking. It is very stable and more resistant than other oils to oxidisation – and to the undesirable chemical changes that can occur when cooking at high temperatures. It's also rich in something called lauric acid, which has anti-bacterial and anti-viral properties. Solid and creamy-white at room temperature, it melts easily to a clear free-flowing oil. You can buy raw coconut oil, which has a delicately coconutty flavour, or an odourless version which has been steam-treated to remove any trace of flavour or aroma. I occasionally use the latter, but if I'm not keen on the prospect of a faint scent of coconut in my baking or frying, I'll often switch to rapeseed oil (see below).

CORNMEAL, POLENTA AND MASA HARINA

Ground from maize, or corn, and consequently wheat-free, cornmeal and polenta are essentially the same thing – the name 'polenta' relates more to the intended finished dish than to the ingredient itself. But do read the pack carefully – quick-cook or instant polentas have been pre-cooked so that they turn very quickly into a thick purée (traditional polenta needs to be simmered and stirred for up to an hour). The grains of quick-cook polenta are relatively big and coarse and are not suitable for use in cakes or cornbreads. For this you need a fine-ground cornmeal or polenta.

You may also come across a form of cornmeal labelled 'maize flour' – for me this is just a little bit *too* finely ground, and gives rather dense results. Always double-check the info on the pack as some cornmeal is handled or packed in a non-gluten-free environment.

For cornmeal tortillas (see page 72), it's essential to use a particular type of cornmeal called masa harina (which is easy to find online). This is made from corn that has been treated with a solution of calcium hydroxide, a process that allows the proteins in the corn to join with each other and form a dough – something that ordinary fine cornmeal will not do.

Cornflour comes from maize too but is much more processed, with more of the original grain removed, leaving it very fine and usually pure white. It's used to thicken sauces and soups, and to give a light, friable texture to biscuits and shortbreads.

DRIED CHILLI FLAKES

These are a brilliant storecupboard standby – they give the same punch you'd expect from fresh chillies but with zero prep involved. Do be aware that, as with fresh chillies, the heat level of chilli flakes can vary considerably from product to product. Test the heat of the ones you're using first (dab a couple on to your tongue if you're brave, or whisk them up in a simple salad dressing and try them that way) and add them according to your taste.

DRIED FRUIT

I'm a massive dried fruit fan – I find the intense sweetness, pleasing chewiness and tangy flavour of these ingredients to be a boost to so many recipes. Apricots, raisins, dried cherries and prunes are always on my shelves – and I choose organic in order to avoid additives such as sulphur dioxide (a preservative) that I consider quite unnecessary. You'll also find a healthy sprinkling of dates in this book. These fudgy little fruits are a godsend if you're trying to cut down on refined sugar. Generally, I choose the large Medjool type, as they are so irresistibly soft and luscious. The firmer, smaller drier form of date – familiar from those 'Eat-Me' boxes – is fine too but you may want to soak them in boiling water before cooking. I sometimes use dried banana chips. Usually these have added sweeteners (often honey, which vegans should be aware of) so they're not an everyday dried fruit for me – but a handful of organic banana chips does turn a bowl of muesli into something particularly enticing.

HONEY

Honey is a wonderful natural sweetener – but it isn't merely sweet. One of the things I love about it is the aromatic complexity of its flavour. This is especially true of unblended honey such as the local Devon or Dorset honeys I like to buy. Small-scale beekeepers usually process their honey only minimally whereas big-brand honeys may have been heated – a process that can compromise flavour. Also, they often contain a blend of several different honeys from different countries in one jar.

The texture of a honey depends on the particular ratio of fructose to glucose within it – the more fructose, the runnier it will be. A free-flowing honey is easier to use in cooking, particularly in dressings or batters. Honey is an excellent ingredient to use in baking and its hygroscopic (water-attracting) nature means it tends to produce nicely moist results. It is also sweeter than sugar, so can usually be added in smaller quantities. Take care when exposing honey directly to heat from the oven – on roasted veg, for instance. It burns very easily and benefits from being combined with oils and liquids such as orange juice.

(Honey, of course, is not suitable for vegans, since it is produced by bees.)

LINSEEDS/FLAXSEED

These are different names for the same thing. The little oval seeds, with their shiny carapaces, can be brown or golden (the brown seeds are supposed to have a stronger flavour but I think you would be hard-pushed to tell). They are prized for their high content of fibre, omega-3 oils and lignans (phytoestrogens). The outer skin of these seeds is pretty tough and it is thought that our bodies may not be capable of breaking it down fully – using ground linseed is one way to ensure you reap the full benefits.

MAPLE SYRUP

This richly flavoured, golden brown liquid is made today much as it has always been – by boiling the thin, clear sap from maple trees until it becomes thick, dark and sweet. I like to use it from time to time because of its distinctive flavour and its unrefined nature. It's mostly sucrose of course but, as sweeteners go, it's relatively nutritious, containing some antioxidants and nutrients including vitamin B2, manganese and zinc.

MUSTARD

With bags of feisty flavour and a very valuable seasoning action that seems to bring the best out of other ingredients, this is a staple for me. I use it in dressings and sauces almost every day, and a good, plain, hot English mustard is my favourite. If you're avoiding gluten completely, check the ingredients list – some mustards may contain wheat flour, though there are plenty that don't.

NUTS, NUT BUTTERS AND NUT MILKS

Nuts have always featured strongly in my recipes – a sprinkling of walnuts, hazels or pecans in so many of my salads. But if you're avoiding wheat or dairy, then nuts really come into their own. Ground down to a meal, they can be used as a flour – or as part of a flour blend. I use ground almonds particularly liberally to add moisture and flavour to wheat-free breads, biscuits and cakes, and ground hazelnuts are quite delicious in baking too.

You can also purée nuts with water to form a thick cream or a milk. I always keep raw cashews on hand – once soaked for a few hours, they can be blitzed with a little water to make a cream (see page 394) or used in soups to add a creamy touch. And almonds make a lovely and refreshing nut milk that I've become very fond of – its delicate, sweet creaminess is a great alternative to dairy milk and it's very versatile (see page 30). If I'm buying ready-made almond milk, I choose an unsweetened one, and I avoid brands that have almond flavouring added. Nut butters, meanwhile, work beautifully in cookie doughs and dressings, saving you the bother of having to chop or process nuts yourself. I go for the no-sugar-added types so I can sweeten or not, as I please.

OATS, OATMEAL AND OAT MILK

Oats are good for much more than porridge. You can use them to thicken soups and smoothies, bake them into a sweet, crunchy granola and even cook them in stock to make a sort of oat risotto. For all these uses, I prefer quick-cooking porridge oats, which are slightly smaller and finer than chunky jumbo oats. Oatmeal, which comes in various grades from coarse pinhead to fine oat flour, is also a great ingredient for porridges and for baking. Oats are naturally free of gluten but, like some other grains, they may be 'contaminated' with gluten if they are grown or processed close to wheat. Completely gluten-free porridge oats are easy to find and gluten-free oatmeal and oat flour are also available. Pure, 'uncontaminated' oats do contain avenin, a protein similar to gluten. A very small number of people are sensitive to this but research has shown that most people with coeliac disease can safely eat it.

Oat milk (usually labelled 'oat drink') is a very useful alternative to dairy milk, with a mild, slightly sweet oaty flavour. Always give it a very good shake before use as it tends to separate while standing. Be aware that most commercial oat milks do contain some gluten.

OILS

For dressing salads and finishing soups, I like to use an oil with bags of character: a local, extra virgin rapeseed oil is often my first choice. I sometimes use rich, grass-green hempseed oil. Pungent – almost astringent – it bears comparison with some of the intense single-estate extra virgin olive oils from Italy and I love it trickled over breads or wraps. (I only tend to finish off a dish with olive oil these days if I want to give it a Mediterranean feel.) Because of its high smoke point, rapeseed is

also my default oil for sautéing, frying and roasting. Coconut oil (see above) is another great frying oil and I often use this if I think a mild background flavour of coconut will be agreeable. Neutral groundnut or sunflower (not cold-pressed) oils are useful if I don't want the frying oil to impart any flavour to the dish.

Toasted sesame oil also deserves a mention here. It has a wonderful, rich 'umami' flavour that gives real depth to salads and is especially good with other aromatic flavourings such as garlic and ginger – but don't cook with it or you'll destroy its flavour.

QUINOA

This is celebrated as a super-grain because it is a 'complete' protein – it contains all the essential amino acids the body needs. Easy to cook, it makes a nutritious alternative to rice, and is great for replacing couscous (which is made from wheat flour). Always rinse the whole grains very well before cooking as they have a soapy coating. Quinoa flakes shouldn't need rinsing (but do check the pack).

RICE FLOUR

This can be bought in white or brown varieties. I've found they behave similarly in recipes, so I tend to plump for brown if I can – to benefit from the whole grain and the slightly richer flavour. Recipes such as tempura spring veg (page 272), where I want a very light result, are an exception.

Rice flour is one of the most neutral tasting of the gluten-free flours so is it ideal in cakes, soda bread, scones, etc. It's a dry, fine, starchy flour and often works best when combined with more protein-rich ingredients. I like it mixed with ground almonds, for instance, in treats such as brownies.

RYE FLOUR

Available in both dark and light varieties, this is very useful if you're avoiding wheat. It contains some gluten, though less than most wheat flours, and it's a weaker type of gluten, so you won't get the same elastic, springy texture as when cooking with wheat flour. But it still works well in soda breads, flatbreads and biscuits, binding the ingredients into a nice dough. Dark rye flour, sometimes called wholemeal rye flour, is widely available. The lighter flour, which has some of the bran removed, is less easy to find, but you can get it from health food shops, and online.

SEEDS

Seeds give amazing crunch and texture, not to mention added goodness, to salads, granola, bread and even pancakes and muffins. Pumpkin, sunflower and sesame are probably my top three but I also like to keep a tub of nigella (black onion) seeds to hand for their dramatic, dark good looks and sweet allium flavour. And poppy seeds feature in my oatcakes on page 47. (See also linseeds, page 400.)

STOCK

Home-made stocks give body and flavour to soups, curries and stews, but there are plenty of quick alternatives that do the job very well too. I like Kallo's organic veg stock cubes, or vegetable bouillon granules such as Marigold's vegan ones. For a free-range chicken stock, Kallo's organic cubes are a good choice. Some cubes contain wheat and/or dairy, so do check the pack. Always taste stock before adding to a dish so you can adjust the levels of saltiness.

SUGAR

I don't have a problem with using sugar if it will make something more delicious – I just try to use the smallest amount necessary and choose the best quality I can find. Unrefined soft light brown sugar, which has lots of lovely flavour, is a favourite, and I use golden caster sugar too, opting for Fairtrade brands in both cases.

You'll see that some of my recipes marked as suitable for vegans contain sugar. For the recipe to be strictly vegan, you should opt for beet sugar, or check with the manufacturer of cane sugar. Many of the most widely available British sugar brands are suitable for vegans, but manufacturers in some parts of the world use charcoal formed from animal bones as part of the filtering process for cane sugar.

TAHINI

This sesame seed paste has a rich creaminess, which is invaluable in dressings when you're not using ingredients such as cream or yoghurt. Tahini has a bittersweet quality that marries beautifully with strong flavours such as garlic and citrus. I generally use a light rather than a dark tahini. Oil separation is normal – just give the paste a good stir before you spoon it out.

TAMARI

This is a Japanese condiment, brewed from soy beans, which has a similar flavour profile to soy sauce but is a little stronger and more intense. I use it often as an alternative to soy sauce, which almost always contains wheat. Clearspring's organic tamari is a good choice.

VANILLA

This exotic, sexy flavouring is a wonderful way to add depth and a subtle sweetness to baking and fruit dishes. Whole vanilla pods give you incomparable flavour but pure vanilla extracts are pretty good and will save you money and time. Avoid anything labelled vanilla flavouring or essence as it won't contain much of the real thing. If you are vegan, it's worth double-checking with the manufacturer to ensure the vanilla extract you are using is completely free of animal products, as some may not be.

VINEGARS

Do not be afraid of the acidity of vinegar: used wisely, this is a vital ingredient that can really bring a dish alive. It's particularly great for giving backbone and definition to salads and sauces. Dressings are usually too oily and/or too sweet without it. Organic cider vinegar is always to hand in my kitchen – I rely on its fruity sharpness pretty much every day. But I also like rich and slightly sweet apple balsamic – which is particularly good with roasted veg. I often use rice vinegar when I'm whipping up a dressing that has an Asian feel, but my ever-dependable cider vinegar will do the job too.

Gluten-free baking

The following recipes for breads, cakes, biscuits and other baked goods, are gluten-free as well as wheat-free (and therefore suitable for coeliacs) *provided* you choose guaranteed gluten-free ingredients. I realise that sounds irritatingly tautological, but the caveat is needed because ingredients like cocoa powder, buckwheat flour and oats, for instance, are gluten-free *in theory*, but, as discussed in the previous section, may in practice be contaminated with traces of gluten from wheat grown or processed nearby. So please always double-check any product for gluten before using it. If in doubt, contact the manufacturer.

Carrot cornbread (page 67)

Buckwheat and almond scones (page 69)

Buckwheat chapatis and cornmeal tortilla variations (page 72),
but not the rye chapatis

Socca (page 74)

Buckwheat galettes (page 77)

Spinachy wraps (page 78)

Linseed and rosemary crackers (page 85)

Seedy bars with chilli and rosemary (page 88)

Castagnaccio (page 366)

Chocolate bean cake (page 368)

Fruity cider loaf (page 371)

St Clements polenta cake with blueberries (page 372)

Hazelnut chocolate cake (page 374)

Chestnut marmalade muffins (page 376)

Ultra choc brownies (page 379)

Chestnut and almond shortbread (page 380)

Coconut macaroons (page 383)

Oaty, nutty, fruity cookies (page 384)

Spiced date and almond cookies (page 387)

Nutty cherry choccy bites (page 388)

Index

Acknowledgements

Writing this book has been a voyage of discovery and I'm indebted to the many people who have helped it reach its destination.

As you can see, I've been exploring exciting new waters. And, thanks to the talented team who've joined me for the ride, the entire venture has been both fun and fruitful.

Anna Horsburgh and Nonie Dwyer – two great cooks I've had the pleasure of working with over the years – have contributed a host of exciting and inspiring ideas, many of which have evolved into fabulous finished recipes.

Nikki Duffy has been my main creative co-conspirator on the recipe front for six books and almost a decade now. It's hard to know how to pay tribute to her continuing brilliance, utter dependability and extraordinary patience except to say that I simply couldn't do it without her – and I really hope I never have to.

Gill Meller, head chef at River Cottage, has been the other lynchpin of the book-making process, firing off brilliant ideas with his characteristic verve, and working tirelessly to make sure the food looks as good in the photographs as it tastes in the mouth.

The book would be a mere shadow of what you now hold in your hands without the superb photography of Simon Wheeler, whose work never fails to surprise and delight me. It can sometimes be the case that very simple recipes don't leap off the page as excitingly as they might – but Simon has not missed a beat in revealing these dishes, even the most pared-back, in all their tasty, tempting beauty.

Thanks also to my wife Marie for her wonderful additional photographs, produced with great patience against very tight deadlines. And thanks to our friend Nick Booker for the brilliant Freddie somersault pic.

Our hugely productive photoshoots have also been facilitated by some very hard work from Alice Meller and Sam Folan, both of whose patience and energy in assisting Gill and Simon has been invaluable.

Quite apart from the stunning photography, much of the visual impact of this book is down to the gorgeous illustrative work of Mariko Jesse. I love the wit and elan of her 'graffiti' and the way it uplifts and transforms these pages. And bringing illustration, photography and type together in seamless harmony – not to mention delightful good humour – has once again been the job of designer Lawrence Morton. It's a job he makes look very easy – so much so that I might have a go myself next time…

The final stages of getting a book to press can lead the whole team into rather choppy waters, but guiding us all through with emollient calm and confidence have been project editor Janet Illsley, whose razor-sharp attention to detail has made everything watertight, and Natalie Bellos, my wonderful editor at Bloomsbury, whose unflappable demeanour and expert navigation have seen us all home safely once again.

Also at Bloomsbury, Alison Glossop has helped the whole process go smoothly, and production manager Marina Asenjo has ensured the book looks shipshape and Bristol fashion in all quarters.

Jess Upton has been my PA for more than ten years now and continues to manage my hectic schedule with a deftness and efficiency for which I am truly grateful. Her many talents include considerable skill in the kitchen, and she's done sterling work testing many of the recipes that appear in this book. Her helpful comments have made them all the tastier. Thank you Jess.

Input from another long-time and stalwart colleague, Antony Topping, has also been indispensable. Antony has an amazing talent for imagining a book in its finished form before it's even off the drawing board and this is just one of the many reasons he is such a brilliant agent.

Various knowledgeable people have helped in my research for this book and I must give special thanks to Nicola Crawford-Taylor, dietitian at Coeliac UK, Chris Young at the Real Bread Campaign for his comments on modern wheat, and Samantha Calvert at The Vegan Society.

Finally, on the home front, for keeping me safe and sane, as well as responding to my daily cooking with unbounded frankness, my endless love and thanks to Marie, Chloe, Oscar, Freddie and Louisa. Thanks to you all, life tastes good.

First published in Great Britain 2014, this edition first published 2017

Text copyright © 2014 by Hugh Fearnley-Whittingstall
Photography © 2014 by Simon Wheeler
Photographs on pages 13, 24, 73 and 345 © 2014 by Marie Derôme
Illustrations © 2014 by Mariko Jesse

The moral right of the author has been asserted.

No part of this book may be used or reproduced in any manner whatsoever without written permission from the Publisher except in the case of brief quotations embodied in critical articles or reviews.

Bloomsbury Publishing Plc
50 Bedford Square
London WC1B 3DP

Bloomsbury is a trademark of Bloomsbury Publishing Plc

Bloomsbury Publishing, London, Oxford, New York, New Delhi and Sydney

A CIP catalogue record for this book is available from the British Library

ISBN 978 1 4088 8847 6

Project editor: Janet Illsley
Designer: Lawrence Morton
Cover design: Greg Heinimann
Photographer and stylist: Simon Wheeler (simonwheeler.eu)
Illustrator: Mariko Jesse (marikojesse.com)
Indexer: Hilary Bird

10 9 8 7 6 5 4 3 2 1

Printed and bound in Italy by Graphicom

MIX
Paper from
responsible sources
FSC® C013123
FSC
www.fsc.org

bloomsbury.com
rivercottage.net

The information included in this book has been assembled by the author to provide general advice in relation to the subject matters dealt with in the text. However, this book is not a substitute for professional medical advice, diagnosis or treatment. To the best of the knowledge and belief of the author and publisher, the information contained in this book is correct as at July 2014.

While every effort has been made to ensure the correctness of the information contained in this book, the author and publisher disclaim all legal liability and responsibility for any loss or damage (including damage to property) to the full extent permitted by English law, whether such loss or damage arises from any error or omission on the part of the author or publisher, or from the failure of the reader to correctly follow any advice or instructions contained in the book. To the full extent permitted by English law, the author and publisher also disclaim all legal liability arising directly or indirectly from the use, or misuse, of the information contained in this book.